# THE KENNEDY ASSASSINATION — 24 HOURS AFTER

This Large Print Book carries the
Seal of Approval of N.A.V.H.

# THE KENNEDY ASSASSINATION — 24 HOURS AFTER

## LYNDON B. JOHNSON'S PIVOTAL FIRST DAY AS PRESIDENT

### STEVEN M. GILLON

**THORNDIKE PRESS**
*A part of Gale, Cengage Learning*

GALE
CENGAGE Learning

Detroit • New York • San Francisco • New Haven, Conn • Waterville, Maine • London

## GALE
### CENGAGE Learning™

**LIBRARY OF CONGRESS CATALOGING-IN-PUBLICATION DATA**

Gillon, Steven M.
  The Kennedy assassination—24 hours after : Lyndon B.
Johnson's pivotal first day as president / by Steven M. Gillon.
    p. cm. — (Thorndike Press large print nonfiction)
  Originally published: New York : Basic Books, c2009.
  Includes bibliographical references.
  ISBN-13: 978-1-4104-2479-2 (hardcover : alk. paper)
  ISBN-10: 1-4104-2479-0 (hardcover : alk. paper)
  1. Kennedy, John F. (John Fitzgerald),
1917–1963—Assassination. 2. Kennedy, John F. (John
Fitzgerald), 1917–1963—Death and burial. 3. Johnson, Lyndon
B. (Lyndon Baines), 1908–1973. 4. United States—Politics and
government—1963–1969—Decision making. I. Title. II. Title:
Kennedy assassination—twenty-four hours after.
E842.9.G55 2010
973.922092—dc22                                    2009052315

Published in 2010 by arrangement with Basic Books, a member of the
Perseus Books Group, LLC.

*This book is dedicated to
the honorable David L. Boren*

# CONTENTS

# PREFACE

President John F. Kennedy has now been dead for more years than he lived, yet his assassination on November 22, 1963, remains one of the most misunderstood events in American history despite being one of the most well documented. Hundreds of people were gathered in Dealey Plaza in Dallas, Texas, at the time of the shooting. Dozens of reporters and Secret Service agents were traveling with the president, filing reports on what they saw and heard. The same television cameras that helped to forge such a strong emotional bond between the young, charismatic president and the nation he led transformed his death into a uniquely personal event for millions of Americans. The nonstop television coverage, which began within minutes of the shooting and continued until after the funeral on November 25, allowed the entire nation to experience the tragedy firsthand.

President Kennedy's death was the defining moment for many members of the massive baby boom generation that was coming of age in the 1960s. Their ongoing fascination with the assassination and their instinctive skepticism toward authority have spawned a cottage industry of conspiracy theories: Did Oswald act alone? Was the fatal shot fired from the grassy knoll? Was the shooting part of a larger conspiracy involving high-level government officials?

The intense public focus on how Kennedy died, and who was responsible for killing him, has obscured other important questions raised by events that day. Kennedy's death resulted in the most violent and sudden transition of presidential power in American history. Yet, of the hundreds of books about the assassination, few address this issue. This book will attempt to fill that void by examining the transfer of power that took place in the twenty-four hours following the assassination. What steps did Lyndon Johnson take to consolidate his hold on power in those critical hours? What problems did he confront? How did the conflicts that emerged on that day set the stage for the rest of his presidency?

On television, great crises are revealed and solved in a twenty-four-hour period. In real life, it takes longer, but the first twenty-four hours are often the most crucial. It is during those first hours that the die is cast. Those critical hours represent a test of presidential character. Dependable information is scarce. Situations are fluid, changing by the minute. A president has little time for reflection. Decisions need to be made. Process is abandoned. It all comes down to the judgment and instincts of one man, forced by circumstance to make momentous decisions that can shape the course of history. Johnson was thrust into that position under the most difficult of circumstances.

Focusing on the first hours of LBJ's presidency allows me to tell a familiar story in an unfamiliar way, providing a refreshing new perspective on the inner workings of the presidency. Sometimes in their desire to tell the sweeping narrative, historians have missed the revealing details that capture the texture of life in the White House. Traditional history writing shows the past as more coherent than it really is. Isolating a twenty-four-hour period captures the fear, chaos, uncertainty, and excitement that often shape history.

In trying to retell this story, I am reminded of the words of Theodore White, who observed that "it is a trap of history to believe that eyewitnesses remember accurately what they have lived through."[1]

Understanding what happened, especially in those first few hours after the shooting, involves sifting through dozens of conflicting accounts. For understandable reasons, chaos, confusion, and a profound sense of loss clouded the memories of the presidential party that rushed to Parkland Hospital on the afternoon of Kennedy's death. Even among the handful of people who were with Lyndon Johnson, there is no consensus about who told LBJ that Kennedy was dead, or at what time. Because of longstanding resentments, there are at least two versions of nearly every conversation Lyndon Johnson had with Robert Kennedy and with JFK appointments secretary Kenneth O'Donnell. Each of these three men worked tirelessly in the years after the assassination to ensure that his own version of events was injected as fact into the historical record.

Most of the eyewitnesses that day have recorded what they saw and heard, and they have done so on numerous occasions. But their stories are not always consistent. In a number of cases, participants have added details to their accounts. At other times they have completely changed the facts and emphasis of their testimony.

Given the many conflicting accounts, it is often difficult to get a clear impression of Lyndon Johnson. For the Kennedy clan, memories of LBJ on November 22, 1963, were corrupted not only by confusion and time but by anger and longtime suspicions about his character. Johnson himself is often an unreliable witness to his own actions. Framed by his hostility toward Robert Kennedy, his recollections of that day are often self-serving and factually inaccurate.

Both the Kennedy family and Lyndon Johnson turned to sympathetic writers to channel their views and frame the debate. As a result, popular accounts of Johnson's actions that day, like the decade itself, have been divided into competing narratives.

William Manchester's *The Death of a President* still stands as the most comprehensive history of that tragic day. Shortly after the assassination, the Kennedy family approached two established authors, Theodore White and Walter Lord, to write an account of the events. Both declined, mostly because the Kennedys demanded final-review rights for the book. Manchester was their third choice. A former correspondent for the *Baltimore Sun,* Manchester had published both fiction and nonfiction works before becoming the editor of the Wesleyan University Press in 1955. He was not a well-known author at the time, but he had written a flattering book about Kennedy, *Portrait of a President.*

When he received the call from Mrs. Kennedy in March 1964, Manchester jumped at the opportunity. He took a leave of absence from his job and worked on the project for the next two years. For as many as fifteen hours a day for the next twenty-one months, the author gathered material, accumulating forty-five volumes of tapes, notes, and documents. Unlike the Warren Commission, which was created to solve a murder, Manchester was a storyteller, hoping to find intrigue and suspense in the day's tragic events. The "goals of the Commission and the historian do not coincide," Manchester wrote in a private letter to Johnson aide Jack Valenti. "Our mandates are different. I shall cover certain events which were irrelevant to the Commission."[2]

In December 1966, Manchester submitted his 1,200-page manuscript to his publisher, Harper & Row. Copies of the book also circulated around Washington. Originally titled *Death of Lancer,* in reference to President Kennedy's Secret Service code name, the manuscript created a storm of

14

controversy. Manchester made little effort to hide his contempt for Johnson, whom he privately dismissed as "someone in a Grade D movie of the late show." Leaning heavily on the accounts of disgruntled Kennedy aides, Manchester painted a portrait of a boorish and overbearing vice president insensitive to the needs of a grieving widow and driven by a combination of megalomania and insecurity.[3]

Even some Kennedy partisans were shocked by Manchester's treatment of Johnson. The historian Arthur Schlesinger Jr. complained about the book's opening scene, which depicted Johnson pressuring JFK to shoot a deer while the two men were at LBJ's Texas ranch in the days following the 1960 election. According to Schlesinger, the scene suggested that "the unconscious argument of the book is that Johnson killed Kennedy (that is, that Johnson is an expression of the forces of violence and irrationality which ran rampant through his native state and were responsible for the tragedy of Dallas)."[4]

As the book neared publication, Mrs. Kennedy expressed reservations about the project. She complained that Manchester had violated her privacy by exposing too many private details about her actions and thoughts in the hours following the assassination. She insisted that he make significant changes to the manuscript, including toning down the criticism of Johnson.

Manchester did make some minor changes, but not enough to satisfy Mrs. Kennedy. She filed suit to block publication. Eventually, the two sides reached a settlement that required him to remove all references to his interviews with Mrs. Kennedy. The published version, although lacking some of the tougher anti-Johnson sections, still offered a very unflattering portrait of the president and a glossy picture of all things Kennedy.[5]

Released in early 1967, *The Death of a President* became an instant bestseller. Manchester's story of presidential arrogance and deception made sense to Americans disillusioned with the war in Vietnam, student protest, and racial rioting.

Johnson had sensed from the beginning that Manchester was going to write a pro-Kennedy book and refused the author's numerous requests for an interview. He viewed the book as part of RFK's effort to undermine his presidency and challenge him in the 1968 Democratic primaries. LBJ complained bitterly in a series of conversations captured by his White House taping system that Manchester was an agent "of the people who want to destroy me." He claimed the book "makes Bobby look like a great hero and makes me look like a son-of-a-bitch, and 95 percent of it is completely fabricated."[6]

Johnson, and his allies, pushed back hard against Manchester's narrative of events. White House aides, who had combed through an early draft of the manuscript, refuted some of Manchester's more exaggerated claims and highlighted how Johnson acceded that day to many "unusual demands" from the Kennedy family. Their assessment reflected LBJ's own views. "From the time of reaching Parkland Hospital after the shooting, no one could have been kinder to Mrs. Kennedy, members of the Kennedy family and the Kennedy staff than were President and Mrs. Johnson," they wrote. "For a man who had just had thrust upon him the responsibilities and burdens of the strongest nation in the World, President Johnson and Mrs. Johnson personally thought of the many kind and considerate acts toward the loved ones of the deceased."[7]

Although complaining that he was not able to compete with the well-oiled Kennedy public relations machine, Johnson followed their example and hired his own writer. He turned to Jim Bishop, a popular author who had written a flattering magazine article about President Kennedy that was later turned into a bestselling book, *A Day in the Life of President Kennedy.*

Just as the controversy over the Manchester book was peaking, Bishop approached the White House asking for access to write a book titled *A Day in the Life of Lyndon Johnson.* "It will be a happy, exuberant book, or nothing," Bishop assured Jack Valenti. "I cannot write a critical book about Lyndon Johnson because I believe that he has done more work, made more good decisions and has faced the harsh realities of this world better than any president I know — and in a shorter span of time."[8]

The flattery worked: LBJ not only agreed to be interviewed, but provided Bishop with an office in the White House and gave him access to all federal agencies. When asked if he wanted to arrange a meeting with Bishop, Johnson scribbled, "I'll cooperate fully."[9]

Both Johnson and Bishop appear to have had other motives, however. Although Bishop would eventually publish the book that he promised, he really wanted to write about the Kennedy assassination. Being at the White House, and having access to

Johnson, would allow him to tell the story that Manchester had been denied. At the same time, LBJ could use Bishop to counter Manchester's account while maintaining a public posture of indifference to the whole controversy.

A week after the assassination, and four days after Kennedy was buried, Bishop had written to White House press secretary Pierre Salinger to inform him that he was writing a book called *The Day President Kennedy Was Shot.* He had already written similar books about the days on which Jesus Christ and Abraham Lincoln had died, and now he planned to adopt the formula to Kennedy. "I am sure that this will be attempted by several writers," he said, but he was hoping that Mrs. Kennedy would designate him as the authorized writer. "If you agree with me that one person — and not several — should write this book, I think you should make a terse announcement to the press to that effect, whether that person happens to be me or someone else. This will have the effect of stopping the others."[10]

Undeterred when the Kennedys announced they had chosen William Manchester to write the authorized version, Bishop declared his plans to write his own book. Mrs. Kennedy begged him "to please not go ahead with your intended book." The family, she wrote, had hired Manchester "to protect President Kennedy and the truth." She told him that "none of the people connected with Nov. 22 will speak to anyone but Mr. Manchester — that is my wish and it is theirs also." Having lost out to Manchester, Bishop complained publicly that Mrs. Kennedy was "trying to copyright the assassination" and proceeded with his plans to produce his own volume.[11]

Not surprisingly, Bishop's account of that day represented the flip side of the Manchester book, channeling LBJ's hostility toward RFK and his sense of grievance toward the Kennedy clan. Bishop described Johnson as "a big, industrious man," while RFK was the beneficiary of "arrogant nepotism." "The Kennedys were effete Europeans, in manner and address," he wrote. "The Johnsons were earthy Americans." He sided with LBJ on nearly every major point of dispute between the two camps. By the time it was released in 1968, however, the nation had soured on Johnson and his presidency, and the book achieved only modest success.[12]

Four decades later, it is time for a fresh examination of Lyndon Johnson's handling

20

of the transfer of power on November 22, 1963. With new information that was not available to either Manchester or Bishop, and with the benefit of historical perspective, it is possible to reach a more balanced assessment of Johnson's actions.

Overall, I believe the record shows that LBJ performed exceptionally well under the most difficult of circumstances. Despite Manchester's claims to the contrary, Johnson was unfailingly sensitive to the suffering of the grieving widow, constantly balancing the demands of the presidency with the needs of a mourning nation and a grief-stricken family. He masterfully choreographed the first few hours of his presidency to underscore the theme of continuity and to reassure a shell-shocked nation.

Yet Johnson also revealed a nagging insecurity, a reluctance to take responsibility for some of his actions, and a penchant for deception that confirmed the worst fears of many in the Kennedy camp.

The actions of many of those close to the slain president are less defensible. While understandably grief stricken, they could barely contain their contempt for the new president. There is also a critical question that needs to be answered: why did it take so long for Kennedy aides to tell Lyndon

Johnson that JFK was dead? This book presents a new time line that challenges the conclusions of the Warren Commission and shows there was an inexcusable delay in informing Johnson that he was now president.

Within a twenty-four-hour period, a president was assassinated and a new presidency was born. While capturing the excitement of the moment and the texture of life on that day, this book will highlight how the decisions made in those first critical hours helped shape the rest of Johnson's presidency. We will also witness the tensions and conflicts that would eventually destroy the Johnson presidency, divide the nation, and produce a civil war in the Democratic Party.

# 1
# "IT ALL BEGAN SO BEAUTIFULLY"

The president and vice president went to Texas in November 1963 for two simple reasons: money and politics. President John F. Kennedy was gearing up for the 1964 presidential campaign and he wanted to keep Texas's twenty-five electoral votes in the Democratic column. It was by no means a sure thing — in 1960, the Kennedy-Johnson ticket had carried the state by only 46,233 votes — despite the fact that LBJ was a native son.

Kennedy also hoped to raise money for the cash-starved Democratic Party and assumed he could rake in a million dollars — a lot of money in 1963 — with a quick swing through the state. Over the past two years, Kennedy's personal popularity had failed to translate into much-needed donations to the Democratic National Committee. The party's financial head, Dick Maguire, pressed JFK to raise funds with a campaign swing through oil-rich Texas. "We've got that four-million-dollar debt to pay off," Kennedy told Johnson.[1]

The state may have been a good source of money, but it was becoming increasingly hostile to JFK's more liberal message. His poll numbers were ebbing in the wake of his decision the previous summer to support a civil rights bill banning segregation in public facilities. Many whites, realizing that the proposed law represented a direct challenge to the engrained system of racial hierarchy in Texas and throughout the South, vehemently opposed the measure. In October, a *Newsweek* poll showed that Kennedy was "the most widely disliked Democratic President of this century among white Southerners." His approval rating in the state stood at a dismal 38 percent. A *Houston Chronicle* survey, scheduled for release after the visit, showed him trailing the likely Republican nominee, conservative Arizona senator Barry Goldwater, by a 52–48 percent margin in Texas.[2]

The visit to Texas would be complicated because the state's Democratic Party was split into feuding factions, preventing it from forming a united front against a rejuvenated GOP. Until the 1960s, Texas had been a one-party state: Democrats won nearly every election and liberals exercised considerable influence within the party. Over the past few decades, however, a thriving oil industry had created an expanding white middle class at odds with the liberal leadership of the Democratic Party in both Texas and Washington. Race also played a central role. Many whites in Texas, opposed to the national Democratic Party's gradual embrace of the civil rights movement, fought to maintain the system of Jim Crow segregation and started defecting to the Republicans.

Lyndon B. Johnson and Governor John Connally, his protégé, were the most visible leaders of the conservative wing of the party. Connally had begun his political career in 1938 as a young staff member to then-freshman Texas congressman Johnson before moving on to become a successful lobbyist for the oil industry. Over the years, Johnson and Connally remained close friends and political allies. Johnson's sponsorship continued when he became vice president: in 1961, President Kennedy appointed Connally as secretary of the navy.

Later that year, Connally resigned his navy post to run for governor. His candidacy was unpopular among Texas liberals, who viewed him as a pawn of the state's booming oil industry and waged a vigorous campaign to defeat him in the primaries. Opponents dubbed Connally "LBJ" — Lyndon's Boy John. Connally managed to outmaneuver and outspend his opponents, however, and won narrow victories in both the primary and in the 1962 general election.

Connally's election highlighted how a rising conservative tide was transforming Texas politics. The governor's supporters controlled all the major state offices, the state party organization, and most of the big Texas money. Although he had served in the Kennedy cabinet and remained close to LBJ, Connally opposed most of the New Frontier domestic program. Earlier that summer, he took the unusual step of appearing on statewide television to criticize a president of his own party when he declared his opposition to Kennedy's proposed civil rights bill. The move was wildly popular in Texas. With an approval rating near 80 percent, it was clear to both Kennedy and Johnson that Connally's tactics had struck a nerve with the white conservative base of the Democratic Party.[3]

While the state shifted to the right, the outgunned liberal forces looked to Senator Ralph Yarborough to energize their base and stem the conservative tide. Over the past decade, Yarborough had won the hearts of Texas liberals with his evangelical rhetoric, energetic style, fiery attacks on big business, and emotional appeals to use government to help "the common man." He ran, and lost, three consecutive races for governor between 1952 and 1956. He finally broke through in 1957, when he won a special election to fill a vacated Senate seat. The following year he was elected to a full term.

Despite the rightward drift of the state, Yarborough remained true to the reform impulse of the New Deal. He broke with the state leadership and supported the Supreme Court decision in *Brown v. Board of Education* (1954), which put an end to the "separate but equal" doctrine. He championed increased federal spending for education, housing, and veterans. Politically, Yarborough was far closer than Connally to the reform-minded agenda of the Kennedy administration. According to *Congressional Quarterly,* he voted for major administration bills 73 percent of the time in 1961, and 69 percent of the time in 1962 and 1963. He managed to build a small but vocal following among organized labor, liberal intellectuals, East Texas populists, the growing Hispanic population, and most blacks who were allowed to vote — all groups that Kennedy would need to turn out on election day.

But Yarborough was sailing against the wind of Texas politics and found himself increasingly isolated as the party lurched to the right. A poll in July showed him favored to hold his seat in 1964 against a weak Republican opponent. However, the battles with the party's conservative wing were clearly taking their toll. After six years in office he commanded the support of less than half of his party — 47 percent. A majority of Democrats, 53 percent, either favored someone else or were undecided.[4]

Yarborough had to contend not only with the spirited opposition of the governor but also with the vice president's open hostility. When Yarborough was campaigning for the Senate in 1957, both Johnson and Connally had endorsed his primary opponent. Traditionally, senators control the flow of federal patronage jobs in their state, but when Johnson joined the ticket in 1960 he made a private agreement with Kennedy, which allowed the vice president to continue to control all federal patronage in Texas — thus bypassing Yarborough. The move infuriated the senator. Just a few months before the Texas trip, Yarborough had called Johnson a "power-mad Texas politician" after

LBJ used his influence to block the senator's appointment to the Appropriations Committee.[5]

The president wanted to avoid taking sides in the Connally-Yarborough standoff. He needed both Connally's machine and Yarborough's coalition if he was going to win in November. Kennedy hoped, for obvious reasons, that Johnson would use his considerable influence in Texas to bang heads together and forge a compromise between the feuding factions. Johnson was the logical man for the job: he was Texan to the core. "If one were asked to construct a stereotypical Texan," Connally later observed, "I suppose you would wind up with someone close to Lyndon Johnson."[6]

Born in 1908, Johnson grew up in the depressed rural area of the Texas Hill Country outside of Austin. His hardscrabble roots instilled in him a passionate desire to help the less fortunate, along with an idealistic faith in the power of government to provide opportunity. But his impoverished upbringing had also left him with a nagging inferiority complex — a fear that people with more refined backgrounds would never accept him.

From childhood, Lyndon was determined

to make his mark in politics. His father, Sam Johnson, a six-term member of the state legislature, took him along on the campaign trail and allowed him to wander around the statehouse. LBJ recalled fondly how, as a nine-year-old, he would sit for hours in the gallery listening to the debates on the floor. Lyndon loved every minute of it and set his sights on someday running his own campaign. In 1937, after completing his education at Southwest Texas State Teachers College, and serving as Texas director of the National Youth Administration (NYA), Johnson won election to Congress.[7]

LBJ started out in politics as a New Deal liberal, but as the political winds shifted after World War II, he trimmed his sails. During the 1930s, with the nation mired in depression and Texans looking to Washington for help, LBJ championed the common man and declared Franklin Roosevelt his hero. After the war, as oil money made white Texans rich and more conservative, Johnson moved closer to the political center. In an effort to appeal to the conservative base, he fought to protect the oil and gas industry and tried to walk the middle ground on civil rights. He developed cozy ties with powerful business interests, which then supplied the cash for his campaigns.[8]

LBJ's rise to power was often character-
ized by political opportunism and ruthless
ambition. In the 1940s and 1950s Texas
politics still resembled the Wild West. Stuff-
ing ballot boxes, accepting bribes, and steal-
ing elections were facts of political life. In
1941, Johnson lost a hotly contested Senate
seat because his opponent stuffed the boxes
after the polls had closed. Seven years later,
in another close contest, it was LBJ who
stole the Senate election from popular
governor Coke Stevenson. The deciding
votes came from the poor, boss-controlled,
Hispanic town of Alice, Texas. On election
night, Johnson received 765 votes to Stevenson's 60. That wasn't enough to win the
election; six days later when the ballots were
recounted, the same town produced 965
votes for LBJ, allowing him to win the election by 87 votes.

LBJ's ability to muster Hispanic votes in
boss-controlled counties inspired a story
that followed him the rest of his career and
cemented his reputation as a corrupt
politician:

Manuel: "Pedro, why are you crying?"
Pedro: "It is because of my poor dead
    father."
Manuel: "But, Pedro, your father died

31

10 years ago."

Pedro: "That's just it. Yesterday, my father came back to vote for Lyndon Johnson, but he no come see me."[9]

The stolen election would cast a shadow of illegitimacy over the rest of Johnson's career and earn him the nickname "Landslide Lyndon." The taint of corruption only made Johnson work harder to earn the respect of his peers. Once in the Senate, Johnson impressed powerful Democrats with his energy and ambition. He learned the rules of parliamentary debate, mastered the details of legislation, and figured out how to count votes. Most of all, he knew how to manipulate colleagues: when to flatter, when to bargain, and when to threaten. He distrusted crusading liberals and moralizing conservatives; Johnson cared about making deals and passing legislation. In 1953, Democrats elected him minority leader. Two years later, after they won control of the Senate, Johnson, at age forty-six, became the youngest majority leader in history.

Johnson was not afraid to twist arms to bend recalcitrant senators to his will. Standing six feet four inches tall, he towered over many of his peers, and he used his size to intimidate his opponents. Two journalists described this process as the "Johnson treatment." "He moved in close, his face a scant millimeter from his target, his eyes widening and narrowing, his eyebrows rising and falling." Minnesota senator Hubert Humphrey once described an encounter with Johnson as "an almost hypnotic experience. I came out of that session covered with blood, sweat, tears, spit — and sperm." Many observers considered him the second most powerful man in Washington behind President Dwight Eisenhower.[10]

Johnson was not only one of the most powerful men in Washington, he was one of the most colorful, controversial, and complicated. "Lyndon Johnson was the most complex man I ever met," recalled veteran Washington insider Clark Clifford. He "also may have been the most difficult." Although often obsequious to superiors, Johnson could be vicious to his subordinates and overbearing with anyone who got in his way. At his Senate office, he fondled, ogled, and overworked his female staff. He boasted of his sexual prowess and had long affairs with at least two women. He demanded unquestioned loyalty from everyone who worked for him. "I want real loyalty," he once said. "I want someone who will kiss my ass in Macy's window, and say it smells like roses."[11]

Johnson was notorious for pushing himself and those who worked for him. He worked long, eighteen-hour days and drove his staff to exhaustion. He was restless and driven, once losing forty-two pounds in forty days while campaigning for a House seat in 1937. He was reckless about his health. He drank heavily — Cutty Sark was his favorite — and chain smoked. His bad habits almost killed him in 1955 when he suffered a serious heart attack. Doctors gave him a fifty-fifty chance of surviving. "Will I ever be able to smoke again?" he asked his physician. On being told that he would not, he muttered, "I'd rather have my pecker cut off." After a short break, Johnson resumed his rigorous schedule but without the cigarettes.[12]

During the lead-up to the 1960 campaign, Johnson started maneuvering for the presidential nomination. In 1957, realizing that he needed to make himself acceptable to the northern, liberal wing of the party, he helped craft a modest civil rights bill. For most liberals, however, it was too little, too late. Dismissing him as a self-serving political operator, liberals viewed LBJ as too closely tied to the powerful Texas oil industry, too anti-union, and too ambivalent about civil rights.

Undeterred, LBJ convinced himself that he could win the nomination the same way he ran the Senate — by making deals and winning the endorsements of influential Washington insiders. LBJ wanted Kennedy and Minnesota senator Hubert Humphrey to split the early primary vote, forcing the party to choose its nominee at the convention. While Humphrey and Kennedy slugged it out in public, Johnson would quietly win the endorsement of the party's movers and shakers who would support him at the convention. [13]

While Johnson worked the halls of Congress, the charismatic Kennedy built a powerful grassroots organization and used his telegenic glamour, and his father's money, to win key victories in the early primary states. In April, he narrowly defeated Humphrey in Wisconsin and then scored a decisive win in West Virginia.

LBJ dismissed John Kennedy and his ambition to run for president, poking fun at his inexperience and his privilege, referring to the Massachusetts senator as "sonny boy." Although he respected Kennedy's intellect and his eloquence, he resented his cavalier attitude toward the hard work of

35

the Senate. In the Senate, he said, there were "workhorses" and "show horses." Kennedy was a "show horse."

As the Democratic Convention opened on July 11, 1960, Kennedy appeared to have an insurmountable lead in delegates, but Johnson refused to accept defeat. "I can't stand to be pushed around by that forty-two-year-old kid," LBJ complained to Adlai Stevenson. Unable to add to his delegate count, LBJ tried to force defections from JFK by spreading rumors about JFK's health, claiming that he was unfit and unprepared to be president. He told a reporter that Kennedy was a "little scrawny fellow with rickets." Johnson surrogates declared that Kennedy was suffering from Addison's disease, a potentially fatal disorder of the adrenal glands. Although true, Kennedy vehemently denied the charge and went on the win the nomination on the first ballot.[14]

Despite Johnson's clumsy effort to block his nomination, the pragmatic Kennedy shocked the convention when he turned around and asked LBJ to join the ticket. It was a highly controversial decision. Kennedy risked alienating his liberal and labor supporters, and many members of his own staff, who were inherently distrustful of having a southerner on the ticket. Many of them viewed Johnson as a representative of the old, corrupt politics that Kennedy had promised to change.

There were compelling arguments in favor of including Johnson on the ticket. Johnson was one of the party's most prominent and skilled legislative leaders. The Massachusetts Catholic realized he needed a southern Protestant on the ticket. Johnson could help in a couple of southern states, especially vote-rich Texas. Kennedy also worried about leaving a disgruntled and temperamental Johnson in the Senate, where he would have the power to block much of his agenda.

There are a number of conflicting accounts of exactly how JFK reached his decision. According to LBJ, on the morning of July 14, Kennedy came to his suite on the seventh floor of the Biltmore Hotel and offered him the vice presidency. Publicly, Johnson had assumed a posture of indifference to being on the ticket. The day before the convention opened, Johnson was asked on *Meet the Press* if he would accept such a position. Johnson said no. "Most vice presidents don't do much," he responded. But privately he feared that his days of dominance in the Senate were coming to an end. Democrats had scored major victories in

1958, but most of the new members were northern liberals who were chafing under his leadership. No matter who won, he would find his power in the Senate curtailed. A Kennedy victory would shift the center of gravity in the party away from Capitol Hill and toward the White House. Republican nominee and former vice president Richard Nixon would also be a more activist president than Eisenhower and depend less on LBJ for support. Although traditionally the vice president had few powers and even less influence, Johnson believed that he could transform the office.[15]

Although he clearly wanted the job, Johnson played coy, telling JFK that he needed time to think about it. "Well, think it over and let's talk about it again at three-thirty," Johnson recalled JFK saying.[16]

Robert F. Kennedy, JFK's brother and campaign manager, vehemently opposed LBJ's selection. Like others in the Kennedy camp, RFK worried that putting Johnson on the ticket would alienate liberals, but his opposition was also personal. While gearing up for the campaign the previous fall, JFK had sent his younger brother to the LBJ ranch to ask Johnson about his intentions. Disingenuously, LBJ told Robert that he was not a candidate, and that he would not try to block JFK's nomination. After the meeting, Johnson took the slightly built RFK on a deer hunt. Instead of giving him a standard rifle, he armed him with a powerful ten-gauge shotgun. The recoil knocked Kennedy to the ground and left him with a gash above his eye. "Son, you've got to learn to handle a gun like a man," LBJ told him. In a matter of a few hours, Johnson managed to lie to RFK and to insult him.[17]

RFK later claimed that JFK had gone to Johnson's suite assuming he would turn down the nomination. "He thought that he should offer it to him, but he never dreamt that there was a chance in the world that he would accept it." According to RFK, after the meeting a flustered JFK returned to his suite. "You just won't believe it," he said to his brother. "He wants it."[18]

RFK's account is not credible, however. People close to Johnson had already given clear signals that LBJ wanted the job and would accept if asked. On the evening of July 13, the day of the presidential balloting, Kennedy met privately with the House Speaker, and Johnson confidant, Sam Rayburn. The Speaker told JFK that he should pick LBJ, and he assured him that if asked, Johnson would accept.[19]

Over the next few hours, the Kennedy

team debated the merits of having LBJ on the ticket. According to RFK, they "spent the rest of the day alternating between thinking it was good and thinking that it wasn't good that he'd offered him the Vice Presidency, and how could he get out of it." When he was unable to change his brother's mind, he made two trips to Johnson's suite to get him to reject JFK's offer. Johnson refused. "I thought I was dealing with a child," Johnson reflected. He claimed to have said to RFK, "The only question is: Is it good for the country and good for the Democratic Party?" According to RFK's version of the meeting, Johnson "just shook and tears came into his eyes, and he said, 'I want to be Vice President, and, if the President will have me, I'll join him in making a fight for it.' " At that point, there was no graceful way of getting Johnson off the ticket.[20]

In JFK's mind the benefits of having LBJ on the ticket outweighed the risks. Kennedy tried to allay the fears of his staff who felt that Johnson was an old-fashioned politician out of sync with his campaign's style and message. "I'm forty-three years old," Kennedy told top aide Kenneth O'Donnell. "I'm not going to die in office. So the vice presidency doesn't mean anything."[21]

Although LBJ was excited at the prospect of being elected vice president, he hedged his bets. He convinced his friends in the Texas legislature to pass a new law that allowed him to seek the vice presidency and run for reelection as senator at the same time. If Kennedy lost, Johnson would return to his old Senate seat and be the front-runner for the nomination in 1964.

Johnson helped to deliver Texas for the Democratic ticket in 1960, but by the summer of 1963 when Kennedy began planning his trip, he was concerned that his vice president seemed to be doing little to help address the state's current political crisis. Frustrated by the lack of progress on the ground, Kennedy decided to take matters into his own hands. In June 1963, during a brief stopover in El Paso, he met privately with both Johnson and Connally to lay the groundwork for a multi-city trip to Texas.[22]

According to Connally, Kennedy stressed the importance of raising money during the trip. "If we don't raise funds in another state, I want to do so in Massachusetts and Texas," JFK said. The president talked about having four fund-raising dinners — in Houston, San Antonio, Fort Worth, and Dallas — and suggested they use LBJ's birthday, August 27, as the excuse for making the trip. Connally balked at the timing. "Mr. President, that would be the worst thing you could do. For the first thing, with you going in four or five places, everyone would say you are just interested in getting money. In the second place, that weekend at the end of August would be a bad weekend. All the rich folks will be up in Colorado cooling off, and all the poor people will be in Galveston and down around the Gulf Coast." The meeting ended with the three men agreeing to find an alternative date for a presidential visit in the fall.[23]

Neither Connally nor Johnson welcomed the presidential intrusion into Texas politics. JFK "was advised by me and by Connally and by several others not to come to Texas," LBJ reflected in a 1969 interview. The governor saw no benefit in being seen campaigning with a northern liberal in a state that was growing more conservative every day. "Many of the people who were Mr. Kennedy's most active supporters in Texas also tended to support my opponent," Connally reflected. It was a no-win situation for him. Campaigning with the president would energize his opponents and anger his base. But he also knew that if he failed to rally support for his own party's president in Texas, "it would be a political embarrassment that I would not be allowed to forget."[24]

For his part, Johnson wished Kennedy would let him manage the state's complicated politics. He believed that, given Connally's immense popularity in Texas, riding the governor's coattails represented the best strategy for keeping the state in the Democratic column in 1964. Johnson worried that instead of uniting the party, the president's presence in the state would only expose the widening political cracks between liberals and conservatives. More important, it would make LBJ appear weak. According to George Christian, who served as Governor Connally's press secretary and would later join the Johnson administration in the same capacity, "A lot of Texas had decided Kennedy was a big eastern liberal and Johnson was his lap dog."[25]

Kennedy likely sensed LBJ's discomfort with the trip and largely excluded him from the planning, choosing to coordinate directly with Connally. On October 4, Kennedy invited the governor to the White House for a private meeting. "How about those fund-raising affairs in Texas, John," he said, greeting him as he entered the Oval Office. Connally suggested that the president arrange for a two-day visit to four cities, but reiterated his earlier concern that multiple fund-raisers would make Kennedy look greedy and make it appear that money was the only reason for his visit. "They are going to think you are trying to financially rape the state," he said. Connally offered to host a single large fund-raising dinner in Austin.[26]

It was clear that the Texas trip was causing tension between Kennedy and Johnson. JFK did not give LBJ advance notice of his meeting with the governor. "I heard Connally was in town and I called him and asked him what it was about," LBJ reflected. That was when he learned that Kennedy was dealing directly with the governor and had cut him out of the loop. "He was distinctly irritated," Connally recalled.[27]

Despite some initial confusion in planning, the trip was scheduled for November 21. The plan was to visit five cities, which together were responsible for 36 percent of the Texas vote. The president planned to dedicate a $16-million aerospace medical center in San Antonio, then go to Houston for a dinner honoring Congressman Albert Thomas. Later that evening, the presidential party would fly to Fort Worth where they

44

would start the next day with a sold-out breakfast sponsored by the chamber of commerce. Then they would fly to Dallas for a brief luncheon address before traveling to Austin for a fund-raising reception at the governor's mansion. The president and First Lady would spend the evening at the LBJ ranch outside Austin.

To help soften his image in Texas, Kennedy asked Jackie to join him on the trip. Cultured, vibrant, and young — only thirty-one years old on inauguration day — the former Jacqueline Bouvier had become a surprising political and diplomatic asset for the president. He had worried that her sophisticated style, along with her elegant and expensive tastes in fashion, would be a liability. Instead, she added to the luster of the Kennedy White House, underscoring that the dowdy Eisenhower days had come to an end. Within a few months of moving into the White House, Jackie had become a cultural icon.

Despite her fame and popularity, the First Lady was a very private person. She never enjoyed the routine of politics, and often refused to attend luncheons with congressional wives and politicians. She focused her attention on redecorating the White House, and on inviting artists and musicians to perform. In February 1962, more than 46 million Americans tuned in to see her understated elegance and hear her whispery voice on a nationally televised tour of the White House. She also enjoyed elaborate state trips to foreign capitals. In June 1961, large crowds had come to see her in Paris, and she even managed to charm the crusty French president Charles de DeGaulle. At the end of the trip, JFK deadpanned, "I am the man who accompanied Jacqueline Kennedy to Paris, and I have enjoyed it."

The First Lady was reluctant to travel to Texas, which would be her first political trip since the 1960 campaign. She went into seclusion after the death in August of their son Patrick, who lived only thirty-six hours after birth. The tragedy did, however, bring the couple closer together, and seemed to be healing a marriage that had been significantly damaged by JFK's perpetual philandering. This newfound closeness seems to have been one of the primary reasons Jackie decided to make the Texas trip despite her abhorrence for politicking. "I know I'll hate every minute of it," she confessed in a letter to a friend. She would go, she said, because it was important to her husband. "It's a tiny sacrifice on my part for something that he feels is very important to him," she wrote.[28]

Throughout the fall, during the planning stages for the trip, the feuding between the two Texas factions plagued every decision and threatened to sabotage the trip before Kennedy stepped foot on Texas soil. White House advance man Jerry Bruno, assigned to work out the details of the presidential visit, had to navigate the huge political egos and bitter turf wars. "The split in the Democratic Party in Texas was obvious from the start," Bruno noted in a summary of the trip.

The problems started the minute he got off the plane on October 20. When he arrived in Texas he was greeted by a representative from the Yarborough camp and one from the Johnson camp. Both expected to be his guide. On October 29, Bruno had lunch with Connally, who insisted on maintaining complete control of the trip. "Either we select the stops and run the trips or the President can stay home," he told Bruno. "We don't want him." That was fine with Johnson. The vice president's point man for the trip, Cliff Carter, "kept insisting that Connally was the best man for Kennedy in Texas and he should be allowed to run the whole trip."[29]

Realizing that he needed the governor's cooperation, the White House initially gave in to his demands. With Connally running the show, Yarborough's supporters found themselves excluded from the planning. They complained about the cost of the $100-a-plate reception in Austin, fearing that the money would go into the coffers of the Johnson-Connally political machine and be used in the 1964 primaries against liberal candidates. They worried that Kennedy would be spending most of his time with well-heeled businessmen and little time meeting "regular" people. "It seems to me the party is making a grave mistake in ignoring the real Democrats," said a local party official. "Kennedy has tremendous loyalty among the lower income Mexicans and Negroes. But the way this trip has been handled, it hasn't gained him any friends among those who worked for him previously." Yarborough was outraged. "You can't just have a luncheon for the fat cats and not let the people see him," he told Connally.[30]

As they moved closer to the visit, the Kennedy advance team altered the original plans to accommodate the Yarborough faction. They asked the state party to agree that all the money raised would be used exclusively against Republicans. They also

48

added an outdoor rally in a parking lot in Fort Worth before the scheduled indoor breakfast meeting. And because Kennedy made it clear that he wanted to be seen by as many people as possible, they included motorcades at every city.

Although anxious about the entire trip, Johnson was especially worried about the Dallas stopover. They would be spending only three hours in the city, but Dallas was a base of right-wing extremism and had never been a welcoming place for him. In the final days of the 1960 campaign, a well-orchestrated crowd had swarmed LBJ and Lady Bird as they walked across the street in downtown Dallas for a planned speech at the Adolphus hotel. They shouted "Traitor," "Socialist," "Judas." Women grabbed Lady Bird's gloves from her hand and threw them into the gutter.

Johnson's fears were reinforced just a few weeks before their scheduled visit. UN ambassador and former two-time Democratic nominee for president, Adlai Stevenson, was attacked in Dallas by an angry mob of right-wing protestors. "There was something very ugly and frightening about the atmosphere," Stevenson noted.[31]

Because of the security concerns, both Connally and Johnson wanted Kennedy to make a quick stopover in Dallas, speak before a luncheon of businessmen, and leave without making any public appearances. The less exposure, the better. It would reduce the possibility of an embarrassing incident and also help Connally, who wanted to limit his association with the more liberal president by cutting back on the amount of time he spent with Kennedy in public. In particular, Connally opposed a motorcade through downtown Dallas. "I wanted to skip the motorcade and go directly to the Trade Mart for the luncheon." The Kennedy team refused to bend on this point. "The president is not coming down," O'Donnell said, "to be hidden under a bushel basket. Otherwise, we can do it from here by television."[32]

The president left the White House for the last time on the morning of Thursday, November 21, boarded *Air Force One,* and arrived in San Antonio early in the afternoon. Even before the plane landed, the feud had intensified. Yarborough, who had been in Washington on Senate business and was traveling back home with the president, was still upset with Connally. He complained that Connally had failed to even invite him to the reception at the governor's mansion. During the flight he issued a statement that sharply criticized the governor for failing to afford him the respect befitting a United States senator. "Gov. Connally is so terribly uneducated governmentally, how could you expect anything else?"[33]

While Kennedy was making his way from Washington to Texas, Johnson was at his ranch outside Austin preparing for the president's visit on Friday night. Late Thursday morning he took a private plane from Austin to San Antonio to ensure that he would be there early in order to welcome the president as he descended the steps of *Air Force One.* Later in the day, the two men traveled together to Houston for the dedication of the aerospace center. Reporters on the scene noted that the president and First Lady "appeared in radiant good humor as they drove in motorcades through San Antonio and Houston."[34]

The crowds were large and welcoming, but the ongoing squabble between Connally and Yarborough was threatening to drown out the message of party unity the trip was designed to promote. In San Antonio and again in Houston, Yarborough complained that Connally was excluding him and his supporters from events. Assuming that Johnson had conspired with Connally, Yarborough refused to ride in the same car with the vice president.

Kennedy was clearly annoyed by the ongoing squabble. That evening at the Rice Hotel in Houston, JFK summoned Johnson to his suite. It is unclear what they discussed. William Manchester claimed there was shouting and Johnson stormed out. Jackie, who was in an adjacent room, told him that she heard loud voices and then walked into the room just as Johnson was leaving. "He sounded mad," she said to her husband. "That's just Lyndon. He's in trouble," Kennedy responded.

Johnson later downplayed rumors that he and Kennedy had argued. He contended that Kennedy invited him to his room for a drink. "Kennedy had a scotch and water or whatever it was he drank. I had a scotch and soda." JFK said he had been told about the incident with Yarborough. "I told my staff people, 'Tell him he either rides in the car or he doesn't ride,' " LBJ recalled him saying. "Mr. President," he responded, "it doesn't make any difference." He said the meeting ended amicably. Later that evening, the presidential party flew to Fort Worth.[35]

The headlines in the local papers on Friday morning, November 22, forced Kennedy to take charge of the situation. The morning edition of the *Dallas News* carried a front-page story with two headlines about the party split:

STORM OF POLITICAL CONTROVERSY
SWIRLS AROUND KENNEDY ON VISIT
YARBOROUGH SNUBS LBJ

Johnson would later dismiss the stories. "It was the biggest [thing] ever since [French president Charles] de Gaulle farted," he said. Kennedy, however, was not amused. "Christ, I come all the way down here and make a few speeches — and this is what appears on the front page," he fumed. "I don't care if you have to throw Yarborough into the car with Lyndon. But get him there," he told White House aide Larry O'Brien.[36]

The presidential threat, along with the intervention of Texas congressman Albert Thomas, led to a temporary truce. Thomas pressured Connally to make some concessions to Yarborough, inviting him to the reception at the governor's mansion. At the same time, Thomas told the senator that his antics were hurting Kennedy more than Connally.

There was no hint of animosity the following morning, Friday, November 22, when the three men appeared in public. At 8:45 a.m., Kennedy, Johnson, Yarborough, and Connally stood in a misty rain in a parking lot across the street from their hotel to speak to a crowd that was unable to secure tickets to the chamber of commerce breakfast inside. They managed to hide their differences. They looked "like they were four fraternity brothers who hadn't met in twenty years," recalled White House press secretary Malcolm "Mac" Kilduff.[37]

The sight of an enthusiastic crowd standing in the rain provided a much-needed lift. "Money and power were represented at the breakfast, but the parking lot audience — made up of workers, mothers, and children — gave me more assurance about the mood of Texas," Johnson recalled. Kennedy was also elated.[38]

It was neither JFK nor LBJ, however, but rather the First Lady who seemed to attract the most interest. When the president initially appeared at the rally without Jackie, the crowd seemed disappointed. "Mrs. Kennedy is organizing herself," he said jokingly. "It takes longer, but, of course, she looks better than we do when she does it."[39]

Afterward, they moved inside for the main event — a breakfast meeting at the Hotel Texas for 2,500 guests. Kennedy returned briefly to the hotel to change and asked Johnson to come by his room. LBJ showed up at 10:02 a.m. and brought his sister, who lived in Fort Worth, with him. He told her to stay in the hallway until he could ask if the president would see her. When Johnson told JFK that his sister was outside the door, Kennedy responded, "Bring her in." JFK thanked her for the Texan hospitality. "You've been awfully good to us in Fort Worth." He then turned to Johnson. "Lyndon, there is one thing I'm sure of — it's that we're going to carry two states in the election if we don't carry any others, and those two are Massachusetts and Texas." Johnson responded, "We're going to carry a lot more than those two." It would be their last private conversation.[40]

At 10:37 a.m., the presidential party left their hotel for the short trip to Carswell Air Force Base and the eight-minute flight to Dallas's Love Field. The president's political advisers had decided to fly the thirty miles to Dallas in order to arrive in time for a midday motorcade through downtown to attract the largest possible crowds.

In keeping with tradition, *Air Force One* took off with the president onboard, followed a few minutes later by the plane carrying the vice president. During the flight, the planes hopscotched so that Johnson could officially welcome the president and First Lady in each city. When they landed at 11:35 a.m., local dignitaries greeted the Johnsons, who immediately joined the reception line to welcome the president and First Lady.[41]

When the president and First Lady stepped off the plane, Johnson noted that "a great roar went up from thousands of throats." LBJ was struck by "how radiant Mrs. Kennedy looked." Presidential aide Dave Powers recalled to William Manchester that they "looked like Mr. and Mrs. America." Jackie was wearing a pink wool suit with a matching pillbox hat. "Someone in the reception line added the final touch by presenting her with a bouquet of dark red roses," Johnson noted. "It all began so beautifully," recalled Lady Bird.[42]

# 2
# "They Do Love This President, Don't They?"

After disembarking from *Air Force One* in Dallas, the Kennedys spent several minutes working the fence line, shaking the hands of the well-wishers who had come to see them. "I touched him! I touched him!" some of the women squealed. As Jackie worked the receiving line, a reporter asked her how she liked campaigning again. "It's wonderful, wonderful," she said in her typically breathless voice.[1]

The Kennedys were all smiles, but LBJ looked miserable. Hugh Sidey, Washington bureau chief for *Time,* later told William Manchester that Johnson appeared "very dour and perfunctory." Johnson and Lady Bird refused to linger with the Kennedys along the fence. Instead, they shook a few hands, then walked to their car and waited for the motorcade to leave. Perhaps LBJ was still smarting from the scolding that Kennedy had presumably delivered the night before; or maybe the president's visit, and the ongoing Connally-Yarborough squabble, was reminding him of his own political impotence. The dispute continued to dampen the mood. When Senator Ralph Yarborough joined the Johnsons in the back seat of their limousine, LBJ refused to even acknowledge his presence. There was no exchange of pleasantries because neither man had anything pleasant to say to the other.

At 11:55 a.m., Kennedy climbed into his car for the nine-and-a-half-mile motorcade through the city en route to the Dallas Trade Mart, where he was scheduled to speak at a luncheon for local businessmen. To guarantee maximum exposure, Kennedy aides chose a circuitous route through the most populated parts of the city.[2]

The motorcade was massive. It consisted of twenty-two cars, three buses, and over a dozen Dallas police motorcycles; it extended more than a half-mile. At the front of the motorcade, in the lead car, were Dallas police chief Jesse Curry and two Secret Service agents. Five car lengths back was the presidential limousine — a specially designed twenty-one-foot-long, midnight blue, seven-passenger Lincoln convertible, which carried the Secret Service designation SS 100X. Agent Bill Greer was behind the wheel. Lead agent Roy Kellerman sat to his right. Governor Connally and his wife, Nellie, occupied the jump seats. President Kennedy sat directly behind the governor with Jackie to his left.

The president's car possessed a number of security features, including a running board, foot stands, and handholds so that agents could ride on the outside to provide an added layer of safety. The car also came equipped with a Plexiglas bubble top, which could be deployed in the case of rain. About thirty minutes before the president arrived, Kenneth O'Donnell ordered that the plastic top be removed. O'Donnell was following JFK's instructions. The president also insisted that the Secret Service stay off the running boards. Since it was a political trip, Kennedy wanted the crowds to be able to see him. He understood his appeal, and that of his wife.[3]

Directly behind the president's car was the Secret Service followup car, a Cadillac dubbed the "Queen Mary." The car carried six Secret Service agents, either in the car or standing on the running boards. Two close aides, Dave Powers and Ken O'Donnell, sat together in the jump seats keeping close watch on the president, the crowds, and the schedule.

The vice president's limousine, a light blue 1961 Lincoln convertible, rolled along about two-and-a-half car lengths behind the Queen Mary. The motorcade organizers kept a reasonable distance between the cars carrying the president and vice president so the crowd would have clear views of both men. A Dallas highway patrolman, Hurchel Jacks, sat behind the wheel while an alert Rufus Youngblood, the Secret Service agent in charge of the vice president's security detail, occupied the front passenger seat. Johnson sat directly behind Youngblood. Lady Bird was to his left, providing a buffer between the vice president and Senator Yarborough.[4]

Carrying Lyndon Johnson's security detail, a car nicknamed "Varsity" trailed a few feet behind. It carried agents Lem Johns, Jerry Kivett, and Woody Taylor, along with aide Cliff Carter. Since this was a presidential trip and a campaign stop, most of Johnson's senior advisers were back in Washington.

Dallas residents were clearly excited about the presidential visit and they turned out in massive numbers to get a glimpse of JFK and Jackie. The police estimated that approximately 150,000 people crowded the sidewalks that day to see the motorcade. Even when driving through the less populated areas, Johnson later recalled how struck he was by "the visible enthusiasm of the people along the route and their obvious good wishes." As they moved closer to the cluster of tall buildings in the downtown area on Main Street, the crowds grew in size and energy, and police officers struggled to keep people behind the barricades. With a bright sun and temperatures in the mid-seventies, many people decided to use their lunch hour to see the visiting dignitaries. The *New York Times* described the crowds as "thick, enthusiastic and cheering." Nearly everyone had been worried about some ugly incident, but the sea of smiling faces and waving hands put the fears to rest. Even Johnson, who had been among the most concerned about the Dallas leg of the trip, later acknowledged that "Dallas was giving the President a genuinely warm welcome."[5]

The president's advisers were relieved to see the large crowds that had turned out to greet Kennedy. As they reached the downtown area, O'Donnell looked at the roaring crowds standing eight and ten deep, and hanging from the windows above. "There's certainly nothing wrong with this crowd," he said to Powers. Riding in the sixth car in the motorcade, Elizabeth "Liz" Carpenter, a Johnson press aide, turned to Jack Valenti, a local advertising executive who had helped organize the trip, and said, "They do love this president, don't they?"[6]

Not everyone in the motorcade was overwhelmed by the greeting. As they moved through the downtown area, Yarborough was looking upward at the people looking down from the skyscrapers. In his mind, most of the office workers had come down to the street level to give Kennedy a warm welcome, while their more conservative bosses stared down from the windows above. "Few of the people up *there* were smiling or waving," he later told William Manchester. Their faces, he said, were "hard and mad as hell at the reception he was getting on the street." It crossed his mind, he revealed in an interview the following year, that "anyone could throw a pot of flowers down on him from up there."[7]

Many people in the crowd roared when the president and First Lady drove past. A few seconds later they caught a glimpse of the car carrying Lyndon and Lady Bird. "There's Lyndon!" some shouted. "There's LBJ."

According to Yarborough, Johnson never acknowledged the well-wishers; instead he "stared glumly, straight ahead." Only a few times did he raise his right hand, offering a perfunctory wave of his large, white Stetson hat to the crowd. At one point, when Kennedy stopped the motorcade to shake hands with an onlooker, Johnson seemed annoyed by the delay. He told the driver to turn on the radio so he could hear the local coverage of the event. "It was turned up loud and was blaring and it was hard for me to hear my friends on the curb," Yarborough complained. The radio would remain on for the entire trip, even after the shots were fired at the presidential motorcade.[8]

Yarborough was not the only observer to comment on Johnson's dour mood that day. According to Ken O'Donnell, Johnson "sulked all through the trip." Veteran reporter Hugh Sidey, who had observed LBJ for many years, believed that the vice presidency had changed Johnson. "He didn't have anything to do," Sidey told Manchester, "and he became much less vital and more mechanical."[9]

On November 22, 1963, Lyndon Johnson was at one of the lowest points in his long political career. A ferociously ambitious man, he felt that his career in politics had hit a dead end. He had accepted Kennedy's offer to join the Democratic ticket in 1960 because he saw the vice presidency as a way for him to escape the taint of sectionalism and emerge as a politician with national appeal. He believed that he could transform the sleepy office of the vice presidency into a power base that would allow him to win over powerful Democratic leaders. This would put him in position for a possible run for the presidency in 1968.

After almost three years on the job, however, Johnson's high hopes had been dashed. Lady Bird later referred to this period as "Lyndon's quiet years, out of the arena." Part of the problem was institutional. The vice president's sole constitutional duty, other than to succeed the president, was to preside over the Senate. He was not even a full member of the executive branch. He could not propose legislation or sign it into law, nor could he veto bills, appoint executive officials, or take over any of the significant duties of the president. As Senate majority leader he had been at the center of the legislative action; now as vice president he was forced to sit on the political sidelines.[10]

Upon becoming vice president, Johnson

had hoped to retain some of the power of his previous role. Scheming to keep his hands in Senate business, he asked his former colleagues to allow him to become chairman of the Democratic Conference. Seeing the move as a clear violation of the separation of powers, his colleagues refused. The rejection stung LBJ. "Now I know the difference between a caucus and a cactus," he said. "In a cactus all the pricks are on the outside."[11]

While clinging to past legislative powers, LBJ hoped to claim new executive responsibilities. Shortly after the inauguration, Johnson sent JFK a memorandum outlining a new role for the vice president, providing him with "general supervision" of a number of executive agencies. JFK chose to ignore the memorandum, but White House aides tried to humiliate LBJ by leaking it to the press. They compared LBJ to William Seward, who had made a similar power grab as Abraham Lincoln's secretary of state.[12]

Although he rejected LBJ's effort to redefine the vice presidency, JFK shared Johnson's desire to expand the powers of the office. Kennedy wanted to keep Johnson happy, if for no other reason than to prevent him from undermining the administration's agenda. "I can't afford to have my Vice

President, who knows every reporter in Washington, going around saying that we're all screwed up, so we're going to keep him happy," he told an aide.[13]

In an effort to appease his vice president's desire to play a more active role in the White House, the president insisted that LBJ be included in all official ceremonies and meetings. He asked him to supervise the space exploration program, which was a top administration priority, and to chair the President's Committee on Equal Employment Opportunity. As a sign of his new power, Johnson became the first vice president in history to have an office in the executive branch — an impressive six-room suite in the Executive Office Building.

Despite his good intentions, however, Kennedy never figured out an effective way to use his vice president. Worried that Johnson's enormous ego could hurt more than help on Capitol Hill, he failed to include him in deliberations on key legislative initiatives. Although LBJ may have been one the most successful legislators of his generation, Kennedy aides rarely asked for his advice or allowed him to do what he did best — twist arms, make deals, and count votes.

Johnson sat helplessly on the sidelines as

the great promise of the New Frontier stalled in Congress. Kennedy had begun his presidency by calling for an increase in the minimum wage, an extension of health insurance for seniors, and expanded federal spending on education, housing, and aid for depressed areas. But by November 1963, Congress had acted on only one of his New Frontier proposals. Johnson, the master legislator, scoffed at the competence of the White House legislative effort but had little power to change it. "They don't have any idea of how to get along and they don't even know where the power is," he complained to an aide in 1963.[14]

Although institutional obstacles blocked Johnson from realizing his hopes of leading a more activist vice presidency, differences in personality and style also played a role. Johnson's background was worlds away from that of the other members of the Kennedy administration. The top Kennedy men — and they were all men — were sophisticated and well mannered. Most had attended elite East Coast preparatory schools, traveled the world, and relished their roles as the "best and brightest" of their generation. They were as comfortable in Manhattan and Palm Beach high society, and the highbrow intellectual centers of Cambridge and New Haven, as they were inside the Beltway.

To them, Lyndon Johnson seemed culturally and socially alien. His manner was antithetical to the sophisticated style that defined the New Frontier. He scratched his private parts, belched loudly at meals, picked his nose in public, and speckled his speech with profanity. At state dinners, he piled large portions of food on his plate and seemed to inhale them. Jackie cringed when she heard LBJ describe UN ambassador Adlai Stevenson as someone who "squats to piss."[15]

Johnson was an endless source of amusement for the Kennedy crowd, the subject of mean-spirited jokes and bitter snipping. "Really, it was brutal, the stories that they were passing," recalled a Kennedy friend, "and the jokes, and the inside nasty stuff about Lyndon." Some refused to call him "Mr. Vice President." Instead they simply referred to him as "Lyndon." Despite the president's stated desire to have Johnson attend all top-level meetings, members of his staff frequently would "forget" to invite the vice president. Tip O'Neill, then a young congressman from Massachusetts, reflected that the Kennedy inner circle "had a disdain for Johnson that they didn't even try to hide, and they relished talking about his crudeness and mocking the vulgarity of his language. They actually took pride in snubbing him."[16]

Robert Kennedy, who secured a position as attorney general in the administration, emerged as LBJ's chief critic in the White House. In many ways, the two men were natural antagonists. Johnson, who was seventeen years older and six inches taller, was a natural politician: an expansive, back-slapping, practical deal maker, always willing to bend facts to serve a larger purpose. RFK was an introvert who loved politics but disliked most politicians.[17]

RFK never forgave LBJ for breaking the promise he had made not to block JFK's nomination or to be a candidate. Johnson, he said, "lies all the time. . . . In every conversation I have with him, he lies. . . . He lies even when he doesn't have to." RFK still bristled with anger over Johnson's last-minute effort to "steal" the nomination in 1960 by spreading rumors about his brother's health."[18]

Johnson, in turn, viewed Robert Kennedy as an ambitious, spoiled lightweight, someone who refused to show him the proper deference. Dismissing RFK as "the snot-nosed little son-of-a-bitch," he resented his sense of privilege and his arrogance. Johnson also deeply resented RFK's access to the president — access which he was himself denied. LBJ had hoped to serve as President Kennedy's closest adviser, but he watched helplessly as RFK usurped many of the powers he had hoped to exercise. Johnson had a strong paranoid streak as well, and was convinced that RFK spent most of his waking hours plotting his downfall. "Johnson had contrived in his own mind a very complex plot against him being led by Bobby Kennedy," observed LBJ's press secretary George Reedy. "Bobby couldn't do anything that would please LBJ," said Reedy, "except commit suicide."[19]

Their antagonism grew as much from their similarities as from their differences. Although he claimed to detest Johnson for his dishonesty, RFK himself did not object to telling lies — about his brother's health, for example — when it served his family's political ambitions. He dismissed Johnson's brokering compromises with unsavory characters to win elections. RFK never had to make those deals because his father took care of much of the dirty work himself. Both men could be ruthless, take-no-prisoners political gladiators who were willing to do whatever it cost to gain the upper hand. They were also men of noble vision and great passion for helping the poor.[20]

In the weeks leading up to the Texas trip, Johnson worried that RFK was orchestrating a campaign to discredit him — to force him off the ticket in 1964 by tying him to an emerging scandal involving an old Senate aide, Bobby Baker. As secretary to the Senate majority leader, Baker had amassed considerable power, even earning the title of "the 101st senator." In 1962, the Federal Bureau of Investigation (FBI) launched an investigation into a luxury motel Baker co-owned in Ocean City with two mobsters. The following year, after more accusations of a possible kickback scheme involving federal defense contracts, Baker was forced to resign his position in the Senate. He eventually spent time in prison. Although there was never any evidence tying Johnson to wrongdoing, and nearly all the crimes that Baker was accused of took place after Johnson became vice president, the scandals tapped into longstanding allegations that Johnson was corrupt.

RFK wanted LBJ off the ticket in 1964, but his brother had the only vote that counted, and he dismissed talk of dumping Johnson. In a news conference on October

31, a reporter, referring to "talk that Lyndon B. Johnson would be dumped next year," asked Kennedy if he wanted Johnson on the ticket and if he expected him to be on the ticket. "Yes to both those questions," JFK said.[21]

By November 1963, despite the frustrations and disappointments, Johnson and JFK had managed to forge a respectful, if distant, relationship. The reporter Charles Bartlett recalled that JFK dismissed LBJ as "uncouth and something of an oaf," but he respected his dedication and skill and appreciated his sardonic humor. The president did not share his brother's animosity toward Johnson. Perhaps JFK recalled that it was Lyndon Johnson who helped him secure a position on the Senate Foreign Relations Committee, an important step in his emergence as a national political figure; or that Johnson, as a member of the Texas delegation, had cast his state's votes for him during his furtive campaign to secure the vice presidential nomination in 1956. If nothing else, Kennedy, the consummate political pragmatist, understood that he needed LBJ to slow Republican gains in the South and allow him to win reelection in 1964.[22]

LBJ found his boss charming and bright, but also resented him. He never lost the sense that he was more qualified than JFK for the job, and he could not appreciate why the public found him so captivating. "He never said a word of importance in the Senate and he never did a thing," LBJ said. "But somehow . . . he managed to create the image of himself as a shining intellectual, a youthful leader who would change the face of the country. Now, I will admit that he had a good sense of humor and that he looked awfully good in the god-damn television screen and through it all was a pretty decent fellow, but his growing hold on the American people was a mystery to me."[23]

Despite his personal feelings, Johnson nonetheless remained fiercely loyal to the president. He never violated the cardinal rule that vice presidents should be seen and not heard, and was careful never to upstage the president. Reporters who had covered him for years were surprised by his refusal, in public or private, to say anything disparaging about JFK. "I do not know of any reporter who got a 'leak' from Johnson that damaged or denigrated the President," observed *New York Times* reporter Tom Wicker. "In fact, Johnson leaks of any kind were few and far between throughout his vice-presidency."[24]

The president delegated the job of "handling" Johnson to his close friend and chief aide, Kenneth O'Donnell. At the age of thirty-six, he had earned the title of appointments secretary, but he really served as a de facto chief of staff. A 1963 *Wall Street Journal* article described O'Donnell as "the first person the president sees in the morning and the last one he sees at night." He oversaw the president's daily schedule, supervised the West Wing staff, and coordinated all travel and security arrangements.[25]

O'Donnell had a long history with JFK and the Kennedy family. Like Kennedy, O'Donnell was a World War II veteran and genuine hero, who won the Distinguished Flying Cross as a bombardier in a B-17 squadron. Like many other veterans, he went to college after the war, enrolling at Harvard, where he met the president's brother, Robert Kennedy. The two men became close friends, and when Robert managed his brother's first Senate campaign in 1952, he asked O'Donnell to serve as his chief lieutenant.

Over the years, O'Donnell won the respect and affection of both JFK and RFK by being tight-lipped, self-effacing, shrewd, tough, and completely loyal. "You see

Kenny there?" Kennedy once said to an aide while O'Donnell slept on a plane. "If I woke him up and asked him to jump out of this plane for me, he'd do it. You don't find that kind of loyalty easily." O'Donnell, along with Dave Powers and Lawrence O'Brien, were the core members of Kennedy's "Irish mafia." All three had worked for Kennedy for many years and shared a deep personal devotion to him. Manchester claimed that O'Donnell ultimately developed a "quiet almost fanatical devotion" to the president.[26]

"Handling" Johnson was not a pleasant task for O'Donnell. He had opposed the decision to put Johnson on the ticket in the first place. "I was so furious that I could hardly talk," he recalled. He never deviated from his original position that offering Johnson the vice presidency was a "disaster" and "the worst mistake" JFK had ever made.[27]

Although sympathetic to his reservations, Kennedy gave O'Donnell explicit instructions to do whatever it took to keep the vice president happy. "I just want you to know one thing," JFK once said to O'Donnell. "Lyndon Johnson was Majority Leader of the United States Senate, he was elected to office several times by the people. He was the number one Democrat in the United States, elected by us to be our leader. I'm President of the United States. He doesn't like that. He thinks he's ten times more important than I am, he happens to be that kind of a fellow. But he thinks you're nothing but a clerk. Just keep that right in your mind." Kennedy went on to say that elected officials had a "code," which required them to show each other deference "whether they like each other or hate each other. . . . You have never been elected to anything by anybody, and you are dealing with a very insecure, sensitive man with a huge ego. I want you literally to kiss his ass from one end of Washington to the other."[28]

O'Donnell and the president worked out a routine for dealing with Johnson's many grievances. Most of the complaints involved Bobby — "that kid brother of yours," as Johnson called him. According to O'Donnell, the president would listen to LBJ's protests in private. He would then call O'Donnell into his office and denounce him "in front of Johnson for whatever the Vice-President was beefing about." O'Donnell would "humbly take the blame and promise to correct the situation, and the Vice-President would go away somewhat happier." O'Donnell, however, rarely followed up on his promises and the problems persisted.

Kennedy realized that keeping Johnson happy would require more than an occasional dressing down of his appointments secretary in the Oval Office. "I cannot stand Johnson's damn long face," Kennedy complained to Georgia senator George Smathers in 1961. "He comes in, sits at the cabinet meetings, with his face all screwed up, never says anything. He looks so sad." Smathers suggested that Kennedy send Johnson abroad as a roaming ambassador. "A damn good idea," Kennedy responded.[29]

Kennedy took the advice to heart and sent LBJ packing. Reflecting on his years as vice president, Johnson remembered "trips around the world, chauffeurs, men saluting, people clapping [and] chairmanships of councils, but in the end, it is nothing. I detested every minute of it." In less than three years, he made eleven foreign trips and visited thirty-three countries. More subdued in Washington, his worse qualities became exaggerated on these trips. Like a spoiled child, he made a long list of demands for each trip: an oversized bed, a shower attachment that guaranteed a strong spray, two dozen cases of Cutty Sark, five hundred boxes of autographed ballpoint pens, and six dozen cases of cigarette lighters.[30]

Foreign travel may have satisfied LBJ's inflated ego, but the time spent on the road further eroded his influence in the White House. By November 1963, Johnson had little contact with the president. The president's secretary estimated that in their first year in office, Johnson spent a total of more than ten hours in private meetings with JFK. By 1963, that number had shrunk to less than two hours.[31]

As he lost direct access to the president, Johnson was forced to find other ways to get messages to him. On one occasion, his press aide, Liz Carpenter, called Kennedy friend and journalist Charles Bartlett: "Couldn't you get him to call the Vice President and ask him more opinions about things because he feels awfully lonely up here?" Bartlett told Kennedy the story. The president responded sympathetically. "I feel so sorry for that guy," he said. "You know, when you get into an exciting one or when you get into a hot one, you just don't think to call people who haven't read the cables."[32]

Inevitably, as early as 1962 the press began writing articles about how LBJ had lost power and influence in the White House. "Whatever has happened to Lyndon Johnson?" asked Copley News Service reporter Robert W. Richards in July 1962. "That's the question traveling the capital cocktail circuit these days about the fall from favor of the Vice President, only rarely heard from and occasionally seen about town." Why, he asked, "has Lyndon gone into eclipse?" The answer was simple: "he's been supplanted by the President's brother, Bobby Kennedy."[33]

As if Johnson was not already aware of the rumors, his supporters photocopied the articles and sent them to him with letters expressing their own anger at the way he was being treated. "In the nine months you've been in office I've seen you in the news exactly five times," a Texas supporter wrote. "If this sounds like sarcasm — it isn't. It's bitterness that you should have allowed yourself to be jockeyed into such an untenable position for 'the good of the Party,' " he wrote. "What has the President done to your executive powers?" asked another. "Why is *Brother Bobby* representing the United States in Foreign Countries instead of yourself?"[34]

Johnson defensively assured his supporters that he was an active member of the administration and key adviser to the president. "If I had the time, I might get a little annoyed with some of the newspaper reports about 'what is Johnson doing?' " After assuring his supporters that no "President and Vice President in history have had the close relationship — both professionally and personally — that President Kennedy and I have had," he went on to list his many important responsibilities in the administration. "I have tried to be the kind of Vice President I would want to have if I had been President."[35]

Despite his claims to the contrary, Johnson was miserable. The stress and strain showed. A man of such enormous energy and ambition simply had difficulty playing second fiddle to anyone. "Every time I came into John Kennedy's presence, I felt like a goddam raven hovering over his shoulder," Johnson said. He suffered from long bouts of depression during which he would have trouble getting out of bed and would sit for long hours staring at the ceiling. He drank too much Cutty Sark. In the summer of 1963, Harry McPherson, a close aide and friend, went to visit LBJ at his home and was shocked by his appearance. "He looked absolutely gross. His belly was enormous and his face looked bad, flushed, maybe he had been drinking a good deal." After looking in Johnson's eyes that summer, the social scientist Daniel Patrick Moynihan observed, "This is a bull castrated very late in life."[36]

Lyndon may have been in a dour mood, but Lady Bird, fifty-one, was as cheerful as ever. Only five feet four inches and weighing 118 pounds, she was overshadowed by the two men sitting on either side of her. As the motorcade snaked its way between the cheering crowds in downtown Dallas, Lady Bird was holding a bouquet of yellow roses and looking for people she might recognize. She had attended junior college in Dallas and still had friends in town. "The streets were lined with people — lots and lots of people — the children all smiling; placards, confetti; people waving from windows," she observed. "As we rode in cars I looked up from time to time and saw smiling faces in the windows of the buildings — I even saw a familiar face of my dress-fitter and we called out to each other."[37]

Her eyes were scanning the crowd, but her mind was probably on the dinner she would be hosting for the president that night at the ranch. Both Lyndon and Lady Bird wanted to make sure that everything went well. Lady Bird had arrived a week earlier to oversee the preparations. No detail was overlooked. They showed the White House Signals Corps, which handled all communications on presidential trips, where the special phones should be installed. They made sure the president had plenty of Poland water and Ballantine's scotch — two of his favorites. The First Lady preferred champagne and Salem cigarettes. Lady Bird made sure she had the terry-cloth towels that the First Lady liked for the bathroom. The president's special horsehair mattress, which he needed to provide support for his aching back, was flown in from Washington. Lady Bird personally prepared the linens and sheets. There would be fruit and flowers in every room.

Claudia Alta Taylor, who was nicknamed "Lady Bird" as a child, grew up in a wealthy, cultured, East Texas family. She fell in love with Lyndon Johnson the minute she saw him. This was in 1934, shortly after her graduation from the University of Texas with a degree in journalism. Meeting Johnson, she recalled, "was just like finding yourself in the middle of a whirlwind." After a ten-week courtship, he insisted she marry him. "I felt like a moth drawn to a flame."[38]

Despite her privileged background, and the access to power that Lyndon provided her, Lady Bird remained modest and down-to-earth. On their wedding day Lyndon forgot to buy a ring. At the last minute he sent his best man to the Sears across from the chapel to buy one for $2.98. Later, as their family fortune grew, Johnson would buy her expensive diamonds, perhaps to compensate for his emotional absence. But Bird, as LBJ called her, always treasured the original one from Sears. That was the one she wore when meeting royalty and entertaining at formal functions.

While Lyndon focused on his political career, Lady Bird took over responsibility for making money and paying the bills. In 1943, she used $17,500 of her inheritance to purchase a small Austin radio station, KTBC. In 1952, she purchased KTBC-7, a local television station affiliated with CBS. Her shrewd instincts, and Lyndon's political connections, allowed her to turn her small investment into a multimillion-dollar enterprise.

LBJ dictated nearly every aspect of Lady Bird's life, even picking out her dresses and telling her whether or not to wear lipstick. She served him coffee in bed every morning, along with the morning newspaper. She paid the bills, did the laundry, and had meals ready whenever he asked for them. She also endured his abuse. Clark Clifford recalled going to the Johnson home for dinner one evening when, in front of a room full of people, Lyndon decided that Lady Bird was wearing the wrong dress. "From the moment she appeared, he began attacking the dress, mockingly asking why she was wearing that 'dreadful yellow thing.' Finally, almost in tears, Lady Bird left the room before we sat down to eat, returning a few minutes later in another dress."[39]

There was an implicit bargain in the relationship between Lady Bird and Lyndon: she provided him with stability and advice; he offered her access to a wider world. LBJ made her feel worthwhile; she gave him the loyalty he required. They complemented each other: he provided the ambition; she offered support. Her compassion and sensitivity balanced his arrogance and ego. She was refined, cultured, and self-effacing; LBJ was crude, bombastic, and egotistical. "Ours was a compelling love," she once said. "Lyndon bullied me, coaxed me, at times even ridiculed me, but he made me more than I would have been. I offered him some peace and quiet, maybe a little judgment . . . I guess you could sum it up by saying we were better together than apart."[40]

It took the motorcade eight minutes to travel down Main Street. At 12:29 the car passed the Old Court House and turned right onto Houston. As they approached Dealey Plaza, Johnson knew that the motorcade was almost over. They had cleared the most congested part of the route and had only two miles left to the Trade Mart. Since most of that would be on a freeway, the crowds would thin out and they would pick up speed. "There was just about 12 to 14 blocks to go and I thought, 'It'll be good to get him out of this,' " Yarborough recalled.[41]

A few car lengths ahead, the presidential limousine had already made the sharp left turn onto Elm Street; it had started down a slope leading to an underpass and the ramp onto the highway that would take them to the Trade Mart. Jackie Kennedy had been uncomfortable sitting in the bright sunlight, but her husband insisted that she not put on her sunglasses. The whole purpose of the motorcade was to allow the crowds to see them and he did not want Jackie's face hidden behind a pair of dark sunglasses. Now she hoped the shade from the underpass would provide a brief reprieve from the sun. "I thought it would be cool in the tunnel," she recalled.[42]

Tragically, her husband would be dead before they made it into the shade.

# 3

# "THEY'RE GOING TO KILL US ALL"

As they turned onto Houston Street, Johnson could see Dealey Plaza on the left and the School Book Depository Building directly in front. A large sign on top of the building listed the time. It was 12:30 p.m. From the vice president's Secret Service car, Lem Johns radioed Rufus Youngblood, "Five Minutes to the Trade Mart." Youngblood turned around and passed the information back to Johnson.[1]

While Johnson continued to stare glumly ahead, Youngblood kept a careful eye on the crowd and listened intently to the Secret Service chatter on his radio. He would be Johnson's constant companion for the rest of the day, rarely more than a few feet away. The soft-spoken Georgia native had joined the Secret Service in 1951, and after a brief stint in the Atlanta field office, Youngblood moved to Washington where he joined the White House detail protecting Harry Truman and, later, Dwight Eisenhower. In 1957, he transferred back to the Atlanta field office to be closer to his family. He returned to Washington and to the White House detail in 1960, just in time for the new administration.

Youngblood first met the vice president in March 1961, when he was assigned to provide protection for Johnson during a trip to Senegal. Although they had never met before, Youngblood was already aware of LBJ's reputation as a demanding and temperamental man.

It was an awkward but revealing first meeting, Youngblood later recalled in his memoir. LBJ and Lady Bird were attending a formal luncheon on the last day of the trip, when Johnson announced that he was tired and wanted to return to the embassy to rest. His driver, however, had decided to take a break so Youngblood had to find another car to transport the vice president back to the embassy. The only car available was an old Plymouth sedan.[2]

Leaving Lady Bird behind at the luncheon, Johnson climbed into the back seat of the car alone. By the time Youngblood approached there were already three people in the front seat. Realizing that four people would be too many, Youngblood told them to go; he would catch up with them later. "Hold it," Johnson said, leaning out the window. "Come on, son, hop in. No use you standing out there in the hot sun." Instinctively, Youngblood opened the front door, but Johnson swung open the back door. "Climb in back here. No use crowding." As he got in and sat down, it occurred to Youngblood that in nearly ten years of riding with presidents "and an occasional Vice President," this was "the first time I had ever shared the back seat with one of them. And one I had not formally met, to boot."[3]

After the initial kindness, LBJ revealed his gruffer side when he started grilling Youngblood. "How'd you fellows get over here?" he asked. Youngblood must have looked puzzled by the question. "Your advance group, how'd you get here to Dakar?" Johnson repeated. Youngblood explained they flew Pan Am. Through pursed lips, Johnson persisted: "What'd your ticket cost?" Youngblood said he had no idea. "Well, you'd better always find out how much your ticket costs and know how much of the taxpayers' money you're spending," Johnson admonished him.[4]

Johnson, however, had good reason to be

concerned about the cost of Youngblood's ticket. At the time, the vice president was not guaranteed Secret Service protection. If LBJ wanted protection, he had to formally request it, which also meant that he would need to defend the expenditure before the appropriate congressional committees. Initially, Johnson followed Vice President Nixon's example of asking for protection only during foreign trips, which became more frequent as his influence in Washington waned. There was rarely much preparation for these trips. One morning, Youngblood called the vice president's secretary to see if there were any upcoming plans that would involve the Secret Service. "Well, we might have a trip to Berlin coming up," she said. "Okay," Youngblood responded. "What's the approximate date? "Today," she said.[5]

The policy changed dramatically in October 1962, at the beginning of the Cuban Missile Crisis, when Kennedy signed into law new legislation giving the Secret Service full-time responsibility to protect the vice president. Almost overnight, the vice president's detail went from an occasional two-man team to a full-blown staff of twenty-six agents working full time.

Even with the added protection, security

for the vice president remained casual and open in a way that seems shocking by contemporary standards. For instance, Johnson often flew commercial when traveling domestically, even though he could request access to a government plane. (Occasionally, the Kennedy White House turned down these requests.) It was not uncommon for passengers waiting for a flight to see the vice president, along with a few Secret Service agents, sitting in the airport waiting area reading the newspaper.[6]

The security arrangements for the Johnsons' private residence were also lax. The Johnsons lived in a private home called the Elms on Fifty-second Street in northwest Washington. It was a French-style house ideal for entertaining, but difficult to protect. There were minimal security measures in place. LBJ's home phone number was listed in the Washington phone book. There were a few alarms, but the front gates were usually open, and friends often just walked up and knocked on the front door.

Johnson chafed under the new security requirements imposed in 1962. On a hot night the following summer, a group of local teenagers jumped over the fence around the Elms in the hope of using the vice presidential pool. Their movements tripped one of the alarms and alerted the Washington, D.C., police. When the story made the local papers, Johnson exploded. He felt the Secret Service and police overreacted to a bunch of kids looking for some relief from the heat. "I want you to get all that damn alarm equipment off the place!" he screamed at Youngblood. It took the Secret Service days to talk him out of removing the security alarms.

Like most people who worked with Johnson, Youngblood found him complicated and difficult. He was "a man of many moods" who possessed an explosive, hair-trigger temper, Youngblood wrote in his memoirs. He could be warm and sentimental, but he "also had the capacity of chewing you out in a way that would have been the envy of a seasoned Marine drill instructor." The key to working with Johnson, he discovered, was to be able to adjust to the pendulum swings. Not every agent could. "There were many agents who would never have flinched under the assault of a thousand assassins, yet who wilted at the thought of LBJ," he wrote.[7]

"We went down Main Street and almost to the end [where] you enter a big freeway," Lady Bird recalled of the seconds before the first shots were fired. "The crowds began to get thinner and I remember we were some 5 minutes behind schedule. There was sort of a long grassy slope on the sides with people standing and I saw a tall red brick building on the hill as we were approaching the underpass. I heard a loud crack — a second passed — and then I heard 2 loud cracks." There had been such a "gala air" to the parade that Lady Bird assumed she was hearing firecrackers.[8]

Sitting next to her, Lyndon heard "an explosion," but did not know what it was and was not initially alarmed. "I just thought it was firecrackers or a car backfiring," he recalled. "I had heard those all my life. Any politician — any man in public life — gets used to that kind of sound."[9]

In the front seat, Youngblood wasn't sure whether he was hearing backfire from a motorcycle, firecrackers, or a gunshot. It was what he saw that alarmed him: unusual movements in the presidential car and bystanders running for cover and throwing themselves on the ground. He turned around toward Johnson and shouted "get down" in "a gruff voice I had never heard him use," recalled Lady Bird. Johnson, perhaps startled, barely moved, only slightly dipping his head.[10]

Senator Ralph Yarborough immediately knew that what he had heard was the blast from a high-powered rifle. He had handled guns since he was ten years old and owned more than a dozen rifles. "At the first shot, I knew right away it was a rifle shot," he told William Manchester in 1964. "I began to smell it before the second shot, and I thought that was odd. The reason I smelled it is that we were right under the trajectory — right in front of the muzzle blast." Even though he knew that everyone in the car was in grave danger, his competition with Johnson prevented him from ducking. "I didn't want to lean too far if Lyndon Johnson and Lady Bird were not going to do it," Yarborough told Manchester. "My first thought was that I am a Senator from Texas and I can't be a coward."[11]

Seeing that Johnson remained upright, Youngblood vaulted over the front seat before the second shot was fired, grabbed Johnson forcefully by the shoulder, and forced him to the ground. "Get down!" he shouted. "Get down!"[12]

The agents protecting President Kennedy were not able to act as quickly as Youngblood. Since he was riding in a standard Lincoln, Youngblood had easy access to

Johnson. Kennedy's car was much bigger. In order to reach the president from his seat in the front of the specially designed car, Roy Kellerman would have had to climb over a large divider and over Governor Connally.

According to the Warren Commission, the first shot missed its mark. The second hit Kennedy in the back, exited through his throat, and then struck John Connally. "My God," Connally cried. "They're going to kill us all!" Kellerman believed that he heard Kennedy say, "My God, I am hit." After the second shot, Nellie Connally pulled her husband into her lap and covered his body. Then a third shot rang out, exploding Kennedy's head and showering her with blood, bone, and brains. Both Nellie Connally and her still conscious husband heard Mrs. Kennedy say, "They've killed my husband, I have his brains in my hand."[13]

Mrs. Kennedy described what she saw to journalist Theodore White a few weeks after the assassination. "They were gunning the motorcycles; there were these little backfires; there was one noise like that; I thought it was a backfire," she said. "Then next I saw Connally grabbing his arm and saying 'no, no no, no, no,' with his fist beating — then Jack turned and I turned. . . . His expression was so neat; he had his hand out, I could see a piece of his skull coming off," she said. "He was holding out his hand — and I can see this perfectly clean piece detaching itself from his head; then he slumped in my lap; his blood and his brains were in my lap."[14]

No one who witnessed the third shot that hit Kennedy ever doubted that he was dead. Agent Paul Landis, riding in the backup car, described to the Warren Commission the sound of the bullet hitting Kennedy's head as "the sound you would get by shooting a high-powered bullet into a five gallon can of water or shooting into a melon." The result was devastating. "I saw pieces of flesh and blood flying through the air and the President slumped out of sight toward Mrs. Kennedy. . . . My immediate thought was that the President could not possibly be alive after being hit like he was," Landis testified.[15]

From their seats in the "Queen Mary," Dave Powers and Ken O'Donnell watched helplessly as the fatal third shot struck Kennedy's head. "Kenny and I not only saw the next one," Powers told Manchester, "we heard it. We just saw that handsome head get blown off. We heard the shot and we heard the impact of the shot. It was the most sickening thing — like a grapefruit thrown against a brick wall." O'Donnell recalled that he was looking at the president when "the third shot took the side of his head off. We saw pieces of bone and brain tissue and bits of reddish hair flying through the air. The impact lifted him and shook him limply, as if he was a rag doll, and then he dropped out of our sight, sprawled across the back seat of the car." After the third shot, O'Donnell turned to Powers and said, "He's dead."[16]

Another agent, Clint Hill, jumped off the backup car, sprinted toward the president, and leaped onto the back of the limousine. "As I lay over the top of the back seat I noticed a portion of the President's head on the right rear side was missing and he was bleeding profusely," Hill wrote in his official report. "Part of his brain was gone. I saw a part of his skull with hair on it lying in the seat."[17]

According to Landis's testimony before the Warren Commission, Hill looked at the president's wound and gave a thumbs-down signal with his hand. Realizing that Johnson may now be the president, Agent Emory Roberts, the shift supervisor, instructed two agents in the Queen Mary to protect LBJ as soon as they stopped. "They got him," he said to Agent William McIntyre. "You and Bennett take over Johnson as soon as we stop."[18]

Within seconds of the third shot, the presidential limousine was racing to the hospital. "We were floating in yellow and red roses and blood," recalled Nellie Connally. "It was a sea of horror." In the back seat, Jackie cradled her husband's body. "All the ride to the hospital I kept bending over him saying 'Jack, Jack, can you hear me. I love you Jack. I kept holding the top of his head down trying to keep the brains in."[19]

Lying on the floor of his limousine with Youngblood spread out on top of him, Johnson heard the second and third explosions but had no idea what was transpiring ahead of him in the presidential limousine.[20]

Desperate to get information about what was taking place and what steps needed to be taken, Youngblood pulled a two-way radio over the seat. Since the president's and vice president's security teams had different radio frequencies, Youngblood immediately switched to "Charlie" frequency to overhear the chatter on the president's Secret Service line. He learned that they were headed to Parkland Hospital.[21]

LBJ was able to pick up fragments of

information, but not enough to give him a clear sense of what was happening. Within a few seconds after the third shot, he recalled overhearing the crackling voices on Youngblood's radio — "Let's get out of here quick" — and he felt the car accelerate. "We wheeled around a corner, careening over the curb — almost, it seemed to me, on two wheels." As they sped to Parkland Hospital he could hear Youngblood shouting instructions to the driver. "Close it up. Follow the car in front." He may have heard Youngblood using code names such as Dandy, Halfback, Varsity, but it would have been gibberish to him. "I still was not clear about what was happening," he reflected about the drive to Parkland Hospital.[22]

Although he was pressed close to the floor, LBJ was concerned about Lady Bird. He glanced over a few times to make sure she was crouched down and safe. No one cared about Yarborough, who kept asking the same question: "Has the President been shot?" No one answered. "They didn't speak," he recalled.[23]

The five lead cars broke away from the rest of the motorcade, hitting speeds of seventy to eighty miles an hour as they raced north on the Stemmons Expressway toward Parkland Hospital. The cars took the Wycliff exit and turned right onto Industrial Boulevard. The driver of the vice president's car, Hurchel Jacks, stayed tight, lingering just a few feet behind the presidential follow-up. As they sped past the Trade Mart where 2,500 people were waiting to hear the president, Johnson still did not know that the president had been shot. "What happened, Rufus?" Johnson asked. "Where are we going?" He knew that something had gone horribly wrong. "Was it a bomb? A bullet? A firecracker exploding in front of someone's face? And who was hurt?"[24]

Youngblood did not know for sure what had happened, but he assumed the worst. "The President must have been shot or wounded, sir," Youngblood told LBJ. "We're being directed to a hospital." He again told everyone to stay down until he received more information on what was happening. "All right, Rufus," Johnson said.[25]

As they approached the hospital, Youngblood received further instructions from Emory Roberts: "Rufe, keep your man covered," he said. Roberts realized that if there was a conspiracy to decapitate the U.S. government, Johnson was still a potential target. Their route to the hospital was predictable, and another gunman could be

100

waiting to take a shot at Johnson. "Simply because the explosions were behind us did not necessarily mean that there could not be more at any moment," Youngblood recalled in his memoirs.[26]

It was incredibly noisy in the car. The radio was at full volume, the wind howled through the convertible as it raced at top speed, and sirens blared all around. To shout more instructions at Johnson, Youngblood had to lean down so he was only a few inches from the vice president's ear. "When we get to the hospital," he told LBJ, "I want you and Mrs. Johnson to stick with me and the other agents as close as you can. We don't know the extent of the emergency in the President's car, but it may be necessary for you to be Acting President." As they approached the hospital, Youngblood went on, "We aren't gonna stop for anything or anybody. Do you understand? We will separate from the other party the moment we stop!"[27]

The car made a sharp left turn into the emergency entrance of Parkland Hospital. "Get ready," Youngblood said, "we're almost there." Johnson looked over to his ashen-faced wife, "You ready, Bird?" "I'm ready," she replied. At 12:35 p.m., less than five minutes after the shooting, the limousine carrying Lyndon Johnson screeched to a halt outside the emergency entrance of Parkland Hospital.[28]

# 4
# "DAVE, HE'S DEAD"

As soon as the car stopped, Secret Service
agents swarmed around LBJ. "Secret Service men began to pull, lead, guide, and
hustle us out" of the car, Lady Bird recalled.
"As we got out of the car a flank of secret
servicemen and policemen closed around
Lyndon and almost made a wall and they
were walking with considerable speed. It
was obvious to me that these men were
protecting Lyndon and that was frightening
to me," she reflected. Other agents escorted
Mrs. Johnson, who hurried to keep up with
her husband.[1]

Because the vice president was surrounded
by so many guards, he was unable to get a
view of the bloodstained presidential limousine parked only a few feet away. Kennedy's
body lay motionless in the back seat, cradled
in the arms of a bloodstained First Lady,
but the vice president never saw him.
"Because of the method which Agent Young-

blood directed for leaving the car and entering the hospital, I did not see the Presidential car or any of the persons in it," Johnson told the Warren Commission. Lady Bird, however, peeked over her shoulder as she entered the hospital and saw "a bundle of pink, just like a drift of blossoms, lying on the back seat."[2]

As he was escorted from the car, Johnson remained very much in the dark about what had transpired. He knew from Youngblood that there had been an assassination attempt and that the president may have been injured. The phalanx of agents that surrounded him when he arrived at the hospital certainly could have tipped him off that the president had been shot. But he knew very little: Was Governor John Connally hurt? What about the First Lady? And, most important, how serious were Kennedy's injuries?

A small group of agents formed a protective circle around LBJ as Youngblood led him into the hospital. Neither he nor any of the other agents knew their way around the hospital, which must have seemed a maze of brightly lit corridors. Youngblood walked briskly, occasionally resting his arm against Johnson's back, pushing him to keep up. Johnson said nothing. "In situations like that, they're in command, and you don't question them," Johnson later explained. He followed Youngblood's instructions as a nurse pointed toward a doorway. There had been no time to prepare a secure space. The hospital staff had only a few minutes' notice that they were about to be invaded by dozens of gun-toting Secret Service agents with high-profile patients.[3]

Youngblood led Johnson through a double door and entered "minor medical," a large, blue-tiled room; illuminated by bright fluorescent lights overhead, it was used to treat walk-in patients. White curtains separated the room into several cubicles, each with a metal examination table.

Frantic Secret Service agents quickly secured the area. They cleared the one patient from the room and closed the blinds to prevent anyone from discovering Johnson's location. Youngblood stationed an agent at the door. "Nobody comes in here unless you know who he is and you know he's got a damn good reason to be here!" He escorted the Johnsons to a cubicle in the far corner of the room, farthest from the door. It was "a quiet room," Lady Bird recalled, "a very small room."[4]

"I'm sticking to you like glue," Youngblood told Johnson. "We're staying right here until we find out what's happened."

Johnson was cut off from the grisly scene that was unfolding just a few yards away.

As soon as they arrived at Parkland Hospital, Roy Kellerman had jumped out of the front seat of the presidential limousine and rushed to open the back door. At the same time, Emory Roberts leaped out of the backup car and ran to the president. Because they made the trip from the scene of the shooting in less than five minutes, no one from the hospital was there to meet them. "Go get us two stretchers on wheels!" Kellerman shouted.

Roberts opened the left rear door, trying to get access to the president. But the First Lady was cradling his body, refusing to let go. "Let us get the President," he said to Mrs. Kennedy. "No," she said. Roberts needed to confirm what he already suspected: Kennedy was dead. If he had somehow managed to survive a direct shot to the head, Roberts would need to get him medical help as quickly as possible. "I lifted her arm and saw the President's head and I knew that he was dead," he reflected.[5]

It was reasonable for Roberts to assume that Kennedy was already dead: a large portion of his head had been blown away, portions of his brain were scattered across the back seat, and his body was limp. The final version of the Warren Commission report, however, stated that JFK was technically still alive when he arrived at the hospital. The commission based its conclusion on the observation of a doctor who reported hearing "a few chest sounds which were thought to be heartbeats." But an earlier draft of the Warren Commission report described Kennedy's condition as "hopeless," stating that "from a practical standpoint, he was dead on arrival at Parkland."[6]

Roberts was not a doctor, but he had seen enough to convince himself that Kennedy was not alive. He immediately switched his mission to protecting Johnson. "My commission book directs me 'to protect the President of the United States,' and I regarded Johnson as the President," he said. "You stay with Kennedy," he told Kellerman, "I'm going to Johnson."[7]

As soon as the president's security car pulled up behind Kennedy's limousine, Dave Powers had jumped out of the follow-up car and, hoping that he would find him still alive, raced to Kennedy's side. When he saw the president lying in Jackie's arms with his eyes wide open, he thought for a second that he was conscious. "Oh, my God, Mr. President, what did they do?" A shell-shocked Jackie looked up at him and said, "Dave, he's dead." Powers broke down and cried.[8]

Senator Ralph Yarborough, who walked over to the presidential limousine as Johnson was being guided into the hospital, later described the scene to William Manchester. "Lace was laying over Lancer's body," he said, using the Secret Service code words for the President and First Lady. "Her body was rent with sobs. There was blood running down her legs. 'They've killed my husband, they've killed my husband,'" she said. Yarborough noted that Kennedy's "brain was shot out. Pools of blood — great globs of blood as broad and as thick as my hand were on the floor of the car."[9]

While everyone was focusing on Kennedy, Governor Connally lay across the jump seat directly in front of the president and First Lady. Nellie Connally, cradling her husband, was growing frustrated that everyone was focused on Kennedy, while her husband was writhing in pain. "How long do I have to sit here in deference to my president, who is dead?" she asked herself. The agents were not interested in helping Connally, but they needed to get him out of the way in order to get to the president. When the first stretcher arrived, agents helped the governor up and rushed him into the hospital, with Nellie stumbling behind him.[10]

With the jump seats clear, Kellerman maneuvered closer to the president, but Jackie refused to let go. Clint Hill took Mrs. Kennedy by the arm and pleaded tenderly. "Please let us remove the President." "No, Mr. Hill. You *know* he's dead. Let me alone." Hill quickly realized that she may have been refusing to let go because she did not want the onlookers who were gathering at the scene to see her husband's gaping head wound. Hill removed his sport coat and placed it over the president's head and shoulders. Only then did Mrs. Kennedy relent. "She fumbled for the flowers and covered his face with them," recalled Yarborough, "and the secret service covered his head with a coat, but his body was so limp — the head and legs were going every which way and they were trying to keep his coat over his head." As they loaded the president's body on a stretcher, a Secret Service agent picked up the purse, hat, and cigarette lighter that Jackie left behind in the back seat.[11]

The agents rushed Kennedy into the hospital, following an endless arrow on the floor, turning left and then right, heading

109

toward the trauma room. Hospital administrator Jack Price recalled that about eight to ten Secret Service agents surrounded the stretcher. Because the patient was covered with a coat, Price recalled, he did not know it was the president, but he recognized Mrs. Kennedy, who was running alongside. "At first I wondered what had happened to Mrs. Kennedy," he reflected. "The right lower part of her dress and her right leg looked as though it had been thickly painted." He was shocked when he "realized that it was not paint, but blood."[12]

It was obvious to the doctors who rushed to the trauma room to treat Kennedy that his wounds were fatal. Had he been just another patient, doctors would have declared Kennedy "dead on arrival." Dr. Malcolm Perry told reporters later that day: "We never had any hope of saving his life." Dr. Charles Carrico, the first physician to see the president, told the Warren Commission that JFK "was blue-white ashen in color" and had "no palpable pulse." Brain matter and tissue were oozing from the large open wound in the back of his head. He was, however, the president of the United States so the team of doctors engaged in a Herculean, but futile, effort to save his life. They performed a tracheotomy to clear his airway, inserted a tube into his chest cavity to drain fluid, poured steroids into his veins, and started closed-chest massage. Nothing worked.[13]

Across the hall in trauma room number two, physicians were having more success treating the governor, whose wounds were less severe than Kennedy's. Connally had "a large sucking wound" in his right chest and a collapsed lung, which was making it difficult for him to breathe. The doctors inserted tubes between his ribs to allow the lung to expand. Once they had the patient stabilized, they prepared to move him to an operating room on the second floor.[14]

While doctors worked on their patients, Mrs. Kennedy and Mrs. Connally stood across from each other in the hallway outside the trauma rooms. "Once or twice our eyes brushed across each other's, but there was no communication in those glances," recalled Mrs. Connally a year later. "We were two women, strangely isolated and curiously linked by a world-shaking event. Both of our pink suits were now bloodstained. Both of us were too shocked to speak or think coherently or grieve. Eventually, someone brought two straight chairs, and we both sat down."[15]

■ ■ ■ ■

Within minutes of the presidential party's arrival at 12:35 p.m., the corridors of the hospital started filling up with politicians, policemen, doctors, and nurses. Members of the press had arrived and were fighting for phone lines. "In the halls, all was chaos," reflected Elizabeth Forsling Harris, who had helped plan the visit for the Kennedy White House.[16]

Johnson, however, was unaware of almost all of it, isolated as he was in the medical examination room. He could hear the heels clicking on the hard tile floors as agents ran back and forth, and the frantic calls for doctors over the hospital speaker system. But he had no idea of the severity of the president's wounds.

At approximately 12:38 p.m., Emory Roberts joined Johnson in the small corner room and gave him his first report about the president's condition. Before speaking, Roberts picked up a plastic hospital chair and set it down for Johnson. Another agent grabbed a chair for Lady Bird. Johnson sat down for a few seconds, but quickly stood up. By all accounts, Roberts painted a grim picture of Kennedy's condition. In his testimony before the Warren Commission, Roberts claimed he said "that I did not think the President could make it and suggested that we get out of Dallas as soon as possible." According to Agent Jerry Kivett, Roberts "informed him that the President had been shot and was critically injured and probably would die." Youngblood recalled him saying, "It looks bad. Both the President and Governor Connally have suffered gunshot wounds. I don't know the Governor's condition, but I have seen the President and I don't believe he can make it." Roberts assured Johnson that both Nellie Connally and Jackie Kennedy were unharmed.[17]

Assuming that Johnson might also be a target for assassination, Roberts immediately urged him to leave the hospital and return to *Air Force One*. "You have got to get in the air," he said, believing that the vice president would be safer at 30,000 feet than on the ground in Parkland Hospital, and safer still back at the White House. Convinced that Kennedy was dead, and that Johnson was now president, Roberts never questioned that LBJ would eventually be returning to Washington on the plane that had carried JFK to Dallas.

Johnson was clearly confused, unsure of

the severity of Kennedy's wounds. "Maybe President Kennedy will need the airplane," Roberts recalled him saying. "He won't need it this day or this week or ever again," an excited Roberts responded, renewing his call for Johnson to leave the hospital. Youngblood repeated the point, adding a sense of urgency. "We should evacuate this hospital right away, get on that plane and get back to Washington," he said. "We don't know whether this is one man, two men, a gang or an army. The White House is the safest place to conduct the nation's business."[18]

As Youngblood and Roberts pressed the case for leaving the hospital, Johnson shook his head in defiance. "It would be unthinkable for me to leave with President Kennedy's life hanging in the balance," he told them.[19]

Of course, it is impossible to reconstruct with certainty what was going through Johnson's mind during these crucial minutes, but a large number of oral histories, memoirs, and contemporary notes give some indication. Obviously, Johnson was traumatized by the suddenness and brutality of the shooting. "My President and leader . . . my confidant and friend . . . both shot," he reflected in his memoirs, "both undergoing emergency treatment just yards from where I stood; both, for all I knew, dying." He felt genuine concern for the fragile Jackie Kennedy and for his friend Nellie Connally.[20]

It is also clear that, from the moment he learned that Kennedy was shot, Johnson assumed that the assassination was part of a larger conspiracy. "What raced through my mind was that, if they had shot our president, driving down there, who would they shoot next?" he told press aide Bill Moyers in a 1966 phone conversation that was captured by the White House taping system. "And what was going on in Washington? And when would the missiles be comin'?" He repeated the point in a 1970 interview with Walter Cronkite. "I think the first thought I had was that this is a terrifying thing that may have international consequences, and the problems that we'd had with Castro and what I had seen in intelligence reports and other things that concerned me, that this might be an international conspiracy of some kind."[21]

Why, then, did Johnson not rush to the airport? If he assumed that the shooting was potentially part of an international plot, the first move in a larger offensive — one in which he might also be a target — then it would have made sense for him to rush to

115

*Air Force One,* use its communications equipment to take control of the situation, then fly back to Washington as quickly as possible. Both Youngblood and Roberts were pushing hard for him to do so. Why, then, did Johnson reject their advice?

LBJ appeared to be thinking clearly, balancing a host of personal and political considerations. Since he was not a witness to the shooting and had not seen Kennedy's wounds, Johnson was being asked to leave the hospital based solely on Roberts's account of the president's condition. It was not unreasonable for him to want more information, or at least to get confirmation from another source, ideally a doctor or a member of Kennedy's staff. He was not going to leave the hospital based on the opinion of one Secret Service agent. According to Congressman Jack Brooks, who soon joined LBJ in his cubicle, it was "obvious that the President was seriously hurt. The Secret Service people were discussing with the VP whether he ought to leave now. They wanted him to leave now. VP thought he should not do that until they got a medical determination rather than a nonprofessional comment."[22]

Johnson was also a sensitive and shrewd politician, aware that the world's media would soon be focused on Dallas and on him. Would it look like he had panicked if he fled the hospital while Kennedy was still alive, fighting for his life? How would the public view his decision to leave the widow behind?

What probably worried him most of all was how the Kennedy loyalists, especially RFK, would interpret his actions. Fear of RFK likely shaped every decision Johnson made on November 22. Aware that the attorney general, and many other members of the Kennedy cabinet, viewed him as ruthless and power hungry, LBJ was determined not to provide them with ammunition that could be used against him. As aide Jack Valenti would later observe, "LBJ foresaw that he would be maligned for being so eager to be President that he left behind his predecessor's body."[23]

In addition, Johnson was aware of the complex legal issues that surrounded presidential succession. Article II, Section 1, of the Constitution spelled out the procedure for presidential succession in the event of death. It stated that if the president died in office, his powers "shall devolve on the Vice President."

History provided some guidance for how the process would take place. In 1841, when

William Henry Harrison became the first president to die in office, Congress debated whether the founders intended for the vice president to assume the title of president or simply the powers of the office. Vice President John Tyler insisted that he deserved both, but many in Congress wanted to refer to him as "Acting President." Because he was never elected, they claimed that he was "Vice President, now exercising the office of President." After a spirited debate, Congress accepted Tyler's assertion and settled the debate over presidential succession.

The Tyler precedent was upheld in all subsequent cases when a president died in office. Less than ten years later when President Zachary Taylor died in office, Congress without debate referred to Taylor's vice president, Millard Fillmore, as the "President of the United States." The following decade, Congress impeached Andrew Johnson as president, even though he assumed the office following the assassination of Abraham Lincoln.[24]

By 1963, seven presidents had died in office and in each case the vice president succeeded them, which meant that Johnson's path to the presidency was clear if Kennedy died. But what if he were disabled? What if the doctors managed to keep his heart beating? What then? The Constitution was silent on the question of presidential disability.

The question came up during Eisenhower's second term. In 1957, after he suffered a mild stroke, President Eisenhower and Vice President Nixon established a procedure for dealing with presidential disability. According to their understanding, the president would, if possible, inform the vice president of his disability. If he were suddenly disabled, the vice president, "after such consultation as seems to him appropriate under the circumstances," would assume the role of acting president.[25]

In a memorandum drafted shortly after assuming office, Kennedy and Johnson had agreed to continue the practice initiated by President Eisenhower. Their understanding, however, established specific criteria about whom the vice president must consult with before assuming the powers of the presidency. They agreed, "as a matter of wisdom and sound judgment, that the Vice President would wish to have the support of the Cabinet as to the necessity and desirability of discharging the powers and duties of the Presidency as Acting President." Probably more important from Johnson's perspective, the memorandum stated that the vice president must seek "legal advice from the Attorney General that the circumstances would, under the Constitution, justify his doing so."[26]

For LBJ, the question of whether Kennedy lived or died was key to how he would assume the presidency. If Kennedy died, the Constitution would make him president. If the president were disabled, however, the transition to power would be more complicated. LBJ would need to consult with the cabinet, but also with the attorney general, before assuming the power of the presidency. Given the animosity between the two men, and the contempt that RFK had for him, it must have crossed Johnson's mind that JFK's younger brother might try to block his ascension or, at the very least, conspire to limit his powers.

Given LBJ's paranoia about RFK, it's possible that he imaged a scenario where Kennedy's aides would attempt to disguise the seriousness of the president's injuries to prevent LBJ from becoming president. Would RFK assume the role of Edith Wilson, acting as de facto president for nearly two years while her stricken husband, Woodrow Wilson, lay in seclusion?

However far-fetched, it is reasonable to assume that these and quite possibly other similarly paranoid thoughts crossed LBJ's mind during these crucial first minutes.

It would seem that a combination of compassion and calculation convinced LBJ to remain at the hospital. He was genuinely concerned about the well-being of President Kennedy and Governor Connally, and still maintained hope that Roberts had exaggerated the extent of Kennedy's injuries. However, if JFK was going to die, there was no reason to risk alienating the attorney general by fleeing the hospital without confirmation that the president was dead. For once, LBJ could advance his career by being passive.

Johnson desperately needed information, and he wanted to get it officially, on the record, from Kenneth O'Donnell. He also wanted to hear from Roy Kellerman, the head of President Kennedy's security detail. At around 12:40 p.m., after hearing Roberts's report about the president's condition, Johnson asked him to find O'Donnell. Roberts rushed out of the room. A few moments later, Youngblood then turned to Lem Johns, who had just arrived at the hospital, and gave a similar order to "find Ken O'Donnell and see what was happening with the President." He left the room and soon encountered Roberts, who was on a similar mission. When Johns asked about the president's condition, Roberts told him that the president was dead — a far more definitive assessment than he had given LBJ a few minutes earlier.[27]

While Johns and Roberts were out searching for O'Donnell, Johnson sent word that he wanted to see the members of the Texas congressional delegation who had been traveling with the president and had accompanied him to Dallas. Most had been in the motorcade when the shots rang out, but made their way to the hospital between five and ten minutes after Johnson. He was soon joined by three Texas congressmen — Jack Brooks, Henry Gonzalez, and Homer Thornberry. Johnson looked at his old friend Thornberry and said, "This is a time for prayer, Homer, if ever there was one." Cliff Carter, who had been riding in the vice president's security car that had rushed to the hospital, also joined the group. Apparently, Johnson was not planning on leaving the hospital anytime soon because he asked Carter to get coffee for him and Lady Bird.[28]

When he first saw Johnson, Congressman Gonzales said he was "leaning against the wall with his head down, inhaling thru each

122

nostril in turn, pinching off the nostril thru which he was not breathing with his fore finger. Lady Bird was standing next to him and she looked white." Gonzalez felt that he was intruding on an intimate, private moment and moved to the other side of the room.[29]

Thornberry recalled the uncertainty that pervaded the room. "There would be three of us sometimes, and then one of the Secret Service men would come in and out. Maybe one or two other members of the delegation would wander in and out. But most of the time it was President Johnson, Mrs. Johnson, a Secret Service man, and me. Very little passed between us. We didn't know what was happening, just did not know what was happening. We did not know about the condition of the President and I remember the Vice President saying that he was just praying that everything was going to be all right." At one point, Thornberry left emergency medical to try and get an update on the president's condition. "Either nobody knew or they didn't tell me," he reflected.[30]

However distraught and confused he may have been, Johnson was, according to all accounts, reassuringly calm during these early minutes. Roberts noted that Johnson was unusually subdued, which should not have been surprising given the circumstances. "Johnson did not say too much at Parkland, although he is normally a very talkative man. He was alert, but stunned — he knew what was going on." Lady Bird said that "Lyndon was remarkably calm and quiet." She knew that he could become easily irritated over little things, but in a crisis he was often quiet. He was "a good man in a tight spot."[31]

While he was waiting for word from O'Donnell and Kellerman, Johnson asked Youngblood to find his children and make sure they were safe. Youngblood had agents check on both Lynda Bird, a student at the University of Texas, and Lucy Baines, a student at Washington's National Cathedral School for Girls. Lady Bird was glad to hear Johnson voice concerns about his daughters. He often took them for granted and rarely spent time with them.[32]

Aware of the historical moment, Johnson turned to Lady Bird and said, "Bird, why don't you make some notes on all this?" Lady Bird took out a small pad that she kept in her purse and started scribbling notes.[33]

# 5

# "THE CONDITION IS NOT GOOD"

At approximately 12:50 p.m. Agent Lem Johns found Roy Kellerman outside the emergency room. "Mr. Johnson wants to talk with you," he said. Kellerman followed Johns back to minor medical where Johnson was eagerly awaiting a report. "Roy, can you tell me the condition of the President?" Johnson asked. "President Kennedy has been hit," he said tersely. "He is still alive. The condition is not good." "You let me know of any developments," Johnson said, as Kellerman turned and walked back to the emergency area.[1]

At roughly the same time, Emory Roberts found Ken O'Donnell in the hallway. While doctors worked frantically on the president, O'Donnell, along with Larry O'Brien and Dave Powers, had been pacing outside the emergency room. They kept a close eye on Mrs. Kennedy, who was sitting on a small folding chair. Very little was said. O'Donnell was "feeling too numb" to talk. By his own admission, he was in a state of shock. Kennedy had been vibrant and smiling one minute, the next he was laying lifeless on a hospital stretcher. People were asking him questions, he recalled, "but I couldn't answer them."[2]

O'Donnell channeled his energy — his grief, his anger, and his sorrow — into protecting Jackie. Many of the men around the president had always viewed her as fragile, unable to cope with the rough-and-tumble of modern politics. Within a matter of a few months she had buried her newborn son, Patrick, and now she had witnessed the violent murder of her husband. From the moment she saw the bullet strike her husband's head, she assumed he was dead. Seeing the doctors rushing around, ordering blood transfusions, gave her fleeting hope that perhaps he was still alive. "Do you think he still has a chance?" Jackie asked O'Donnell. "I did not have the heart to tell her what I was thinking," he wrote years later. "If he's got a chance, it's a thousand to one," he whispered to Powers.[3]

Roberts told O'Donnell that Johnson wanted to see him and to receive an update on Kennedy's condition. Reluctantly, O'Donnell decided to walk the roughly sixty feet to see the vice president. According to Agent Johns, O'Donnell reported that Kennedy was in a "bad way" and advised Johnson to return immediately to Washington.[4]

By this point, Johnson had talked to three people who had witnessed the shooting — O'Donnell, Kellerman, and Roberts. Two of them, Roberts and Kellerman, had also seen the president's massive head wound. At a time when the operating assumption was that the shooting was part of an international conspiracy, and that America's national security could be at stake, it would seem imperative to guarantee a functioning chain of command. The obvious question is, Why did no one tell LBJ that JFK was dead or close to death? Even Roberts, who offered the most detailed and pessimistic reports on Kennedy's condition, stopped short of telling the whole truth. He later bragged to William Manchester that Johnson "did not know what I knew — that Kennedy was dead."[5]

O'Donnell and his statements about Kennedy's status were all that mattered to Johnson during this critical period. O'Donnell was not only Kennedy's top aide on the trip, he had been Johnson's main contact person in the White House. As long as Kennedy was alive, Johnson wanted to avoid appearing overeager to assume the presidency. He deferred to O'Donnell as the representative of the president. Johnson was also being cautious: if any questions were raised about the decisions made that day, he wanted to be able to say that O'Donnell approved them. It was part of a disturbing pattern — for the first twenty-four hours after Kennedy's assassination, Johnson hesitated to take action on any front without first securing the blessing of either O'Donnell or RFK.

Although O'Donnell's approval was crucial to Johnson that day, LBJ was certainly not O'Donnell's top priority at Parkland Hospital. He recalled that his "real duty" was to take care of Mrs. Kennedy. O'Donnell was most likely also in denial, unwilling or unable to bring himself to say what he knew — there was nothing doctors could do to keep JFK alive. O'Donnell struck a compromise in the report he gave to Johnson: he tried to ensure the safe transfer of power by encouraging Johnson to return to Washington. However, he stopped short of acknowledging that his beloved president was on the brink of death. He could have simply stated the obvious: "The President is probably going to die, if he is not dead already. Even if he survives, he has suffered a massive head wound. You need to assume the powers of the presidency immediately." Instead, he referred cryptically to Kennedy's condition as "bad," and told LBJ to fly back to Washington.[6]

It was a psychological standoff: O'Donnell would not say that Kennedy was dead and Johnson would not leave the hospital until he did. At some level, O'Donnell could not bring himself to acknowledge two painful realities: JFK was gone and Lyndon Johnson was now president. If O'Donnell had had more respect for the vice president, if he had believed that LBJ would be a worthy successor to his fallen hero, would he have been more willing to provide a realistic assessment? If Johnson had been more secure, and less paranoid about RFK, would he have been more decisive in assuming the reins of power?

While they were waiting for more reports on the president's condition, both Lady Bird and Lyndon wanted to see Mrs. Kennedy and Nellie Connally. "Rufus," LBJ asked in a low voice, "would it be all right if Mrs. Johnson and I went to see Mrs. Kennedy and Mrs. Connally?" Youngblood had no problem with Lady Bird leaving the room, but he wanted Johnson to stay in a secure area. "We don't want you out of this room until we're ready to leave the hospital," he said. Although he rejected the Secret Service recommendation to leave the hospital, LBJ acceded to the request that he not leave minor medical.[7]

Roberts left the room to track down Mrs. Kennedy to see if she was willing to meet with Lady Bird. She said yes. A few seconds later, Lady Bird found herself face-to-face with Jackie outside trauma room one. "You always think of her — or someone like her as being insulated, protected — she was quite alone," she noted a few days after the assassination. "I don't think I ever saw anyone so much alone in my life." Lady Bird held out her arms to support and comfort Jackie. As they embraced, medical personnel were moving equipment out of the emergency room. According to Congressman Jack Brooks, who accompanied Lady Bird, "Kennedy was lying there under a sheet and he was dead."[8]

Lady Bird and Jackie were as much a study in contrast as their husbands. Jackie Kennedy was young, beautiful, the epitome of sophistication and culture. Lady Bird was attractive but never glamorous. She wore the conservative straight skirts and bright colors that Lyndon picked out for her. Lady

Bird had always viewed Jackie as fragile and frail. She once commented that Jackie was a "girl born to wear white gloves." Jackie held Lady Bird in some degree of contempt, once noticing how Lady Bird carried a spiral pad and took careful notes whenever LBJ said something that might be important. She joked that Lady Bird would crawl naked down Constitution Avenue for Lyndon. Many in the Johnson camp were furious when they learned that Mrs. Kennedy had once referred to the Johnsons as "Senator Cornpone and Mrs. Pork Chop."[9]

In one significant way, however, the two women were remarkably similar. Both suffered from being married to men of enormous ambition and raw appetites. Both LBJ and JFK had numerous extramarital affairs. Kennedy's affairs were the worst-kept secret in Washington, especially after he started seeing actress Marilyn Monroe in 1959. It was Monroe, not Jackie, who had accompanied him to the Democratic Convention in Los Angeles. At the same time, LBJ was involved in a long-term affair with movie star and former congresswoman Helen Gahagan Douglas. Jackie and Lady Bird developed similar mechanisms for ignoring or rationalizing their husbands' various indiscretions. They had made implicit bargains:

they offered their loyalty, and in return they received status and access to power and privilege.

Lady Bird stayed only a minute with Jackie, before she was escorted up a flight of steps to see Nellie. About ten minutes after he had been brought to the hospital, doctors had transferred Connally to an operating room on the second floor. "There it was different," Lady Bird reminisced, "because Nellie and I have gone through so many things together." They once shared an apartment together while their husbands served in World War II. They had vacationed together at San Jose Island near Galveston, building sand castles on the beach with their children. When the Connallys' oldest daughter, Kathleen, committed suicide in 1958, Lady Bird was at Nellie's side, offering support. They remained friends even though their husbands were now often political rivals. "I hugged her tight and we both cried," Lady Bird recalled. "Nellie, it's going to be all right," she assured her friend. Seeing Lady Bird was a welcome sight for Mrs. Connally. "She opened her arms wide and I flew into them," she recalled. "And I cried and cried for the first time.[10]

While Lady Bird was out of the room,

Youngblood continued to pressure Johnson to leave the hospital as quickly as possible. According to Youngblood, Johnson "was adamant about staying put until there was some definite word on the President." According to notes that Cliff Carter dictated later that day, Johnson responded to the pleas by saying that "he thought those wishes ought to come from both Ken O'Donnell and Secret Service." But the Secret Service had been pressuring him to leave the hospital almost since he arrived, and O'Donnell had already weighed in by telling Johnson that he should fly back to Washington immediately.[11]

By this point, it is clear that Johnson would not leave Parkland Hospital until he had received a definitive report on Kennedy's condition. Given the information he had received from Roberts, Johnson probably assumed that Kennedy was going to die. "The reports on the President's condition became more discouraging by the minute," he observed in his memoirs. LBJ likely feared that fleeing the hospital with JFK apparently still fighting for his life would reinforce the old stereotype that he was too eager to assume power, potentially complicating his already troubled relationship with the attorney general. But Johnson was also motivated by genuine concern for JFK, and compassion for Jackie Kennedy and his old friend Nellie Connally. He did not want to leave them behind to deal with the tragedy alone.[12]

Realizing that he would have to leave the hospital eventually, Johnson focused the discussion on developing an exit plan. Still worried that another gunman might be waiting to take a shot at him, Johnson suggested moving the plane from Love Field to a more secure location at Carswell Air Force Base. Youngblood sent Agent Johns to look into the logistics. Johns checked with a local policeman, who told him that it would be too long a drive and impossible to secure the highways. He came back with the news and joined Youngblood once again in making the case for a quick exit. "The faster we can get out of here, the sooner we can leave here, the better."[13]

Their conversation was briefly interrupted by a nurse, her white hospital gown splattered with blood. She was carrying two brown bags containing Governor Connally's clothes. One contained the governor's pants, shirt, and socks; the other his coat. Hospital rules required someone to sign for patients' personal effects. For some reason, the nurse decided not to ask Nellie Connally and took the bags, which were seeping blood from the bottom, down to the vice president's room. Cliff Carter signed for them. "How about his money?" Carter asked. "It's at the desk," the nurse replied.[14]

The blood-soaked bags were surely a painful reminder for Johnson of the grave tragedy he was confronting.

# 6
## "HE'S GONE"

Exactly when did doctors give up their efforts to save Kennedy's life? And when did Lyndon Johnson learn that he was dead? These are the central questions that need to be addressed in understanding the transfer of power on November 22, 1963. The questions may be obvious; the answers are not.

The standard narrative states that doctors declared Kennedy dead at 1:00 p.m., approximately twenty-five minutes after the presidential party had arrived at Parkland Hospital. Johnson was notified shortly afterward. According to the official Secret Service report about the assassination, "At 1 p.m., ASAIC Kellerman was advised of the death of the President by Doctor Burkley and Vice President Johnson was notified of the death of the President by members of the President's Staff in the presence of Secret Service Agents Kellerman, Youngblood and Kivett." In his testimony before the Warren Commission, O'Donnell offered a similar account. "As soon as I was assured that he was dead, and it was definite, I went back to the Vice President and informed him the President was dead, and that in my opinion, he ought to get out of there as fast as he could."[1]

Most authors who have written books about the assassination accept this time line. With typical melodrama, William Manchester wrote, "It was 1 P.M. on the IBM clock. The ekg needle was still motionless, and Kemp Clark heaved up from it and said heavily, 'It's too late, Mac [Dr. Mac Perry].' " Clark then turned to Mrs. Kennedy. "Your husband has sustained a fatal wound." She responded, "I know." Author Vincent Bugliosi claimed that at 1:00 p.m. Dr. Clark started "external heart massage" on the president. Only after this procedure failed to produce any cardiac activity did the team of doctors accept the inevitable. The Warren Commission is willfully vague on the time of death, saying that it was "fixed at 1 p.m., as an approximation, since it was impossible to determine the precise moment when life left the President."[2]

The real story, however, is more complicated. It is difficult to fix an exact time for Kennedy's death. For all practical purposes, he was dead when he arrived at Parkland Hospital. But at what time were doctors prepared to stop their efforts to save his life?

New sources suggest that Kennedy died about ten minutes earlier than these accounts claim. Hospital administrator Jack Price, who detailed his actions that day in a long memorandum he wrote and turned over to William Manchester, stated that Dr. Clark came out of trauma room one "and told me that the president was dead and that he would sign the death certificate." Price left and went back to the triage area where an FBI agent whispered to him, "Don't let anyone know when the President died — security." Although Price did not record the precise time of his conversation with Dr. Clark, he did note that just after they finished speaking he saw a priest come in the door. Price asked his assistant to escort the priest to the trauma room.[3]

The priest was the seventy-year-old Reverend Oscar Huber. Only two hours earlier, he had watched on television the president's arrival at Love Field and then walked three blocks from his Holy Trinity Church to watch the motorcade as it passed Lemmon Avenue. "It was a thrilling moment for me as I had never before seen a President of the United States," he reflected in a memorandum he sent to William Manchester a few weeks after the shooting. He then went back to the rectory and was eating lunch when one of his assistants, Father James Thompson, told him the president had been shot and was being taken to Parkland Hospital.[4]

Since the hospital was part of their parish, Huber and Thompson drove to Parkland to offer their assistance. When Huber entered the emergency room, he saw Kennedy lying on the operating table with his face and body covered by a white sheet. He remembered seeing the president's white feet sticking out from the bottom. "There is no blood in this man," he thought to himself.[5]

Father Huber began to perform last rites. Normally he would have knelt, but the floor was covered with blood. Jackie Kennedy was standing next to the body, and later described the scene to journalist Theodore White. "There was a sheet over Jack," she told him. "His foot was sticking out of the sheet, whiter than the sheet . . . I took his foot and kissed it. Then I pulled back the sheet. His mouth was so beautiful, his eyes were open. They found his hand under the sheet, and I held his hand all the time the priest was saying extreme unction."[6]

Huber held up his right hand and began

the prayer in Latin, which translated is "If you are living, I absolve you from your sins. In the name of the Father and of the Son and of the Holy Ghost. Amen." He then reached into his pocket and pulled out a vial of holy oil. He placed a small amount on his right thumb and then made the sign of the cross on President Kennedy's forehead. "Through this holy anointing may God forgive you whatever sins you may have committed. Amen." When he finished, someone asked him to continue praying. For those in the room the ceremony probably seemed too brief for the gravity of the moment and the stature of the man for whom they were praying. "Eternal rest grant unto him, O Lord," he said. Mrs. Kennedy responded, "And let perpetual light shine upon him."[7]

When Huber arrived at the hospital is crucial to fixing an approximate time for when doctors had given up working on Kennedy. Manchester claims that he pulled up to the hospital at 12:57 p.m. Vincent Bugliosi sets the time at 12:58 p.m. But there is strong evidence to suggest that in fact Huber arrived several minutes earlier.[8]

The most reliable source for establishing the time of Huber's arrival is Dave Powers. A certified member of the "Irish mafia,"

Powers's relationship with Kennedy dated back to 1946, when the aspiring congressional candidate knocked on his door in the working-class neighborhood of Charlestown, Massachusetts, and asked him to join the campaign. Powers agreed, and spent the next seventeen years at Kennedy's side.[9]

As a special assistant to the president, Powers played many roles — receptionist, gatekeeper, greeter, and repository of trivia. On trips like this one to Texas, he was responsible for keeping track of the schedule, and constantly checked his watch to make sure they were on time.

As they were running into the hospital with the president's body, Powers had instructed Secret Service agent Jack Reedy to find a priest. For the next few minutes he kept checking his watch, asking the Secret Service, "What's the story on the priest?" Standing outside the emergency room with Mrs. Kennedy, he occupied himself by writing down everything he saw, including the names of the doctors as they responded to the call for help. "Now I was carrying the President's schedule and I was writing this thing down in pencil or ink," he told NBC newsman Sandor Vanocur.[10]

When Powers saw the priest coming down the hall he noted the time: 12:50 p.m. "It seemed maybe like a half hour" from the time the presidential limousine arrived at the hospital until the priest arrived, Powers recalled with Vancour. "But it was probably only ten or fifteen minutes later." Powers estimated that it "may have been five minutes of one when Father Huber administered the Last Rites of the Church."[11]

Dr. Fouad Bashour, chief of cardiology at Parkland Hospital, supported this time line in a handwritten statement that he turned over to the Secret Service a few hours after the assassination. Bashour claimed that when he arrived at the trauma room at 12:50 p.m., "The President had no pulsations, no heart beat, no blood pressure. The oscilloscope showed a complete standstill." He added, "The President was declared dead at 12:55 p.m."[12]

If the doctors were ready to declare Kennedy dead between 12:50 p.m. and 12:55 p.m., why then was the official time listed as 1:00 p.m.? Quite clearly, the time of death was a fiction created to satisfy Mrs. Kennedy. According to Catholic doctrine, the last rites had to be given before the soul left the body. If her husband was already officially dead before Father Huber had a chance to administer the sacrament, it would not have been valid. "Father, do you

think the sacrament had effect?" she asked
Huber in the emergency room. He tried to
allay her fears. "I am convinced that his soul
had not left his body," he said. "This was a
valid last sacrament."[13]

According to author Jim Bishop, Mrs.
Kennedy then followed Huber outside into
the hallway, where she sat in a small metal
chair next to O'Donnell. Press Secretary
Mac Kilduff approached them and said that
he needed to know the exact time of death
to tell the press. Mrs. Kennedy requested
that the official time of death be listed after
the president had been given the last rites.
O'Donnell asked Kilduff for the time. He
said it was a minute or two before 1:00 p.m.
O'Donnell approached Dr. Malcolm Perry
and asked if he would say the time of death
was 1:00 p.m. Perry agreed.[14]

The Warren Commission later accepted
this time line, and stated that the last rites
were administered before the official time
of death. "At approximately 1 p.m., after
last rites were administered to the President
by Father Oscar L. Huber, Dr. Clark pro-
nounced the President dead." Whether doctors had stopped working on JFK around
12:50 p.m. or at 1:00 p.m. no doubt seemed
like a minor point to the commission. It was
not relevant to their central mission of

building a case against Lee Harvey Oswald. The issue is vitally important, however, to understanding the timing of the transfer of power.[15]

For the first few minutes after they arrived at Parkland Hospital, O'Donnell was able to maintain false hope that doctors could save Kennedy. But by roughly 12:50 p.m., when Father Huber entered the room and saw Kennedy covered in a white sheet, it was clear that doctors had stopped trying to save his life. The president was dead, and everyone knew it. Within a few minutes, the Secret Service notified its office in Washington. Shortly after 1:00 p.m., Robert Kennedy would get a phone call at his home in Virginia (where it was 2:00 p.m. EST) informing him that the wounds his brother suffered had proved fatal. Yet, Lyndon Johnson, standing in a cubicle a few yards away, was still in the dark.[16]

When did Johnson finally learn of Kennedy's death? There are numerous conflicting accounts of who told LBJ that Kennedy was dead, and at what time.

Johnson told the Warren Commission that O'Donnell, accompanied by Roy Kellerman, informed him at 1:20 p.m. He recalled O'Donnell's precise words: "He's gone."

Johnson wrote in his memoirs that "a minute or two later Emory Roberts confirmed the tragic news." The Warren Commission accepted this version of events. "At approximately 1:20 p.m., Vice President Johnson was notified by O'Donnell that President Kennedy was dead." Once again, however, the truth is more complicated. O'Donnell managed to push back the official time of death to 1:00 p.m. It appears that Johnson may have pushed back the clock as well.[17]

Emory Roberts directly contradicted LBJ's testimony. Roberts claimed that he was the one who broke the news. "At 1:13 pm I told Lyndon Johnson that President Kennedy was dead," he told Manchester. "One of my agents had told me that the President was dead and I checked with the agent outside the door of trauma room 1. I went to Johnson. Cliff Carter, Rufus Youngblood, Mrs. Johnson, and the President were there. I said, 'the President is dead, sir.' " According to Roberts, Johnson turned to Cliff Carter and told him to make a note of the time. "Someone mentioned that the time was 1:13 p.m.," he noted. Roberts included these details in his daily log of activity for November 22. "1:15 p.m. I notified V.P. Johnson that the President was dead. SA's Youngblood, Johns, Kivett and Taylor were also with Johnson."[18]

Cliff Carter's recollections support Roberts's account. On the ride back to Washington on *Air Force One,* Carter dictated notes about the events he witnessed at Parkland Hospital. He observed that Roberts was the first to deliver the news, and that two minutes later O'Donnell and Agent Kellerman entered the room and made the announcement again. He suggested that O'Donnell mentioned Kennedy's death almost as an afterthought. "Ken O'Donnell had come in and was giving the VP the estimate of the situation, and the VP asked what was the President's condition." It was then that O'Donnell said, "He's gone."[19]

Carter repeated the story to Manchester. "There have been many wrong accounts of this." Roberts "did the notifying," he recalled. "He just said, 'Mr. Johnson, the President is dead.' "[20]

Youngblood backs Johnson's account that O'Donnell and Kellerman delivered the news first, followed a few minutes later by Roberts. Like Johnson, he recalled O'Donnell telling them, "He's gone." The problem with Youngblood's story is that he claimed Roberts entered the room after O'Donnell, but the White House appointments secretary distinctly recalled Roberts being in the room. "Roberts jumped up" as he walked in, saying, "What'll we do, Kenny, what'll we do?"[21]

O'Donnell believed that prior to his arrival in the examination room with Kellerman, someone else had given Johnson news of Kennedy's death. He was convinced that Johnson "had already heard of the President's death" by the time of his encounter. Roberts's question suggests as much — that everyone in the room knew by now what had happened, and they were looking to O'Donnell to explain the next steps. O'Donnell recalls telling Johnson, "You'd better get the hell out of here and get back to Washington right away." Johnson, he observed, "was nervous and excited, and so were the Secret Service agents with him."[22]

Johnson's account is wrong on two key points: it was Roberts, not O'Donnell, who told Johnson that Kennedy was dead, and he delivered the news earlier than LBJ claimed. Despite the evidence to the contrary, the Warren Commission accepted Johnson's version of events.

How could Johnson have been mistaken about such important details? It's possible that, given the extraordinary pressure he was under, he simply misremembered the sequence of events. More likely, Johnson created a narrative designed to insulate him from charges that he was overeager to assume the presidency; one that gave O'Donnell a central role and moved back the clock by at least five to seven minutes.

Technically, the powers of the presidency transferred to Johnson at 12:30 p.m. when the fatal third bullet shattered Kennedy's brain. But because of confusion at the hospital, the understandable grief of Kennedy's close advisers and friends, and LBJ's insecurity, the United States was without a functioning head of state for nearly forty minutes. During this time, LBJ had no contact with any advisers in Washington, or with any members of the Kennedy cabinet. What if the shooting had been part of a coordinated international conspiracy? For three-quarters of an hour the functioning commander in chief was sitting in the corner of a hospital emergency room, isolated from the levers of power.

Most people at Parkland Hospital, even reporters, were simply too traumatized by the brutality of Kennedy's death to give much thought to the problem of succession. Journalist Charles Roberts claimed that "even after we realized that Kennedy was

perhaps dying — and we got thi
— we weren't thinking about su
talked to a nurse who burst into t
realized that she wasn't crying ove
ficial flesh wound or something. W
priest come, and that indicated last rites. So
we were getting the idea gradually that Kennedy was dead or dying. But I still remember no discussion of — I don't remember anybody saying, 'My God, Johnson is president or is about to become president.' " Roberts recalled that there "was almost no focus of attention on him, and this was true as he left the hospital. He left the hospital after Kennedy was dead but before Kennedy's body was removed, and nobody made any attempt to follow him, although he was then president of the United States."[23]

Not only was there a power vacuum at the top of the government, but more than half of the cabinet was away from Washington. At the time of the assassination, six members of the Kennedy cabinet were onboard a government plan en route to Japan. About an hour west of Hawaii, the pilot received a one-line flash saying that the president had been shot. He summoned Secretary of State Dean Rusk, who then contacted the White House and received confirmation. Shortly

rd came the word that President
nedy was dead. Rusk made the announcement on the plane's speaker: "Ladies
and gentleman, we have received official
confirmation that President Kennedy is
dead. I am saddened to tell you this griev-
ous news. We have a new president. God
bless our new president and our nation."[24]

Rusk ordered the plane to return to Hawaii and wait for further instructions. He
recalled that the stunned passengers "sat for
perhaps fifteen to twenty minutes in complete silence" before pulling themselves
together. They gathered in the front cabin
and talked about the future. "My greatest
concern during that long return flight home
and in the assassination's aftermath," Rusk
recalled in his memoir, "was whether or not
Kennedy's murder had international ramifications. Was it a conspiracy involving the
Cubans or the Russians? We just didn't
know."[25]

Rusk was not alone in his fears. Most of
official Washington assumed the assassination was part of an international communist
plot to overthrow the American government. The questions that went through his
head, recalled Under Secretary of State
George Ball, were, "Was it a plot? The
beginning of a Soviet move? The first step

in a coup attempt?"[26]

As soon as word reached Washington that the president had been shot, the Central Intelligence Agency (CIA) set up a "watch committee" that monitored foreign intelligence and assembled information from every possible source. "We all went to battle stations," recalled Richard Helms, chief of the CIA's covert operations. "It worried the hell out of everybody. Was this a plot? Who was pulling the strings? And what was to come next?" At the Pentagon, Defense Secretary Robert McNamara called the chairman of the Joint Chiefs of Staff, General Maxwell Taylor, and suggested that they place all troops on alert because they did not know whether a foreign power had been involved in the shooting. Adding to the anxiety, about thirty minutes after the assassination the Washington, D.C., phone system crashed from the extraordinary demand placed on it.[27]

The fear was understandable. Although after the Cuban Missile Crisis in October 1962, Kennedy initiated a number of high-profile moves designed to reduce tension between the United States and the Soviet Union, relations between the free and communist worlds remained tense. In September, after learning of U.S. efforts to assassinate him, Cuba's Fidel Castro vowed revenge. "We are prepared," he declared in September, "to answer in kind. United States leaders should think that if they are aiding in terrorist plans to eliminate Cuban leaders, they themselves will not be safe." New Soviet ICBMs were capable of striking the American heartland within fifteen minutes of launching.[28]

Within minutes of arriving at Parkland Hospital, the White House Signals Corps had established secure phone lines to the White House. Warrant Officer Art Bales, the Signal Corps technician for the Dallas trip, moved quickly and efficiently to set up the phones. In the case of an international crisis there would have been no difficulty receiving information and sending orders. The question that no one could answer in either Dallas or Washington was, who was in charge? If there was a Soviet move somewhere in the world, who would coordinate the American response?

Adding to the confusion, Ira Gearhart, the "bagman," who carried the "football" containing the codes for launching a nuclear attack, kept getting separated from the president. Like most other members of the presidential party who were riding in the motorcade, he had continued on to the

Trade Mart. As soon as Gearhart learned that the president had been shot and was at Parkland Hospital, he jumped in a car and rode to the hospital. When he arrived, however, the Secret Service agents guarding Johnson did not recognize him. They stuck him in a separate room until Emory Roberts identified him and placed him in a room near LBJ. It was a measure of everyone's distraction or disinterest in the issue of succession that when Johnson eventually decided to leave the hospital, he once again left Gearhart behind holding the nuclear codes.

Rarely has the United States government been so vulnerable. The confusion surrounding the transfer of power raised a serious question: if a lone gunman like Oswald could bring the government to a standstill, what could a well-coordinated attack have accomplished?

# 7
# "MR. PRESIDENT"

Johnson may not have been forthright about who told him that Kennedy was dead, or at what time, but his response to the news was unambiguous. "I found it hard to believe that this nightmare had actually happened," Johnson recalled in his memoirs. "The violence of the whole episode was unreal, shocking, and incredible. A few hours earlier I had been having breakfast with John Kennedy — alive, young, strong, and vigorous. I could not believe that he was dead. I was bewildered and distraught. Along with grief I felt anguish, compassion, and a deep concern for Mrs. Kennedy and the children."[1]

Johnson had little time, however, to wallow in his grief. There were decisions to be made — decisions he had put off while waiting for the definitive word that JFK was dead. With Ken O'Donnell and Agent Roy Kellerman still in the room, LBJ discussed what steps he should take next. O'Donnell reiterated the point everyone had been making since Johnson first arrived at the hospital: he needed to get to Love Field and fly back to Washington. "Don't you think it might be safer if we moved the plane to Carswell Air Force Base, and took off from there?" Johnson asked yet again, even though Agent Lem Johns had already pointed out the logistical problems with that suggestion. O'Donnell also rejected the idea, pointing out that it would take too much time to move the jets, and it would be risky for Johnson to make a thirty-five-mile-drive over the roads from Dallas to the air force base. "Get the police to seal off Love Field, and go there right now," O'Donnell repeated. "And take off for Washington as soon as you get there."[2]

Johnson asked about Mrs. Kennedy and how she would be getting back to the White House. O'Donnell explained that she would not leave without the body. "A casket has been ordered but it isn't here yet," O'Donnell told him. "We must get her out of there," O'Donnell said. "If she sees the casket, it's going to be the final blow." O'Donnell then left the room, hoping to distract Mrs. Kennedy while they placed her husband's body in the casket.[3]

155

This brief, two-minute conversation about seemingly minor details would have dramatic ramifications. Given the traumatic events that had just transpired, it was understandable that misunderstandings would arise. But O'Donnell, and others close to the late president, would transform every disagreement into an indictment of LBJ's character.

There are two different versions of what LBJ and O'Donnell discussed in those few minutes. O'Donnell later claimed that as he walked back to the trauma room, he assumed LBJ had accepted his advice. "I figured that Johnson, who had flown to Texas separately from the Kennedys on *Air Force Two*, the second 707 jet plane in our party, which was identical to *Air Force One*, would be taking off for Washington immediately." Johnson, however, disputed O'Donnell's account of the conversation. LBJ claimed that O'Donnell had specifically instructed him to take *Air Force One* for the flight back to Washington. Johnson also rejected O'Donnell's claim that they had all agreed Johnson should fly back to Washington without Jackie. LBJ insisted that he made it clear he would "board the airplane and wait until Mrs. Kennedy and the President's body were brought aboard the plane." Although he understood why the Secret Service and O'Donnell were so insistent that he return to Washington, "I was determined that we would not return until Mrs. Kennedy was ready, and that we would carry the President's body back with us if she wanted."[4]

Youngblood, as usual, supported Johnson's account. He testified before the Warren Commission that O'Donnell had specifically instructed Johnson to take *Air Force One:* "O'Donnell told the Vice President that Mrs. Kennedy would not leave the hospital without the President's body. And O'Donnell suggested we go to the plane and that they just come on the other plane. And O'Donnell told us to go ahead and take *Air Force One.* I believe this is mainly because *Air Force One* has better communications equipment and so forth than the other planes." Youngblood also supported Johnson's recollection that he had made it very clear he would wait for the former First Lady before taking off. "President Johnson said that he didn't want to go off and leave Mrs. Kennedy in such a state. And so he agreed that we would go on to the airplane and board the plane and wait until Mrs. Kennedy and the body would come out."[5]

O'Donnell flatly and vehemently denied that he and Johnson discussed whether he should wait for Mrs. Kennedy at the airport, or that LBJ would be taking *Air Force One* back to Washington. "That he might wait at the airport for Jackie and the body of President Kennedy before he left for Washington," was never raised, O'Donnell wrote later. "He never discussed with me whether he should use *Air Force One* instead of *Air Force Two,* a question which would have seemed highly unimportant at the time."[6]

O'Donnell was angry that Johnson and Youngblood's testimonies contradicted his own account of the conversation. The Warren Commission investigators, struck by the stark disagreement, assumed that the grief-stricken O'Donnell misremembered the conversation, and asked him if he wanted to change his testimony. He declined to do so. As he said to William Manchester, "My recollection of my conversation with President Johnson in Parkland Hospital is vivid and clear. The commission implied that I might be mistaken with respect to the airplane, but they are wrong," he said. "The President and I had no conversation regarding *Air Force One.* If we had known that he was going on *Air Force One,* we would have taken *Air Force Two.*" He declared that the statements Johnson and Youngblood made to the Warren Commission were "absolutely, totally, and unequivocally wrong."[7]

The disagreement was, on one level, totally meaningless — any plane carrying the president is automatically designated *Air Force One,* so in that sense it did not matter which plane Johnson chose. But on another level it was profoundly symbolic, because one plane — designated *Air Force 26000* — was the plane Kennedy always used. His pictures hung on the walls. It was filled with family memorabilia. Kennedy had personally picked out many of the colors. Mrs. Kennedy told General Godfrey McHugh, Kennedy's air force aide, "There are two things the President adores. One is 'Hail to the Chief,' he adores that song, and he adores *Air Force One.*" O'Donnell surely assumed Jackie would be more comfortable on this plane, and that she could seek solace in the bedroom, which contained many of her personal items.[8]

Otherwise, the planes were identical — as O'Donnell insisted at the time, and in subsequent interviews. "One plane was just like another," he told Manchester. Press reports later suggested that O'Donnell was mistaken; that the president's plane had been recently upgraded with new, more sophisticated communications equipment that would allow him to talk with officials in Washington, monitor any new intelligence information, and supervise a potential military response. If this was the case, it would make perfect sense for Johnson to take *26000* rather than the plane he had previously used, *Air Force 86970*. "What orders the new President would have to give during that return flight no man knew. It would have been feckless for LBJ to take any but the best-equipped plane," observed the journalist Charles Roberts, who often flew on the plane with the president.[9]

A recently declassified oral history with General McHugh, however, makes it clear that O'Donnell was correct in thinking the two planes were identical. McHugh supervised the presidential fleet, approved all requests for use of the flights, and oversaw all upgrades and changes in equipment. McHugh stated, "When the President was killed and we were going to fly him back, President Johnson refused to fly in *Air Force Two* because he said the communications were not the same as *Air Force One*, which of course was not the case. He just wanted to be on *Air Force One*. But they were identical," McHugh stated.[10]

Like many in the Kennedy camp, McHugh assumed the worst about Johnson. In fact, the available evidence suggests that Johnson never asked to take the Kennedy plane, that the Secret Service made that decision for him. Twice while they were waiting for news on the president's condition, Johnson sent Emory Roberts to talk with O'Donnell. The first time, Roberts asked, "Johnson wants to go. Is it okay if he uses the plane?" According to Roberts, O'Donnell responded, "Yes." Roberts reported back to LBJ, "Ken said it was okay." When Johnson still refused to leave, Roberts went back a second time. "Is it all right for Mr. Johnson to board *Air Force One* now?" O'Donnell, growing annoyed, answered, "Yes." Roberts told Manchester that shortly after the announcement came that Kennedy was dead, he alerted Washington that Johnson would be flying back on *Air Force One.* "I was told by ATSAIC Roberts, White House detail, to call the Dallas White House switchboard and have them notify AF-1 to prepare for an immediate takeoff," Agent Warren Taylor noted in his official Secret Service statement.[11]

Roberts, typically, was unsentimental about the issue of which airplane to take.

When Manchester asked Roberts why the sense of "urgency" to take *Air Force One* when the Johnson plane was available, Roberts said, "Yes, we knew there were two planes there but I was thinking only of the presidential plane . . . I was thinking only of *Air Force One.*" In his mind, *Air Force 26000* was the president's plane. Kennedy was dead and Lyndon Johnson was now president. It was now his plane.[12]

Although Johnson had done nothing wrong, his dispute with O'Donnell over *Air Force One* created the situation that he had worked so hard to avoid. Kennedy loyalists would view Johnson's decision to take *Air Force One* as part of the larger narrative of the day — an example of LBJ's insensitivity and his megalomania. He was so desperate to surround himself with the trappings of presidential power that he hijacked the Kennedy plane, they charged. Worse still, they claimed, he refused to take responsibility for his decision and instead claimed that it was O'Donnell's idea.

Even before Lyndon Johnson received the official word of Kennedy's death, rumors were already circulating around the hospital. At 1:16 p.m. Eddie Barker, the news director of the local Dallas CBS affiliate, told viewers, "The word we have is that President Kennedy is dead." At around the same time, hospital officials ordered the flag lowered to half mast.[13]

The press, gathered in a room at the hospital, were growing restless for confirmation. At roughly the same time that CBS was reporting rumors of the president's death, Press Secretary Malcolm Kilduff tracked down O'Donnell outside the emergency room where doctors had worked to save Kennedy's life. "Can I make the announcement?" O'Donnell seemed surprised by the question. "Don't they know?" he asked. Then he told Kilduff to "check with Mr. Johnson."

A Secret Service agent directed Kilduff to the room where LBJ had been in seclusion since the shooting. "I looked at him, very frankly I didn't know what to call him," he admitted later. So he just blurted out, "Mr., Mr. President." It was the first time that Johnson was addressed as "president." LBJ remembered the moment. "I must have looked startled," he reflected. "I certainly felt strange." Kilduff said later that he would "never forget the look on his face." Johnson, Kilduff recalled, "turned and looked at me like I was Donald Duck."[14]

"I have to announce the death of President

Kennedy," Kilduff told him. "Is it all right with you?" Johnson reacted immediately, saying, "No, Mac, I think we had better wait for a few minutes. I think I had better get out of here and get back to the plane before you announce it. We don't know whether this [is] a worldwide communist conspiracy, whether they are after me as well as they were after President Kennedy, or whether they are after Speaker [John W.] McCormack or Senator [Carl] Hayden. We just don't know." Johnson continued, "I had better get out of here and back to the plane," he said, and "as soon as I leave you announce the death."[15]

"And we're leaving now," Youngblood announced as soon as Johnson finished talking with Kilduff. At 1:26 p.m., the Secret Service formed a phalanx around Johnson, followed the red stripe down the same corridor they had raced through less than an hour earlier, and walked out through the ambulance bays toward the awaiting cars. "Our departure from the hospital was similar to our arrival," Johnson told the Warren Commission. "Swift and tense." Lady Bird recalled it in the same way: "Getting out of the hospital into the cars was one of the swiftest walks I have ever made."[16]

The Secret Service had lined up two unmarked police cars for the trip. In order to help confuse a potential assassin, they decided that the president and Mrs. Johnson should ride in separate cars. Johnson slumped into the back seat of the lead car, which was driven by Police Chief Jesse Curry. Youngblood followed and sat next to him. Congressman Homer Thornberry climbed into the front passenger seat. Once both of the Johnsons were loaded into the cars, Youngblood gave the order: "Let's go!"[17]

As they made their way down the narrow drive, Congressman Albert Thomas emerged from between two parked cars and saw his friend Homer Thornberry in the front seat. He started waving, asking him to pull over. "Wait for me," he shouted. Youngblood told Curry to keep driving, but Johnson, still slumped down in the back seat, countermanded the order. "Stop and let him in," he said. "It's alright." Thomas slipped into the front seat. "Hurry up, Albert!" Johnson declared. "Close the door!" Johnson told Thornberry to climb over the seat and join him in the back: "Homer, come back here and sit with me."[18]

The road was temporarily blocked by a delivery truck coming in the opposite direction, but they managed to maneuver around it and, eventually, pick up a few motorcycle escorts. At one point, the lead motorcycle turned on its siren; both Johnson and Youngblood told Curry to radio ahead and have it turned off. On this trip they were trying to attract as little attention as possible.

It was an inauspicious beginning to the Johnson presidency. Watching the scene unfold from the hospital, Congressman Henry Gonzales noted with a tone of sadness, "Suddenly I saw the might and power of the United States government in complete confusion."[19]

"The journey to Love Field took less than ten minutes," Johnson later recalled. "But those few minutes were as crucial as any I have ever spent." Although still in shock and mourning, "I knew I could not allow the tide of grief to overwhelm me. The consequences of all my actions were too great for me to become immobilized now with emotion. I was a man in trouble, in a world that is never more than minutes away from catastrophe." On route to the airport Lady Bird noticed a flag at half mast. She later said this was the moment when the enormity of the events that had taken place dawned on her, and how much her life was about to change.[20]

No American president had ever assumed the office under such difficult circumstances. Johnson was the eighth vice president to succeed to the presidency upon the death of the incumbent. Three others had been killed by assassins — Abraham Lincoln (1865), James Garfield (1881), and William McKinley (1901) — and four had died of natural causes: William Henry Harrison (1841), Zachary Taylor (1850), Warren G. Harding (1923), and Franklin D. Roosevelt (1945).

Never before, however, had the transition been so dramatic or so tragic. Kennedy was the first president to die instantly from an assassin's bullet. Charles Guiteau shot President Garfield on July 2, 1881, just four months after he took the oath of office. Garfield lingered between life and death for two and a half months before finally dying of blood poisoning. Johns Wilkes Booth dashed into Abraham Lincoln's box at the Ford's Theatre on the evening of April 14, 1865, pulled a small pistol from his pocket, and placed it within six inches of the president's head before pulling the trigger. Despite the massive head wound, Lincoln lived until the next morning. On September 6, 1901, Leon Franz Czolgosz stuck a .32-caliber Iver-Johnson revolver into William McKinley's stomach and fired two shots while the president stood in a receiving line. He died five days later.

Most presidents who died of natural causes also had lingered for days. William Henry Harrison contracted pneumonia after just a few weeks in office. He died nine days later, on April 4, 1841. Less than a decade later, the nation lost another chief executive, Zachary Taylor, who became ill after eating milk and cherries at an Independence Day celebration in 1850. He died five days later. Warren Harding had been sick for a week before a heart attack ended his life on August 2, 1923.

In every one of these cases, the vice president had the chance to think about the job, and to consult with friends and colleagues. "I walked the floor all night long feeling a responsibility greater than I had ever felt before," Andrew Johnson wrote to a friend after learning that Lincoln had been shot.[21]

Franklin D. Roosevelt was the only other president who had died suddenly, on April 12, 1945. Yet FDR had grown old and frail, and there had been widespread speculation

168

that he would not be able to complete his fourth term in office. He also died out of public view in the privacy of his Warm Springs Cottage, which allowed the White House to control the flow of information. Presidential aide William Hassett and Press Secretary Steve Early agreed that his wife, Eleanor, needed to be told first, and they allowed her to break the news to her children and to Vice President Harry Truman before the public learned that Roosevelt was dead.[22]

Johnson did not have the luxury of preparing himself or the nation for the transition: he assumed the presidency in the full glare of the media. Even before Johnson left Parkland Hospital, Americans were learning of the unfolding tragedy. At 1:39 p.m. (EST) — 12:39 (CST) in Dallas, or less than ten minutes after the shooting — the United Press International (UPI) wire service carried the word "flash," a designation reserved for the highest priority news.

"DALLAS — KENNEDY SERIOUSLY
WOUNDED. PERHAPS FATALLY."

One minute later, after being alerted by the UPI wire, CBS News anchorman Walter Cronkite broke into *As the World Turns* with an audio announcement: "In Dallas, Texas, three shots were fired at President Kennedy's motorcade in downtown Dallas. The first reports said that President Kennedy has been seriously wounded by this shooting." A few minutes later, Cronkite appeared on camera relaying live reports from Dallas and reading news bulletins from the Associated Press (AP) and CBS Radio.

Even the White House staff were hearing the news from the media. A minute after their wire went out, the UPI called Helen Gnass, an aide to presidential press secretary Pierre Salinger, to ask for clearance so one of their reporters could go to the White House. "Why does he want to come?" she asked. "There's nothing happening." "The President has just been shot," the reporter said. That was when the White House learned the news. Gnass rushed to turn on the television set and was quickly joined by other members of the White House staff, who stood in stunned silence.[23]

Never before had a news story spread so widely, so quickly, to the American people. Thirty minutes after the shots rang out at Dealey Plaza, a full 68 percent of Americans had heard of the shooting. Most people learned of the shooting from friends or colleagues. A study in Denver found that only

13 percent heard the news from radio and 9 percent from television. The majority learned of the shooting from "a good friend" (30 percent), from "a casual acquaintance" (35 percent), or "a stranger" (11 percent).[24]

Most Americans learned about the shooting by word of mouth, but they were sitting in front of television sets or radios when news came of Kennedy's death. At 1:33 p.m., a few minutes after Johnson left, Kilduff walked into the makeshift press room at Parkland Hospital. Holding a piece of paper in one hand and an unlit cigarette in the other, Kilduff stood in front of a classroom blackboard and read this statement: "President John F. Kennedy died at approximately one o'clock Central Standard Time today here in Dallas. He died of a gunshot wound in the brain. I have no other details regarding the assassination of the President. Mrs. Kennedy was not hit. Governor Connally was not hit. The Vice President was not hit." (Reporters would soon discover that Kilduff had misspoken when he said that Connally was not hit.)

Two minutes later, UPI teletype machines around the world reported, "flash President Kennedy Dead." Two minutes after that, at 2:37 p.m. (EST), Walter Cronkite made the announcement on CBS: "From Dallas,

Texas, the flash, apparently official. President Kennedy died at 1:00 P.M. Central Standard Time, two o'clock Eastern Standard Time." He paused for a moment and looked at the studio clock. "Some thirty-eight minutes ago." The sight of Cronkite fighting back tears as he removed his eyeglasses and cleared his throat would be ingrained into the consciousness of an entire generation of Americans.[25]

Although there had been unsuccessful assassination attempts against Franklin D. Roosevelt and Harry Truman, Kennedy was the first president gunned down since William McKinley in 1901. It had been a different world then. The stakes seemed lower — the United States was not a global power and there were no nuclear-tipped missiles aimed at American cities. But, more important, the United States had not entered into the age of mass media. Newspapers had spread word of the McKinley assassination, but the reporting was slow, consisting of daily updates on the attack and the president's condition. The Kennedy assassination took place at a time when the nation was connected by a network of instant communication through ever-present television cameras and radio microphones.

The news of Kennedy's death poured into American homes via the airwaves: A study in northern California found that although 50 percent of those surveyed were informed of the shooting by other people, 84 percent learned of Kennedy's death through radio or television. Within two hours of the assassination, 92 percent of the public knew what had happened. By 6:00 p.m., nearly every adult in America — 99.8 percent — knew that Kennedy had been assassinated.[26]

Kennedy's death paralyzed the nation. The phone system crash that started in Washington spread across the country as people called friends and family to share the news. On street corners and in department stores, crowds gathered around radios and televisions sets to follow the news. In New York City, traffic came to a halt as drivers stopped cars and sat hunched over dashboards listening to their radios. The garish brilliance of Times Square was replaced by darkness as the massive advertising displays were turned off. Broadway performances were cancelled. Nightclubs closed. "In many respects the biggest city in the nation turned into something of a ghost town," reported the *New York Times.*[27]

In Washington, by dusk more than a thousand people had gathered in a silent vigil outside the White House. Across the nation, hospitals reported increased traffic in emergency rooms, from patients complaining of various psychosomatic illnesses. Churches and synagogues filled with people praying for the president, his family, and the nation. "I feel like I lost a real friend," a shoeshine man in Los Angeles said. Four of five people "felt deeply the loss of someone very close and dear." Nearly half of those polled reported problems sleeping and a loss of appetite in the days that followed.[28]

Television transformed President Kennedy's death into a personal tragedy for the millions of Americans who watched the nonstop coverage. In the hours that followed the assassination, the networks juxtaposed pictures of a triumphant JFK at key points in his career — winning the election, his inaugural address — with the tragic scene at Parkland Hospital. One minute viewers saw a smiling Kennedy, his beautiful wife, and two young children; the next they were listening to witnesses describe the president's fatal wounds.

Americans were glued to their television sets on the day of the assassination and for many days after. The three major networks cancelled all commercial broadcasting for the weekend. More than 90 percent of homes watched the assassination coverage over the weekend, and they watched for an average of 31.6 hours — more than 10 hours a day. "When President Franklin D. Roosevelt died, there were memorable radio reports, but the person at home mourned through the eyes and ears of the unseen commentator," observed the *New York Times.* "On this occasion the involvement of the individual carries the total intensity of being a numb eyewitness to the train of events."[29]

Americans growing up in the 1940s and 1950s had experienced a number of big news stories: the dropping of the atom bomb and the end of World War II, the commitment of troops to Korea, the Army-McCarthy hearings, the Soviet launch of Sputnik. These stories grabbed headlines and became the focus of public discussion at work and at the dinner table, but they lacked the shock value of the Kennedy assassination. People did not stop their daily routines to follow them. They did not leave work, cry, or lose sleep over these events. Americans experienced them largely as spectators. Kennedy's death, however, was personal.

The presence of television and the immediacy of news complicated the situation for Johnson, forcing him to deal with the crisis in real time. From the first minutes of the crisis, Johnson seemed to understand the power of the media to shape the public's perception of his actions. Over the next twenty-four hours he would be acutely aware of the media presence, and worked hard to influence the way it covered the day's events.

Many of the initial stories coming out of Dallas had been wildly inaccurate. Within minutes of the shooting, rumors were circulating suggesting that both Kennedy and Johnson had been killed. As he hurried into Parkland Hospital, Johnson rubbed his shoulder, flexing and bending his arm, which was sore from his uncomfortable position during the recent ride to the hospital. Youngblood had pushed him to the floor and had been sitting on top of him the entire time. In the panicky minutes following the shooting, it was reported that Johnson either had been shot or had suffered another heart attack.

When reporter Charles Roberts arrived at the Trade Mart, he overheard a Mexican American woman listening to events on her car radio announce, "I hear they got Johnson too."[30] As far away as Omaha, Nebraska, the manager of a local movie theater interrupted a movie to announce, "President Kennedy has been assassinated, Governor Connally shot, and Vice-President Johnson has suffered a severe heart attack."[31]

Even Johnson's own staffers were confused by the muddled reporting. Back in Washington, George Reedy, Johnson's press secretary, was sitting in his office when he first heard that Kennedy had been shot. He and other staffers stood over the AP ticker trying to get information. "We were getting some very wild stuff," he recalled, "about a secret service man being shot and about the Vice President having had a heart attack." A secretary said she heard a rumor that Johnson had been shot. They would have to wait more than an hour to learn for sure that he was safe and healthy.[32]

# 8

## "ANYBODY CAN SWEAR YOU IN"

It is a clear indication of the confusion that reigned that day that there is no agreement about when Johnson left Parkland Hospital, how long it took to drive to Love Field, and what time he boarded *Air Force One*. Homer Thornberry said they left the hospital at 1:30 p.m. Agent Emory Roberts and Cliff Carter both claimed it was 1:35. The official Secret Service log book listed the time as 1:40. According to Roberts and Thornberry, they arrived at Love Field at 1:40. The secret service said it was 1:50.[1]

As they approached Love Field, Young-blood radioed ahead, "Get ready for us, we're only a couple of minutes away." Johnson asked that his personal steward, Paul Glynn, who had been on *Air Force Two,* move to *Air Force One.* Now that they were flying back on a different plane, LBJ and Lady Bird would need to have their clothes and other personal items transferred.[2]

As the car pulled up toward *Air Force One,* Youngblood remained worried about the possibility of a sniper with a high-powered rifle taking a shot at Johnson. The rings of police officers surrounding the plane provided little comfort. As the car came to a halt by the back door of the plane, Youngblood rushed Johnson out of the car and up the ramp. Lady Bird hurried behind them. Aboard *Air Force One,* Captain James Swindal stood ready to greet his new commander in chief. A gray-haired veteran of World War II, Swindal had been Kennedy's personal pilot since he became president. He had learned of the assassination by listening to Secret Service chatter. "I felt I had been hit in the head with a sledgehammer," he recalled in his interview with William Manchester. Until the moment Johnson boarded the plane, Swindal was unsure whether the new president would be flying back on his plane or the other one parked right next to it, but he had prepared for Johnson's arrival nonetheless. While waiting for updates from Parkland Hospital, he added fuel for the flight back to Washington and requested more police officers to surround the plane. As soon as Johnson arrived, Swindal put on his hat, walked to the rear entrance, and prepared to greet him.

As Johnson ran up the stairs, Swindal saluted him. Johnson nodded and hurried onboard. Youngblood followed right behind him, shouting to the crew to close all the window shades.[3]

As he entered, Johnson passed a small compartment on his right. This area, which would soon carry the president's casket, served as a private family room, a place where Kennedy, his family, and friends could relax on long flights. As he moved forward down a narrow corridor, he passed the presidential bedroom. The blue-carpeted room contained two twin beds, a desk, and chair. There was a small closet for clothes and a bathroom. Pictures of the president and his family hung on the walls. The staff referred to the bedroom as "Mrs. Kennedy's room," because she enjoyed the privacy that it provided. "I want this kept strictly for the use of Mrs. Kennedy," Youngblood recalled Johnson telling him. "See to that."[4]

Johnson then moved forward to the next area on the plane, the stateroom, which served as the president's office. The presidential seal hung on the wall; the room was furnished with a desk, a large work table, a sofa, and a television set. By the time Johnson arrived, the compartment was crowded with people — Johnson aides who had been asked to join him on the plane, Secret Service agents, and crew members. Johnson could not help but notice the reaction as he entered the room. Everyone stood at attention. "It was at that moment that I realized nothing would ever be the same again," he reflected. "A wall — high, forbidding, historic — separated us now, a wall that derives from the Office of the Presidency of the United States. No one but my family would ever penetrate it, as long as I held the office."[5]

It was a striking moment for a man who had languished in obscurity for the past three years. He had never been comfortable being out of the limelight. Now he was the center of attention, but under the most awful of circumstances.

Many in the room were apprehensive about how Johnson would handle the burden that had fallen on him. Few vice presidents were as qualified as Lyndon Johnson to take over the responsibilities of the presidency. But it had never been his qualifications that concerned people — it was his mercurial temperament, inflated ego, and unrestrained ambition. Nearly everyone was worried about his health. Would his damaged heart be able to handle the enormous stress of the day? Even his closest aides, those who knew him best, were unsure how he would handle the stress. Johnson was a complicated man who could be petty, cruel, and easily come unglued when faced with adversity. He was a strong but intemperate man, capable of bouts of self-pity and uncontrolled rage. But he could also be calm, measured, and deliberate.

Which Lyndon Johnson would greet them today?

Congressman Albert Thomas was the first person to speak when Johnson entered the stateroom. He and Johnson had been friends for twenty-five years, and during all that time he had called him "Lyndon." Not today. "We are ready to help you in any way, Mr. President." Johnson smiled briefly, then motioned for everyone to be seated. He then sat down on a chair in front of the table, carefully avoiding sitting on the desk chair that Kennedy used.[6]

Johnson noticed the television set was tuned to the CBS coverage of the events, with anchorman Walter Cronkite. He asked that the sound be turned up. For the past hour, he had been cocooned in a booth at Parkland Hospital. He knew only that the president had been assassinated, but by whom? And why? How was the story being covered, and how was the rest of the nation responding to the tragedy? These were questions he needed answered; as of now he had precious little information.

As he watched, a local station interrupted the broadcast to read the announcement that JFK was dead. "President John F. Kennedy died at approximately 1:00 pm, Central Standard Time, today, here in Dallas. He died of a gunshot wound in the brain. There are no other details at this time regarding the assassination of the President." Lady Bird remembered the announcer saying, "Lyndon B. Johnson, now President of the United States."[7]

It was suffocatingly hot in the stateroom, and Johnson asked for water.

Because he was told to be ready to leave at a moment's notice, Swindal had disconnected the plane from the ground power supply that provided air conditioning and lighting. The plane had been baking in the sun for hours. Press Secretary Liz Carpenter, who boarded a few minutes after Johnson, noted that "the stewards and everybody were aboard weeping. It was very still on the plane and very close and warm."[8]

Perspiring in the stuffy stateroom, LBJ quickly drank two bottles of Kennedy's

Poland water. While quenching his thirst, he instructed Youngblood to tell his agents to keep notes on everything they saw and heard. He understood the significance of what had taken place. Perhaps, at some level, he also realized that because the assassination had taken place in Dallas, questions would be asked about his own involvement in the president's death.

Youngblood continued to pressure Johnson to leave immediately for Washington, but LBJ insisted that he would not leave with out Mrs. Kennedy and President Kennedy's body. He told Youngblood to post a lookout to watch for her arrival.

For Johnson, the first order of business was the oath of office. Article II of the Constitution, which deals with the executive power of the presidency, stipulates that before the president "enter on the execution of his Office" he needs to take an "oath or affirmation." What Johnson did not know, and no one on the plane seemed to know, was whether it was necessary to take the oath before he assumed the responsibilities of the presidency. Was the oath a purely ceremonial act, designed to convey a sense of unity and symbolize the power of the presidency, or was it constitutionally mandated that he take the oath before becoming president? And who could administer the oath?

Even among constitutional scholars there was, and remains, no clear consensus about the oath. Some have argued that Johnson became president in title only until he took the oath; that he could not initiate any action or sign any laws. Others claim that it was unnecessary because he had taken an identical oath when he became vice president.

Johnson was no constitutional scholar, and abstract debates about the oath would have been of little interest to him. What he did know was that every vice president who assumed the office following the death of the president had recited the oath as quickly as possible. Doctors declared Lincoln dead at 7:22 a.m. on the morning of April 15, 1865. Vice President Andrew Johnson was sworn in by the chief justice of the Supreme Court later that morning. Teddy Roosevelt rushed back from a camping trip when he received word that William McKinley's condition had worsened. McKinley died early on the morning of September 14, 1901, and Roosevelt took the oath of office later that day. Calvin Coolidge had his father, a local justice of the peace, administer the oath a few hours after learning that Warren G. Harding was dead. LBJ was a congressman when Franklin D. Roosevelt died suddenly on April 12, 1945. He remembered how Harry Truman was rushed to the White House, where he took the oath of office two hours and thirty-four minutes after FDR's death.

LBJ may have believed that he automatically became president as soon as Kennedy was declared dead, but he did not want any ambiguity or uncertainty about his presidential powers. He also understood the symbolic value of the oath: it would send a reassuring signal to the nation that he was in charge and the government was still functioning. For these reasons, he wanted to take the oath sooner rather than later.

During his years in the Senate, Johnson had perfected the art of making a decision and then convincing other people that it had been their idea. It is likely that he solicited the opinions of those gathered in the room because he knew they would tell him what he already believed. "You've got to take the oath now," Thomas told him, according to Youngblood. "Suppose we were to run into bad weather? It could take three or four hours to get to Washington. I don't think it's fair to the country to delay. The world must know that we do not have a break in leadership."[9]

Both Homer Thornberry and Jack Brooks agreed. They informed Johnson that panic selling in the minutes after word about the shooting reached New York had forced the closing of the Stock Exchange. "My position was he ought to be sworn in right away," Brooks later recalled. "Right then, not wait one minute; that the country was too important to wait for a big ceremony in Washington or do it there on the steps of the Capitol or something or other like that. No, sir, I wanted it done *then!*"[10]

Lady Bird knew, however, that it "was Lyndon's idea" that the oath "should be as soon as possible — but not be before he could talk to the Attorney General." Since this conversation would be delicate, Johnson asked, "Is there someplace that I can make a phone call or two?" He removed his jacket and signaled to the communications staff that he would be using the phone in the presidential bedroom. According to the White House Communications Agency, Johnson placed a call to the Attorney General at 1:56 p.m. (CST).[11]

RFK, who had just celebrated his thirty-eighth birthday two days earlier, first learned about the shooting a little over an hour earlier when he received a call from FBI director J. Edgar Hoover at 1:45 p.m. (EST). Kennedy had met with his Organized Crime Task Force that morning and then invited Robert Morgenthau, the U.S. attorney in the Southern District of New York, to join him at his home at Hickory Hill in Virginia for lunch. Kennedy was sitting by the pool eating clam chowder and a tuna fish sandwich when the call came.

Kennedy knew something had to be wrong. Hoover never called him at home. The FBI head hated the Kennedys. He resented what he considered their arrogance, as well as their glamour and their lack of deference to him. Since he spied on many leading politicians in Washington, he knew about the Kennedys' sordid private lives. Hoover's and RFK's differences went beyond personality: over the years, Hoover had turned the FBI into his private fiefdom; he disliked taking orders from anyone, especially a man half his age. A cultural generation gap also separated the two men. The formal Hoover complained that RFK came to work in his shirtsleeves, put his feet up on his desk, and threw darts, which would occasionally miss the board and lodge in the wood walls. RFK was "desecrating government property," Hoover fumed. RFK often brought his dog, Brumus, to work — "a large and ill-tempered beast who relieved himself on carpets and bit strangers," according to RFK biographer Evan Thomas.[12]

"I have news for you," Hoover said in a matter-of-fact tone as soon as RFK took the call. "The President's been shot. I think it's serious." Hoover promised to call back as soon as he had more information and then hung up. There were no expressions of sorrow, no condolences.

Morgenthau saw Kennedy clap his hand to his mouth with a look of "shock and horror" on his face. Ethel, RFK's wife, rushed to his side. Kennedy was unable to speak for a few seconds, then forced out the words, "Jack's been shot. It may be fatal."[13]

Kennedy quickly went into his house and dressed, wondering whether he should fly to Dallas or wait until the presidential party arrived home. He called the White House switchboard and asked to speak with the Secret Service in Dallas. He was connected to Clinton Hill at Parkland Hospital. "He asked me what the situation was and I advised him that the President had been injured very seriously and that I would keep him advised of his condition," Hill wrote in his official report.[14]

Although shocked and numb, Kennedy was still thinking clearly and strategically. Even before he had received official word that the president was dead, RFK was focused on protecting his brother's legacy and blocking Johnson's access to information. He called National Security director McGeorge Bundy and instructed him to change the locks on his brother's private files. The most sensitive files were moved to the Executive Office Building and kept under twenty-four-hour guard. He also instructed the Secret Service to dismantle the taping system installed in the Oval Office and the cabinet room.

CIA head John "Jack" McCone was having lunch in his office in Langley, Virginia, when his assistant interrupted him to say that the president had been shot. President Kennedy had tapped McCone, whom *Newsweek* magazine described as a "strait-laced, right-wing businessman," to head the CIA following the Bay of Pigs fiasco in September 1961. Although he presided over the nation's most sophisticated intelligence network, McCone, like everyone else in Washington, tuned in to CBS's coverage to learn more details. While waiting for word on the president's condition, he picked up the phone and called Robert Kennedy. The call was forwarded to RFK at his home, which was only a five-minute drive from CIA headquarters. "Jack," RFK said, "can you come over?"[15]

When he arrived, McCone found RFK and Ethel alone in the library on the second floor. "All three of us were speechless," he recalled. Then the news came: at 2:05 p.m. (EST), Captain Tazewell Shepard, JFK's naval aide, called with the report from Parkland. "Oh, he's dead," Bobby cried out. According to McCone, "his tone was one of a man aghast." Kennedy spoke with Shepard for a few more minutes, trying to learn more about his brother's death and the preparations that were being made to take him back to Washington. McCone and Ethel moved to the other side of the library to give him some privacy.

Kennedy made a series of phone calls to family members while Ethel left to pick up the children from school. RFK asked McCone to stay with him, and the two men walked around the Hickory Hill estate, with Brumus trailing behind. "The attorney general and I then went into the yard and walked a long time and talked of many things. The walk was punctuated by phone calls which came in," McCone told Manchester. There were White House phones by the swimming pool and by the tennis courts. Kennedy used whichever one was closest.

One of the calls was from J. Edgar Hoover. "The President is dead," he said dryly. Kennedy recalled afterward that Hoover's voice was "not quite as excited as if he were reporting the fact that he had found a Communist on the faculty of Howard University."[16]

Forty minutes after learning of his brother's death, Bobby took Lyndon Johnson's call from aboard *Air Force One.* The first conversations between RFK and LBJ after the assassination would become the source of intense disagreement and add to their already strained relationship. It must have been a difficult conversation for both men. LBJ was now president, but he feared that the younger Kennedy, who had tried to sabotage him before, would now undermine his presidency. RFK, in turn, had to deal not only with the death of his brother but also the realization that a man he detested now occupied his office.

Johnson started the conversation by offering his condolences. "I tried to say something that would comfort him," he recalled. He was surprised by RFK's businesslike tone. "Perhaps," he speculated, "the full impact of his brother's death had not reached him." RFK assured Johnson that "the FBI had no indication as to the extent of the plot — if, indeed, there was a plot." Johnson then came to the point of the call: he wanted to know about the oath. According to Youngblood, LBJ asked "questions about who, when, and how he should take the Presidential oath." McCone remembered, "There was a question of the procedure of swearing in the new President."[17]

Johnson later claimed that he simply wanted to get RFK's opinion on whether he should take the oath in Dallas or in Washington. RFK and other members of the Kennedy camp deny that Johnson ever posed this question. "First he expressed his condolences," RFK told Arthur Schlesinger Jr. "Then he said . . . this might be part of a worldwide plot, which I didn't understand, and he said a lot of people down here think I should be sworn in right away." According to RFK, Johnson did not ask his opinion about whether he should take the oath in Dallas. Clearly, LBJ had already made up his mind about taking the oath and simply wanted to know if the attorney general had "any objection to it." RFK claimed that he was "taken aback at the moment because it was just an hour after . . . the President had been shot and I didn't think — see what the rush was. And I thought, I suppose at the time, at least, I thought it would be nice if the President came back to Washington — President Kennedy. . . . But I suppose that was all personal." LBJ, he recalled, wanted to know "who could swear me in?"[18]

Whatever his private doubts about the rush to take the oath, Kennedy did not express them to Johnson. "I'll be glad to find out and call you back," Kennedy replied. According to the official log, the conversation lasted only three minutes.[19]

After getting off the phone with Johnson, RFK pressed the hook switch and asked the operator to reach Deputy Attorney General Nicholas Katzenbach, who later recalled the conversation for Manchester. According to Katzenbach, Kennedy said, "Lyndon Johnson wants to be sworn in in Texas and wants to know who can administer the oath." Katzenbach responded, "My recollection is that anyone can administer the oaths under federal or state laws. Anyone who can do that can administer a presidential oath. Do you want to hold on while I check?" While RFK waited on the other end, Katzenbach phoned Harold Reis in the Office of Legal Counsel and asked his opinion. Reis confirmed Katzenbach's view and reminded him that Calvin Coolidge had been sworn in by his father, who was a notary public. Katzenbach conveyed the information to RFK. "Then any federal judge can do it?" RFK responded.[20]

While Kennedy was on the line with Katzenbach, Johnson was making calls of his own. The first was to his trusted aide Walter Jenkins. Except for a brief stint in the military and an unsuccessful campaign for Congress in 1951, Jenkins had worked for Johnson since 1939. "Do you know whether or not this is some sort of plot?," LBJ asked. "Are they out to get a lot of us?" The second was to McGeorge Bundy. "I talked briefly to the new President to say that he must get back to Washington where we were all shaky," Bundy wrote in a memorandum a few weeks after the assassination. "He agreed, and I now know that he immediately reached the same conclusion himself."[21]

In the middle of Johnson's conversation with Bundy, RFK got back on the line. What the two men discussed in this conversation is also disputed. If Johnson was being disingenuous about his intentions on the first call, it was Kennedy who stretched the truth now. RFK claimed that he simply provided Johnson with the information he had requested about taking the oath. "Anybody can swear you in," he told LBJ. "Maybe you'd like to have one of the judges down there whom you appointed. Any one of them can do it."

Johnson remembered the conversation differently: Kennedy insisted "that the oath should be administered to me immediately, before taking off for Washington, and that it should be administered by a judicial officer of the United States." McCone, who was with RFK at the time, substantiates Johnson's story. He recalled RFK insisting "that Lyndon Johnson be sworn in immediately; he did not want the country without a President during the 2 1/2 hour flight, and Lyndon Johnson agreed."[22]

With the issue settled, Johnson asked RFK for the exact wording of the oath. "Well, I'll have it given to you right away," RFK said. Johnson asked Jack Valenti, who had boarded the plane a few minutes after LBJ, to call Katzenbach for the oath. "We want to swear Vice President Johnson in as president. The attorney general said you would have a copy of the oath," Valenti said. Katzenbach walked over to his bookcase and pulled out a copy of the Constitution and read the relevant sections of Article II.

Both at the time of the phone calls, and in the later accounts each man gave of them, RFK and LBJ sought to construct narratives that served their own interests. LBJ, fearful of seeming overeager to assume the powers of the presidency, manipulated their first conversation in such a way that RFK would accede to the idea of taking the oath in Dallas. In subsequent retellings, Johnson lied to give the impression that the decision had in fact been Kennedy's idea. RFK played into his hands, offering the support Johnson desired in their second conversation. But soon RFK would change his story and deny that he had ever endorsed LBJ's request to take the oath in Dallas, painting a portrait of Johnson as selfish and power hungry, the very image Johnson had so strenuously sought to avoid.

For all of their personal animus, RFK and Johnson agreed on one thing: the assassination was part of a conspiracy. Johnson saw the plot in global terms as part of the struggle against communism. He suggested on a number of occasions that the assassination may have been a "payback" for American policy, but he was unclear about who was responsible. "I can't honestly say that I've been completely relieved of the fact that there might have been international connections," he later told Walter Cronkite, challenging the conclusion of the Warren Commission.[23]

RFK believed that the assassination was part of a personal vendetta. As he had paced disconsolately around Hickory Hill that afternoon, he confided to an aide, Ed Guthman, "There's been so much bitterness. I thought they would get one of us. But Jack, after all he's been through, never worried about it. I thought it would be me."[24]

But who were "they?"

The Kennedys had no shortage of enemies. In November 1961, RFK had assumed control of the administration's covert plan, code named Mongoose, designed to destabilize the Castro regime. Was the assassination retribution for their efforts to kill Castro? If not, perhaps anti-Castro forces, who believed that the president had abandoned them at the Bay of Pigs, were responsible for the murder. And there was always the Mob, who felt betrayed by the Kennedys. The Mob believed they helped elect Kennedy, flexing their muscle in battleground states such as Illinois, only to be rewarded with a crusading attorney general leading highly publicized campaigns to root out organized crime. RFK knew that Teamster chief Jimmy Hoffa had discussed hiring a gunman equipped with a rifle and a telescopic sight to kill him.

Kennedy never accepted the Warren Commission conclusion that his brother was killed by a lone gunman. In a conversation with Arthur Schlesinger Jr. a few weeks after the assassination, Kennedy mumbled his fears that his brother had been killed by the Mafia or the Cubans. But he never told the Warren Commission investigators about the administration's secret plans to kill Castro, or his private fears about the Mafia. When this information was forced into the open years later, it raised new questions about a possible conspiracy and a potential cover up. What difference did it make now? RFK would say to Nick Katzenbach. Jack was dead; nothing would bring him back.[25]

Just as he was finishing his second conversation with Kennedy, Marie Fehmer walked into the stateroom. Ostensibly, Fehmer was Johnson's secretary. A slender, twenty-six-year-old brunette, Johnson had hired her fresh out of the University of Texas in 1962. He interviewed her one day over lunch, she started working that afternoon, and she stayed with him until his last day at the White House. According to LBJ biographer Randal Woods, Johnson "quickly fell in love with Fehmer." At one point, he asked her to have his child, but she refused the offer and turned down his many requests for sex.[26]

Fehmer carried a small note pad with her as she entered the room. "I went in and he was sitting on the bed and I sat in the chair at the end of the bed where the telephone is," she recalled. Johnson began to construct his version of the conversations with Kennedy, and she scribbled notes as he dictated. "Write this down," he insisted. "I talked to the Attorney General. Asked him what we should do . . . where I should take the oath . . . here or there . . . said he would like to look into it . . . and would notify me whether we should take it here or not." Johnson said that he had talked to both McGeorge Bundy and Walter Jenkins. They "thought we should come to Washington as soon as could. Told them I was waiting for the body and Mrs. Kennedy. The Attorney General interrupted the conversation to say that I ought to have a judicial officer administer the oath here."[27]

Now confirmed in his decision to take the oath in Dallas, Johnson turned his attention to finding a local judge to administer it.

Johnson knew exactly whom he wanted. "Let's get Judge Sarah Hughes," he said. Fehmer, who always carried a small book with phone numbers, gave Johnson the number for her office.

The choice of Sarah Hughes to preside over the swearing in revealed how quickly power had shifted in Washington. In the spring of 1961, Johnson had asked Robert Kennedy to appoint Hughes to a federal judgeship. After the Justice Department informed him that at sixty-five she was too old, Kennedy rejected her. An embarrassed Johnson had to call her and explain why she did not get the job and then offer the position to another Texas lawyer in her stead.

A few weeks later, however, while he was out of the country, the Justice Department reversed its decision and announced Hughes's appointment. Johnson was furious that he had been undermined and took his complaint directly to the president. As O'Donnell told the story, LBJ pleaded with the president. "Mr. President, you realize where this leaves me? Sarah Hughes now thinks I'm nothing. The lawyer I offered the job to after your brother turned Sarah down, he thinks I'm the biggest liar and fool in the history of the State of Texas. All on account of that brother of yours!" According to O'Donnell, Kennedy was amused by Johnson's grand display of self-pity and started laughing.

Hughes gained the appointment because of the sponsorship of another powerful Texas politician, House Speaker Sam Rayburn. Robert Kennedy had met with Rayburn in August 1961 to find out when a number of key administration bills would make it to the floor for a vote. Rayburn hinted that the bills might move faster if his friend Sarah Hughes received a judgeship. RFK pointed out that Johnson had nominated her but they considered her too old. "Son," Rayburn said, "everybody looks old to you. Do you want those bills passed, or don't you?" Hughes received her judgeship the next day.[28]

Hughes, who had been at the Trade Mart waiting for Kennedy's speech, called back at 2:02 p.m., saying that she could get to *Air Force One* in about ten minutes.

As Johnson continued to work the phone, he could hear the sounds as the crew removed seats from the back of the plane. They were making room for President Kennedy's coffin.

# 9

# "I HAVE ONLY ONE PRESIDENT"

While Johnson was arranging for the oath onboard *Air Force One,* another drama was playing out at Parkland Hospital. The Secret Service and Kennedy aides were in a struggle with a local coroner over the president's body. By 1:40 p.m., the president's body had been loaded into a casket ready for transport back to Washington. As the aides awaited the death certificate so they could depart, a very pale and agitated Dr. Earl Rose, the Dallas medical examiner, approached Agent Roy Kellerman. "There has been a homicide here," he said. "You won't be able to remove the body. We will have to take it down to the mortuary for an autopsy."[1]

Kellerman, who had just witnessed his president's assassination, had no intention of leaving his body behind in Dallas. "There must be something in your thinking here that we don't have to go through this agony," Kellerman said. "We will take care of the matter when we get back to Washington." Rose held his ground. "No, that's not the way things are. You're not taking the body anywhere." Kellerman was not impressed. According to his testimony before the Warren Commission, he responded, "You are going to have to come up with something a little stronger than you to give me the law that this body can't be removed."[2]

Rose went in search of a judge to provide some legal support, and returned with a local justice of the peace, Theron Ward. "It's just another homicide case as far as I'm concerned," Ward explained, meaning the body would have to stay in Dallas until the autopsy was complete. The president's men had heard enough at that point. They devised a plan to force their way out of the hospital. "Ken O'Donnell called a quick huddle with the Secret Service, Dave Powers and Larry O'Brien," Powers recalled. "It was decided in the huddle that Mrs. Kennedy must be spared any further delay. Ken O'Donnell said, 'Let's go, we're getting out of here now.' "[3]

With heavily armed Secret Service agents leading the way, they forced their way past a big Dallas cop. Hospital administrator

Jack Price observed Mrs. Kennedy "walking on the left side of the casket with her right hand encased in a bloodstained glove resting on the casket near the head." *Newsweek* reporter Charles Roberts, who watched as the bronze casket was wheeled out of the hospital, wrote that his "most vivid recollection of that moment is of the dazed look on Jackie Kennedy's face."[4]

Outside, there were a hearse and an ambulance waiting. Mrs. Kennedy, who hated hearses, insisted that the casket be loaded into the back of the ambulance. General Godfrey McHugh, President Kennedy's air force aide, who had rushed to the hospital in the minutes after the shooting, was now among the small group of aides surrounding the casket. "As we got there, the men from the hearse tried to grab the casket. We pushed them politely and gently aside," McHugh recalled. Mrs. Kennedy and McHugh rode in the back of the ambulance with the casket. O'Donnell, Powers, and O'Brien rode in a backup car. At 2:14, according to the official Secret Service log, the presidential party arrived at Love Field.[5]

There is considerable debate about what happened in the minutes after Mrs. Kennedy boarded the plane. Not surprisingly,

Johnson placed his actions in the most gracious light. In his memoirs, LBJ claimed that he walked to the back of the plane and greeted her as she boarded. At the end of the conversation, he and Lady Bird escorted Jackie "to the bedroom and then left her alone. Privacy seemed the only kindness at such a time." Afterward, he said, the casket "was brought up the ramp and placed in the rear of the plane."[6]

Johnson's account does not, however, hold up to scrutiny. First, White House photographer Cecil Stoughton took a series of pictures of the Kennedy group boarding the plane. They clearly show that Mrs. Kennedy boarded the plane after the coffin had been carried up the stairs. Second, no one in the Kennedy group recalled seeing LBJ as they boarded the plane, and given his size, he was hard to miss.

The true story, and the one Johnson no doubt wanted to repress, even in his own mind, is much more awkward. Marie Fehmer, who was with LBJ in the bedroom, claimed in her oral history that the Secret Service failed to alert Johnson when Mrs. Kennedy boarded the plane. LBJ was still working the phone when he learned that Jackie had arrived. They quickly gathered up their belongings and tried to leave, but it was too late. "I picked up my things and opened the door and there was Mrs. Kennedy standing there in the doorway," recalled Fehmer. "I'll never forget it. There was that great lady with blood on her suit and most of all I remember the blood on her stockings . . . I just stepped out of the way." An embarrassed Johnson followed behind her, apologizing to Mrs. Kennedy as he moved hastily past her.[7]

Johnson made no mention of this encounter in his memoirs or any of the other accounts of his actions that day. It was not his fault that the Secret Service failed to notify him that the Kennedy group had boarded. He probably had wanted to greet Jackie the moment she arrived. His concern for her was genuine and heartfelt. Instead of acknowledging the confusion and misunderstanding, however, LBJ chose to distort events. For many of the Kennedy people, these little lies tapped into underlying doubts about LBJ's character. They also distracted attention from the larger story of Johnson's skillful handling of one of the most difficult situations ever to confront an American president.

After scurrying out of the bedroom, Johnson proceeded to the forward cabin to find Lady

Bird. He asked her to go back with him to offer condolences to Mrs. Kennedy. It was, he said, "the moment against which I had been steeling myself — and dreading to the depths of my being." With the exception of their brief encounter as he fled her bedroom, he had not seen Jackie since they arrived at Love Field in Dallas and got into the motorcade. Johnson was shocked by her appearance. Her "beautiful, unsoiled, nicely pressed pink garment" was now "streaked and caked and soiled throughout with her husband's blood." Lady Bird noted that "Mrs. Kennedy's dress was stained with blood. One leg was almost entirely covered with it and her right glove was caked, it was caked with blood — her husband's blood. Somehow that was one of the most poignant sights — that immaculate woman, exquisitely dressed, and caked in blood."[8]

Johnson claimed not to recall much of the conversation. "It was not really a conversation, just clumsy, aching words of condolence and some half-finished, choked sentences in reply." In delicate moments such as these that required sensitivity and emotion, he allowed Lady Bird to take the lead. "I tried to express how we felt," she noted in her diary. "Oh, Mrs. Kennedy," she remembered saying, "you know we never even wanted to be Vice President and now, dear God, it's come to this." She wanted to do something to help the grieving and shell-shocked widow, but realized "there was nothing I could do . . ." The conversation was awkward and disjointed. Mrs. Kennedy responded by saying, "Oh, what if I hadn't been there! I was so glad I was there."[9]

At a loss for words, Lady Bird sobbed, "What wounds me most of all is that this should happen in my beloved State of Texas." She immediately regretted the comment, realizing that Texas pride was not appropriate for the moment. She asked if she wanted someone to help her change into clean clothes. "Oh, no," Jackie replied. "Perhaps later I'll ask Mary Gallagher but not right now." According to Lady Bird, "Then with almost an element of fierceness — if a person that gentle, that dignified, can be said to have such a quality — she said, 'I want them to see what they have done to Jack.' " Although she did not change her clothes, she did use a tissue to wipe the president's blood and hair that was stuck to her face.[10]

After a brief pause, Johnson mentioned the swearing in. "I've arranged for a judge — an old friend of mine, Judge Hughes — to come," he told her. "She'll be here in about an hour. So why don't you lie down and freshen up and everything? We'll leave you alone." With that Lyndon and Lady Bird left the room.[11]

All the simmering tensions between the Kennedy and Johnson camps now came to the surface in the confusion aboard *Air Force One.* There had been no contact between the two groups since Johnson left Parkland Hospital. Kennedy aides did not know about LBJ's plans to take the oath. In fact, they did not even know that he was on the plane. They were about to find out.

When they finally made it back to *Air Force One,* the Kennedy group assumed that they would have the plane to themselves. O'Donnell believed that he and Johnson had agreed back at Parkland Hospital that Johnson would take *Air Force Two* back to Washington and leave the Kennedy plane for the First Lady and the coffin. For Mrs. Kennedy and the slain president's aides, the flight home was going to be a wake, a distinctly private time. "I assumed that he had left the airport at least a half-hour before and was now on his way to Washington," O'Donnell reflected. The Kennedy party pulled up in such a rush that O'Donnell did not see the other 707 sitting alongside *Air Force One* at Love Field.[12]

O'Donnell and the other aides were desperate to get the plane off the ground. Given the legal tussle at the hospital over the president's body, O'Donnell feared the Dallas police would either rush the plane or use their cars to block access to the runway. In a 1969 interview, O'Donnell recalled how on edge he was as he boarded the plane: "I'm concerned that the Dallas police are going to come and take the body off the plane and Jackie Kennedy's going to have a heart attack right in front of us there. I'm petrified. We get on the airplane and I'm urging them to take off." He wanted to get off the ground as soon as possible. "We've got to go," he said. "We've got to get out of here."[13]

As soon as the Kennedy aides secured the casket, O'Donnell told General McHugh to order Captain Swindal to get into the air. McHugh was born in France and spoke with a noticeable accent. As the president's air force aide, it was his job to oversee the details of the new president's transportation and make sure he made it safely back to Washington. His relationship to the First Family, however, went far beyond his official duties. He had once dated Jackie before she met JFK, teaching her to water ski on the Chesapeake Bay.

Like many in the Kennedy camp, McHugh treated Johnson with contempt. Twice at Parkland Hospital the Secret Service asked him to meet with Johnson to discuss logistical arrangements for returning to Washington. Twice he refused. Later, speaking to William Manchester, he justified his actions. Johnson, he said, "had his own Air Force plane nearby . . . I saw no reason for that." Even with Kennedy dead, McHugh's loyalty remained with the slain leader. "My job when the President was aboard the aircraft was to get airborne. The fact that he was dead did not seem to make any difference."[14]

McHugh described the tense scene aboard *Air Force One.* It was standard practice for the plane to take off as soon as the president was onboard; instead, after several minutes "nothing happened." As they sat on the ground in the hot, stuffy plane, Mrs. Kennedy turned to him and asked, "Why don't we leave?" McHugh, ever loyal, rushed to the cockpit and confronted Captain Swindal: "Let's leave, now that the president is aboard." Swindal seemed confused by the question, likely because he assumed that McHugh was referring to Johnson, not Kennedy. He responded, "No, we can't because

212

Mr. Kilduff says we can't." McHugh must have found it galling that his orders were being countermanded by an assistant press secretary. "It didn't matter what anybody else says," he blustered, repeating his orders to get the plane in the air.[15]

McHugh marched back to his seat, but still the engines did not start. Mrs. Kennedy was becoming desperate to leave. "Mrs. Kennedy was getting very warm, she had blood all over her hat, her coat . . . his brains were sticking on her hat. It was dreadful." Again, she pleaded with him to get the plane off the ground. "Please, let's leave," she said. McHugh jumped up and used the phone near the rear compartment to call Swindal. "Let's leave," he said. Swindal responded, "I can't do it. I have orders to wait." Not wanting to make a scene in front of Mrs. Kennedy, McHugh again rushed to the front of the plane. "Swindal, what on earth is going on?" Swindal told him that "the President wants to remain in this area."[16]

The response puzzled McHugh. "I have only one President, and he's lying back in that cabin," he shouted pointing toward the coffin. McHugh's words echoed throughout the plane. It is unclear whether Johnson heard the exchange, but the general's dis-

213

tinctive French accent carried all the way to the rear compartment, where O'Donnell and other members of the Kennedy group were maintaining their vigil. The words must have been startling to those who knew that Johnson was onboard. Was this insubordination? Was McHugh, a brigadier general, refusing to acknowledge his new commander in chief?[17]

Most likely, McHugh was not being intentionally disrespectful; he simply did not know that Johnson was aboard the plane. Like everyone one else on *Air Force One,* he was unclear about the laws governing presidential succession. Thus when Swindal told him that Johnson was issuing the orders, McHugh responded, "But he's the vice president." Perhaps he believed that Kennedy remained president until Johnson took the oath? Swindal was also unsure, but he appreciated that a transfer of power was about to occur. "Well, he's going to be president," Swindal said. "He's ordered for me to wait until his luggage is transferred from *Air Force Two* to here, and I'm told that there's going to be [a] swearing in. I don't know because we were told to call a judge and that she's coming, so we're going to have to wait."[18]

Deflated, McHugh returned to the rear

compartment with other members of the Kennedy camp. O'Donnell told the general he was proud of him for the comments he made about President Kennedy. But although he may have been pleased with McHugh's theatrical performance, he was not thrilled with the results. After sitting for a few more minutes, a "furious" O'Donnell exploded. "Didn't we tell you to leave?" McHugh then explained the predicament. "I can't get the crew to do it because they say President Johnson is aboard." O'Donnell, who was still operating under the assumption that Johnson was already on his way to Washington aboard *Air Force Two,* was incredulous. "Obviously he isn't," he replied.[19]

McHugh decided to find out for himself. He launched himself from his seat and marched up and down the cabin. To some of the other passengers, McHugh seemed out of control. Malcolm Kilduff dismissed him as "galloping General McHugh." According to Jack Valenti, the general "stormed down the aisle, threatening anyone who came near him." Soon after McHugh left the rear compartment, Jackie Kennedy returned from the bedroom and informed O'Donnell about her encounter with LBJ. Now everyone except McHugh knew that

LBJ was onboard.[20]

During his marches through the plane, McHugh encountered Kilduff and once again demanded to know why the plane was not yet airborne. Kilduff seemed puzzled, no doubt because he assumed that McHugh, like everyone else, knew Johnson was on the plane. Kilduff explained to McHugh that "we're waiting for newspaper people." The answer infuriated McHugh. "The hell with the newspaper people, we're going to go." Realizing that argument was not very convincing, Kilduff said, "We have to wait for Lady Bird's luggage which had not arrived." Although Swindal had already told him that Johnson was on the plane, McHugh still was not convinced. "She's on her own plane with LBJ," he said. Kilduff pushed back, "Then you go back and tell that big six-foot Texan he is not Lyndon Johnson."[21]

Now McHugh was confused. He had already been up and down the aisle twice and had not encountered Johnson. McHugh then assumed that he must be in the bedroom, but when he checked there Johnson was nowhere to be seen. The only room McHugh had not explored was the private bathroom in the president's bedroom.

What McHugh claimed to have witnessed

was shocking. The details of his bathroom encounter with LBJ are contained in an oral history the general conducted for the Kennedy Library on May 19, 1978. The transcript was declassified in 2009.

"I walked in the toilet, in the powder room, and there he was hiding, with the curtain closed," McHugh recalled. He claimed that LBJ was crying, "They're going to get us all. It's a plot. It's a plot. It's going to get us all.'" According to the general, Johnson "was hysterical, sitting down on the john there alone in this thing." He walked out and reported what he saw to O'Donnell. "My God, he's there. Yes, you're right. He seems very, very upset." O'Donnell responded, "I don't want to upset him any more." So McHugh explained to Mrs. Kennedy the reason for the delay. "Mr. Johnson is here and he's asked that the plane not leave right away," he told her.[22]

McHugh told a similar story a week before sitting down for an interview for the JFK Library, when he spoke by phone with Mark Flanagan, an investigator with the House Select Committee on Assassinations. "McHugh had encountered difficulty in locating Johnson but finally discovered him alone," Flanagan wrote in his summary to the committee. Quoting McHugh, the investigator noted that the general found Johnson "hiding in the toilet in the bedroom compartment and muttering, 'Conspiracy, conspiracy, they're after all of us.' "[23]

If true, the story is explosive — and reveals a completely different side of Johnson than the collected, calm presence he otherwise managed to convey throughout the hours and days following Kennedy's death. But how credible is McHugh's account? It is, of course, impossible to confirm or deny whether a private encounter took place between the two men, both of whom are now dead. It is true that the general intensely disliked Johnson and was fiercely loyal to JFK; he therefore had some reason to invent such a story. He is, however, generally a very credible source. That said, McHugh's description of a hysterical Johnson cowering on the toilet runs counter to the eyewitness testimony of nearly everyone who observed him that day. Most witnesses described Johnson as cool, calm, controlled, almost subdued. Could Johnson have disappeared long enough to fall apart, compose himself, and leave no trace of his hysteria except for a chance encounter with McHugh?

There are a number of reasons to doubt McHugh's claim. Most glaring, McHugh made no mention of what was surely a very memorable encounter in his long interview with William Manchester in 1964. "On the third trip back and forth through the plane I opened the bedroom door and no one was there," he said. "I never dreamt there would be anyone in the powder room." After pacing the plane a few more times, he "decided that the President must be in the powder room." He did not, however, volunteer any more information and Manchester did not pursue the line of questioning.[24]

It also stands to reason that if McHugh had witnessed Johnson in a state of utter breakdown, he would have told the story to O'Donnell or others within the Kennedy camp. Surely, given how potentially damaging the story would be to the new president, O'Donnell, or other Kennedy partisans, would have leaked it.

The story has taken on new and even more explosive elements since the original telling in 1978. Author Christopher Anderson included an exaggerated version of the story in his bestselling *Jackie After Jack,* published in 1998. He claimed his account came from an interview he conducted with McHugh shortly before his death. In the book, McHugh quotes Johnson as saying, "They're going to kill us, they're going to shoot down the plane, they're going to kill us all." The general, Anderson wrote, "got LBJ to snap out of it by slapping him."[25]

The suggestion that a general would "slap" the commander in chief struck most people as preposterous and called into question the entire encounter. At the time, Johnson loyalists condemned the story. "That's not true. That did not happen," said Bill Moyers. "I was in the room with him the whole time. It didn't happen." Jack Valenti called Anderson "a bloody liar." Johnson, he insisted "was the coolest man on the plane." Oddly enough, all the criticism was directed at Anderson and not at McHugh, who was apparently the source of the quote.[26]

It is possible, however, that McHugh was telling the truth in the 1978 interview. Johnson was a man capable of dramatic mood swings, and occasional fits of hysteria were not unusual for him. McHugh's account of LBJ's behavior is similar to RFK's description of a trembling and tearful Johnson at the 1960 Democratic Convention, when it appeared that JFK might renege on his promise to include him on the ticket. It was not surprising behavior to those who knew him best. Throughout his career, LBJ had suffered from fits of paranoia and serious bouts of depression. These moments would become more common later in his presidency, as he was forced to struggle with an unpopular war and relentless criticism from the press.[27]

We also know from some eyewitnesses that Youngblood stood outside the door to the bedroom and controlled traffic into the room. Aides went in and out, but it is possible that McHugh could have found LBJ alone in the room.

If true, though, why did McHugh wait until 1978 to tell this story? When Manchester interviewed him in May 1964, McHugh was still in the military, although only a few months away from retirement. Is it possible that he worried the story would be too damaging to his commander in chief? We will never know.

Once they learned that Johnson was on the plane, O'Donnell and Larry O'Brien went forward to make the case to him for taking off right away. But before O'Donnell had a chance to explain the urgency created by the standoff with the medical examiner, Johnson announced that he had talked to "Bobby" — the attorney general wanted him to be sworn in in Dallas. According to O'Donnell, LBJ said, "We can't leave here until I take the oath of office. I just talked on the phone with Bobby. He told me to wait here until Sarah Hughes gives me the oath." According to General Chester Clifton, who was listening in on the conversation, O'Donnell kept saying, "We've got to get out of here. . . . We can't wait." Each time, Johnson responded, "No, I have word from the Attorney General."[28]

O'Donnell was "flabbergasted." None of it made sense to him, he later recalled. First, there was no need, he felt, for LBJ to take the oath so soon after the assassination. "He is the president of the United States the minute they say, 'You're dead,' with all the powers of the presidency. He never has to be sworn in ever in his life." Second, if there was a conspiracy, the safest place for him was in the sky on *Air Force One,* not sitting exposed on the ground in Dallas. Third, he did not believe that Robert Kennedy would have instructed Johnson to have the oath administered in Dallas. "I could not imagine Bobby telling him to stay in Dallas until he had taken the presidential oath."[29]

O'Donnell's most serious accusation, however, was that Johnson was failing to show compassion for the First Lady. "Johnson could have waited until he got to Washington and spared all of us on *Air Force*

*One* that day, especially Jackie, a lot of discomfort and anxiety."[30]

Once again, Johnson was being deceptive in claiming that he was simply following RFK's orders that he take the oath in Dallas. He could have simply said that he was president now and in his opinion it was necessary to reassure the nation that the government was still functioning. Instead, as he would do so many times that day, he hid behind either RFK or O'Donnell to justify his actions.

Both the confusion over the oath and the decision to take Kennedy's plane confirmed O'Donnell's worse fears about LBJ — that he was an extraordinarily insecure, insensitive man who was incapable of telling the truth. In his later recollections of those first hours after the assassination, O'Donnell challenged almost every claim Johnson made. O'Donnell convinced himself that LBJ was not in fact waiting for the First Lady before flying back to Washington, and that it was only a coincidence that they showed up before the judge. "I am convinced in my own mind if Judge Hughes had arrived on that aircraft before we did, Johnson would have taken off without us," he told Manchester. Johnson, O'Donnell was certain, was not taking the oath because

Bobby insisted on it. He wanted to take it as soon as possible because "he was afraid somebody was going to take the thing away from him if he didn't get it quick."[31]

O'Donnell's contempt for Johnson may have led him to an extreme and inappropriate degree of paranoia about the man, but he did get something right. Years later, describing that day in *"Johnny, We Hardly Knew Ye,"* the book he coauthored with Dave Powers, O'Donnell shared this crucial insight into LBJ: the man refused to take responsibility for his own decisions. "He was trying to shift the blame for his being on *Air Force One* to me, just as he insisted that he has waited in Dallas to take the oath on the plane because Bobby had told him to do so, which was not true at all."[32]

O'Donnell was bristling with contempt, but for now he kept his feelings to himself. Johnson, apparently unaware of the anger directed toward him, established a very different tone as he pleaded with O'Donnell and O'Brien to stay on and help with the transition. "The Constitution of the United States is putting me into the White House," he said. "But there's no law to make you stay there with me." He urged them "to stay and stand shoulder to shoulder with me."

Both men assured him that he would have their support, but did not indicate for how long. LBJ understood that the two men were "in no mood to discuss the future," but he "wanted them to know that they were on my mind and important to me."[33]

While Johnson was talking with O'Brien and O'Donnell, Kilduff interrupted to ask how he planned to handle press coverage of the swearing in. Kilduff told him it was essential to have press coverage of the event. "Then," Johnson said, "we should ask everyone on the plane who wants to come to be present."[34]

# 10
# "I Do
## Solemnly Swear"

As Johnson's conversation with O'Brien and O'Donnell was winding down, Youngblood alerted Johnson that Judge Sarah Hughes had arrived in her car, cleared the gate, and would be onboard in a few minutes. The Secret Service logged her time of arrival at 2:30 p.m.

The press pool for the event was also arriving and boarding the plane. Merriman Smith of UPI, Charles Roberts of *Newsweek,* and Sid Davis of Westinghouse Broadcasting had raced from Parkland Hospital in an unmarked police car, reaching speeds of up to seventy miles an hour. "Without benefit of a siren (cut off so as not to attract attention to the airport) we had crossed median strips and plowed through red lights," recalled Roberts. The plane, which by now had been sitting in the sun for three hours without air conditioning, was according to Roberts both dark and "suffocatingly hot." The scene was grim; entering the cabin was "like bursting breathlessly into a wake. Johnson and Kennedy secretaries, their faces grotesquely streaked with mascara, were weeping openly and audibly. Strong Secret Service men, slumped into their seats in the forward cabin, were shielding their eyes from view."[1]

Bill Moyers, a former newsman and divinity school graduate, also boarded shortly before the judge arrived. Moyers had worked as a summer intern in LBJ's Senate office, and later returned as a personal aide and as Johnson's traveling companion during the 1960 campaign. After the election, Kennedy offered Moyers a position as deputy director of the Peace Corps.

Born in Oklahoma and raised in Texas, Moyers had seemed to JFK like an ideal person to help organize the November trip. Moyers was having lunch in Austin when he learned of the shooting. He quickly rented a private plane and flew directly to Love Field, where he boarded *Air Force One.*

In a speech a few weeks after the assassination, Moyers recalled the bleak scene aboard *Air Force One.* "My impressions of those first few minutes aboard that plane are blurred. I remember General Clifton, the White House military aide, telling the radio operator to get Washington. I saw Mrs. Evelyn Lincoln, who had been President Kennedy's personal secretary. She was sobbing quietly. Rear Admiral Burkley, Physician to the President, was sitting at the rear of the forward cabin, shocked and stunned . . . And standing at the door which separates the private Presidential compartment from the forward compartment was the familiar but not strained face of the Secret Service Agent. His face was taut."[2]

While everyone was waiting for the swearing in, Johnson "inhaled" a bowl of vegetable soup and some crackers. He looked at Dave Powers and said, "It's been a year since I got up." Marie Fehmer said he seemed "to be speaking more to himself than to the person."[3]

When Hughes arrived, she embraced both the president and First Lady. She was ready to administer the oath, but Johnson said, "Mrs. Kennedy wants to be here. We'll wait for her." Johnson asked Ken O'Donnell to see if Mrs. Kennedy would stand with him. O'Donnell, who was trying to move things along, still fearing that the Dallas police would try to prevent the plane from taking off, was shocked by the request. "You can't do that! The poor little kid has had enough for one day, to sit here and hear that oath that she heard a few years ago! You just can't do that, Mr. President!" Johnson, however, insisted. Although sensitive to her private suffering, LBJ also understood the symbolic power of having the First Lady standing by his side.[4]

This decision, like so many others in the twenty-four hours following the assassination, would be a source of tension between the Kennedy and Johnson camps. Among Kennedy partisans, LBJ's request would be viewed as further evidence of his insensitivity toward the former First Lady. The story that circulated around the White House during the next few days, and which Kennedy aide Arthur Schlesinger Jr. recorded in his diary, was that when O'Donnell initially balked at the idea, Johnson said sternly, "When I tell you to do something, I want it done — and *fast*." It is unlikely that LBJ, who was trying so hard to court O'Donnell, would speak to him that way. But he did insist, and O'Donnell backed off.[5]

O'Donnell went to the bedroom searching for Jackie, but found the door closed. He was reluctant to open it. "You don't break into a lady's bedroom quite often, and the President of the United States' wife," he recalled. Finally, he walked in and found her combing her hair. "Do you want to go out there?" he asked. "Yes, I think I ought to. At least I owe that much to the country," she said.[6]

Moments later, Mrs. Kennedy walked into the cabin. The room went silent. Smith described the former First Lady as "white-faced but dry-eyed."[7] "Her pink blouse was splattered with blood and white flecks of her husband's brain," recalled Jack Valenti. Johnson took both of her hands in his and positioned her to his left and Mrs. Johnson on his right. "She stood beside the new president, eyes opaque, unseeing, cast downward, her hands clasped in front of her, her whole figure a resolve cast in grace and dignity."[8]

Johnson then introduced Hughes, telling Mrs. Kennedy that she was a district judge appointed by JFK. Hughes leaned over to Mrs. Kennedy and said, "I loved your husband very much." Johnson then nodded to Judge Hughes indicating that he was ready.[9]

The scene in the main cabin was chaotic. Merriman Smith, who eighteen years earlier had filed reports on the death of Franklin D. Roosevelt, and Charles Roberts counted "27 perspiring bodies" jammed into the sixteen-foot-square stateroom "in addition to the President's desk and chair, a sofa bed and several bulky lounge seats." A few Kennedy aides crammed into the cabin, but some chose to boycott the ceremony. "I did not belong to the Lyndon Johnson team," James Swindal told Manchester. "My President was lying in that casket." Godfrey McHugh also did not attend. Before the ceremony began, Mrs. Kennedy had asked General McHugh to stay with the body. "Don't leave him," she pleaded. "Stay with him." For the next few minutes, McHugh stood at attention with the slain commander in chief. "I felt I was his military honor guard," he reflected, "that I should stay with him."[10]

"Everybody's in," Johnson said, looking at White House photographer Cecil Stoughton. "Where do you want us, Cecil?"

Cecil Stoughton's pictures of the Kennedys — he took more than 8,000 during JFK's time in office — had been instrumental in creating the public image of a vibrant young family that helped forge an enduring emotional bond between the president and the public. There was the memorable shot of Caroline and John Jr. dancing in the Oval Office, as their father clapped and smiled; the family portrait in Hyannisport showing a beaming Kennedy next to Caroline while a radiant Jackie held

John Jr. on her knee. Just two years earlier he had recorded President Kennedy's swearing in on a cold but joyful January day. Now he was recording another oath under very different conditions.

Stoughton had raced from Parkland Hospital as soon as he learned that Johnson had left for *Air Force One*. He recalled the scene as he boarded the plane a few minutes before the oath: "It was dark. All I could see was just dull images and hear the sniffing of ladies crying." As he walked down the aisle, he encountered Malcolm Kilduff. "Thank God, you're here, Cecil," he said. "The President's going to take the oath on the plane, and you're going to make the pictures."[11]

Stoughton knew the photos would go out on the wire services, so he had to shoot them in black and white. He stripped the Koda-color film from his Hasselbald magazine and loaded a 35 mm camera with Tri-X film. He had two cameras around his neck. "In case one didn't work, I'd have another one."[12]

Just as he finished loading the camera, the judge boarded the plane. Stoughton had only a few minutes to set up the most important picture he would ever take. Once Mrs. Kennedy entered the stateroom, he positioned her close to the camera so her bloodstained suit would be out of the frame. There were too many people in the room and Johnson had moved too close to Stoughton, who was perched on top of the sofa to get the widest angle possible. "You'll have to move back a bit," Stoughton told LBJ. When he went to snap the first picture, the camera malfunctioned. "I almost died," he recalled. "I had a little connector that was loose because of all the bustling around, so I just pushed it in with my finger, and number two went off on schedule."[13]

At 2:40 p.m., just a little more than two hours after the first shots were fired, Judge Hughes, her voice shaking and her hands trembling, asked Johnson to recite the oath. Malcolm Kilduff held a Dictabelt, a dictating machine, to record the sound.

"Hold up your right hand and repeat after me," the judge said, gripping a Roman Catholic missal retrieved from the president's bedroom. Johnson placed his left hand on the missal, slowly raised his right hand into the air, and recited the thirty-four-word oath. "I do solemnly swear I will faithfully execute the office of president of the United States . . ." In a firm voice Johnson declared after the judge, ". . . and will to the best of my ability, preserve, protect and defend the Constitution of the United States. So help me God."

"There," Lady Bird wrote in her diary, "in the very narrow confines of the plane — with Jackie standing by Lyndon, her hair falling in her face but very composed, with me beside him, Judge Hughes in front of him, and a cluster of Secret Service people, staff, and Congressmen we had known for a long time around him — Lyndon took the oath of office."[14]

As Johnson was taking the oath, the only sound on the plane was that of Stoughton's camera shutter and the whine of the plane's engine number three in the background. It all seemed like a bad dream to Lady Bird: "I remember during the swearing-in I thought this was a moment that was unreal and that we were just characters in a play. I thought this was the beginning of something for us that is dreadful and heavy. We were stepping into a strange new world."[15]

The ceremony took only two minutes. And yet the three reporters witnessing the ceremony from only a few feet away nonetheless managed to disagree about the details of how it played out. Smith claimed that Johnson leaned over and kissed Mrs. Kennedy after he took the oath. Roberts reported that he kissed his wife but only embraced Mrs. Kennedy.[16]

Once the ceremony was over, members of the congressional delegation in the room moved to congratulate the new president. Recognizing this was not a moment for celebration, Johnson backed away. The new president spotted Kennedy's secretary, Evelyn Lincoln. He leaned over and gently kissed her hand. A few seconds later, Johnson issued his first order: "Now, let's get airborne."[17]

Mrs. Kennedy returned to the small compartment to sit by the coffin. Bill Moyers, who went back for the takeoff, saw her pause beside the casket. "It's going to be so long and so lonely," she said. Her voice was barely audible.[18]

One of the reasons Johnson took the oath so soon after the shooting was to reassure the nation that he was in charge. As the plane prepared for liftoff, his aides scrambled to make sure the physical evidence of the ceremony — the photos and tape recording — were left behind in Dallas so they could be broadcast to the nation while *Air Force One* was speeding back to Washington.

With the ceremony complete, Kilduff handed Stoughton the Dictabelt recording of the swearing in. Kilduff had charged Stoughton with getting the pictures developed and out to the wire services as quickly as possible. Stoughton rushed to get off the plane before it took off. As he descended the stairs, he handed the Dictabelt recording to a Signal Corps officer. "Colonel, I'm going to give you this and make you responsible to see that it gets dubbed by our Signal Corps guys and given to the networks, because it's the oath, and I've got to take care of the pictures."[19]

Stoughton raced to the Associated Press office at the *Dallas Morning News* building to get the pictures developed. He held his breath the whole time. He worried that the flash, which had failed the first time, would not be synchronized with the pictures. Would his photographs of one of the most important moments in history end up as little more than a series of blurred, unrecognizable images? "I went into the darkroom with the guy," he recalled. "I could do nothing to help them. I just wanted to be there because that was it, until he got them out of the soup and into the hypo, and we spread them out before a transparent light in the darkroom and saw that I had images. And then I breathed."[20]

Stoughton picked out the one photo of

the oath that would be sent over the wire services. He handed the picture over to the UPI courier, who carried it a few blocks to the UPI wire photo service. Stoughton wanted to coordinate the release so that AP and UPI would send the photo at the same time. Once UPI had the photo loaded onto their drum, Stoughton conducted a countdown, 3–2–1 "Roll your drums."[21]

Stoughton's still photograph made it onto the national news as the presidential party was speeding back to Washington. At 5:40 p.m. (EST), NBC became the first news organization to broadcast the picture. The next morning, the picture appeared on the front page of nearly every newspaper in the nation.[22]

The picture of that moment, one of the most iconic in American history, delivered a public message that the government survived, Johnson was in charge, and the transition of power, though violent, had been smooth. "LBJ understood how crucial it was to photograph the swearing-in so that the picture could be flashed around the world quickly," Jack Valenti noted. "This photo would proclaim that while the light in the White House may flicker, it never goes out."[23]

According to *Life* magazine picture editor

Barbara Baker Burrows, the photo "provided the essential evidence of the continuity of government. In the confusion that followed the assassination," she observed, the "photograph told the world that there was a new President, and the country that it was safe."[24]

# "There Was Tenseness on That Plane"

*Air Force One* lifted off at 2:46 p.m. (CST), just 8 minutes after Lyndon Johnson completed the oath, and 136 minutes after Kennedy had been shot. For the first and last time, the plane would be carrying two American presidents. LBJ sat quietly as the jet climbed over the clouds. Initially "no one moved," recalled Cliff Carter, "everyone was just sitting there in a state of shock." The shades remained down for the entire trip. Johnson watched television coverage of the day's events until the reception faded.[1]

The new president had about two hours to collect his thoughts and prepare for his arrival in the nation's capital as the new commander in chief. When asked by Walter Cronkite in 1970 what was going through his mind during the ride back to Washington, Johnson said that he "thought and thought and thought and tried to anticipate what would confront me." He considered the issues he needed to deal with and the priorities he must establish. He decided on the people he wanted to have around him who would "give me the best judgment and most strength."[2]

Johnson had dozens of decisions to make in those critical first hours, including a great many about the protocol of the next few days. What was the appropriate mourning period for the slain president? At what point was it suitable for him to take control of the symbols of the presidency? Should he give an address to the nation that evening when he arrived in Washington? Johnson knew that he had to walk a fine line. He needed to project strength and continuity to the nation, while being respectful of the Kennedy family and sensitive to a nation mourning its fallen leader. It was important for the nation and the world to know that he was in charge, but how did he convey that message without appearing overeager? He needed to balance strength with humility.[3]

One of Johnson's top priorities was to make sure the Kennedy people did not abandon him. He needed to avoid a flood of grief-stricken resignations. His interest in retaining the Kennedy advisers was bred of several factors, including personal compassion, shrewd instincts, and nagging insecurity. By keeping familiar names and faces close to him, Johnson knew he would send a reassuring message to the public. At some level, Johnson had convinced himself that he needed the slain president's team in order to legitimize his presidency. "I needed that White House staff," he confided to Doris Kearns Goodwin. "Without them I would have lost my link to John Kennedy, and without that I would have had absolutely no chance of gaining the support of the media or the Easterners or the intellectuals. And without that support I would have had absolutely no chance of governing the country."[4]

But Johnson also knew what it felt like to be an outsider in the White House, and he was determined not to allow that to happen to the Kennedy people. "The White House is small, but if you're not at the center it seems enormous," he told Goodwin. "You get the feeling that there are all sorts of meetings going on without you, all sorts of people clustered in small groups, whispering, always whispering. I felt that way as Vice President, and after Kennedy's death I knew that his men would feel the same thing. So I determined to keep them informed. I determined to keep them busy."[5]

Not surprisingly, O'Donnell was the first

person that Johnson asked for after the plane took off. As he changed his sweat-soaked shirt, LBJ again pleaded with O'Donnell to stay on. "You can't leave me. You're the only one that I really get along with there. You know that I don't know one soul north of the Mason-Dixon Line," O'Donnell recalled LBJ saying. "You know that I don't know any of those big city fellows. I need you. My staff doesn't know anything, they don't know anything. They don't know anyone outside of Texas." The conversation lasted about ten minutes. Afterward, O'Donnell was "noncommittal." It was too early for him to even think about his future, although he could not foresee ever working for Lyndon Johnson. For now, he was focused on comforting Kennedy's widow. "I wanted to stay with Jackie," he reflected. "So I went back and sat with Jackie."[6]

After O'Donnell left, LBJ asked for the three Texas congressmen who had been with him all day — Albert Thomas, Homer Thornberry, and Jack Brooks — to join him in the stateroom. He also invited staff members Jack Valenti, Cliff Carter, Liz Carpenter, and Bill Moyers.

The first order of business was to set up

meetings in Washington. LBJ wanted to send a clear message to the public that the government was consolidating around his leadership. "He was concerned about the American people; they had responded before to crisis; how would they respond now? He knew they would be watching him — he must show them leadership and purpose, but he must also show compassion and understanding," recalled Bill Moyers. "He knew, too, that eyes were watching from the Kremlin. They would be watching to detect any weakness — any hesitancy — any sign of indecision which might be exploited," Moyers observed. "Above all, he said, there must be continuity — continuity without confusion. That was to be his objective."[7]

As soon as they arrived at Andrews Air Force Base, Johnson demanded that the Kennedy foreign policy team be assembled. He told Moyers that he wanted Defense Secretary Robert McNamara, Secretary of State Dean Rusk, and National Security Adviser McGeorge Bundy to join on the helicopter flight from Andrews to the White House. Johnson did not realize that Secretary of State Rusk, and most of the cabinet, had been en route to Japan at the time of the assassination. The plane had been ordered back to Washington, but it would not arrive until late that night. In place of Rusk, it was agreed that Under Secretary George Ball would be there to greet him.

It is likely that Johnson wanted to meet with the foreign policy team because he was still concerned about the international implications of the assassination. Were the Soviets trying to take advantage of the death of the president? Although he felt comfortable, even confident, in his ability to handle most domestic legislation, and to push Kennedy's stalled agenda through Congress, he was less sure-footed in his handling of foreign affairs. He also needed to make certain that all key members of the president's team stayed on in his administration. Meeting with the Kennedy team face-to-face would allow him to deliver the message of continuity clearly and forcefully.

Mac Kilduff and General Chester Clifton were enlisted to relay LBJ's wishes to Washington using the communications equipment on *Air Force One*. They had their hands full — innumerable messages were going back and forth: friends and family members in Washington trying to contact Mrs. Kennedy, government officials hoping to reach the new president. Some of the passengers were trying to send private messages to family, to alert them of their whereabouts. Many of the people accompanying Johnson back to Washington were based in Texas and had planned to be home that night for dinner. Now they were speeding to Washington without even a change of clothes. Congressman Thomas asked Clifton to contact his secretary and tell her to leave the key to his apartment under the mat. Brooks asked that someone call his wife in Austin and tell her to meet him in Washington. General Clifton prioritized the calls: any message to or from the president received the highest priority.[8]

The communications system on *Air Force One* was supposed to be the most sophisticated in the world, capable of serving as a command center for waging nuclear war. On this day, however, it was difficult to convey even the simplest of instructions. There were no established procedures for returning the body of a dead president to Washington. It took repeated messages for the White House command center to understand that *Air Force One* was carrying both President Johnson and the body of President Kennedy. Once that was worked out, White House officials needed to arrange for an autopsy, which had to be conducted on a military base. But who was responsible for making the plans? The Secret Service sched-

uled the autopsy at Walter Reed Army
Medical Center; Kennedy's military aide
was setting it up at the Bethesda Naval
Medical Center. Through it all there was
constant interference on the telephone lines,
with voices fading in and out. Adding to the
confusion, Kennedy's personal physician,
Dr. Burkley, on the phone with the White
House, referred to Kennedy as "the president." In Washington, they were wondering,
was he talking about Johnson or Kennedy?[9]

The handling of Kennedy's body was one
of many details that needed to be worked
out before the plane landed in Washington.
Johnson understood that when he stepped
off the plane, the nation would be seeing
him for the first time as president. He
wanted to make sure the moment was carefully choreographed to convey a clear message to the public that he was now in charge.

There were discussions about whether the
press would be allowed at Andrews. The
Kennedy family preferred that the arrival
be private, with only a handful of family
and aides at the airport. Johnson understood
the family's desire for privacy, but he realized that the entire world would be watching his every step, listening intently to his
every word. Johnson "felt that if the press
was barred it would look as though we had

panicked," Kilduff told William Manchester. "I want the world to know," Johnson said, "that while the leader has fallen, the nation isn't prostrate."[10]

While Johnson was conferring with aides, Lady Bird sat on a small sofa behind him, trapped in her own thoughts. She asked for Liz Carpenter, telling her that she wanted to go over the notes she had taken. But Carpenter thought "she really wanted someone just to sit with her." Carpenter told Lady Bird that the press would expect a statement from her when they arrived in Washington. Lady Bird could not find the words to describe what had happened. "I just feel it's all been a dreadful nightmare and that somehow we must find the strength to go on," she said. Carpenter wrote down her words. "Well, that will be your statement."[11]

Johnson asked Moyers, Carpenter, and Valenti to draft a speech for him to deliver upon landing at Andrews. "I knew that I would be expected to say something when we touched down at Andrews Air Force Base," he wrote in his memoirs. "The nation would not want to hear a lengthy speech from me, but I felt the people would want to know there was leadership and purpose and continuity in their government," he reflected. "As far as the rest of the world was concerned, there must be no sign of hesitancy or indecision."[12]

The three aides jotted down ideas, which they cobbled together into draft form for Johnson to review. "He took the typewritten page, double-spaced, and began to scrawl, in that full-flowing handwriting I came to know so well," Valenti recalled. Their draft concluded with the line "I will do my best. I ask for God's help." Johnson scratched out the line and wrote, "I ask for your help — and God's." Valenti remembered thinking that it "was not the flourish that any of the three of us might have finally gone with, but it was simple, to the point and LBJ liked it."[13]

Kilduff called ahead to Washington to make sure they knew that Johnson planned to make a statement. "Will you please advise press that normal press coverage, including *live TV,* will be allowed at the [Andrews Air Force] Base," he said. Using Johnson's Secret Service name, he continued: "VOLUNTEER, repeat, VOLUNTEER will make a statement on arrival; will make statement on arrival. Did you read that? Over."[14]

LBJ was also managing the media onboard the plane. Aware that the reporters flying with him would be recording the first draft of history, Johnson made two separate trips to the press table where *Newsweek*'s Charles Roberts and Merriman Smith of the UPI were sitting. "The first time," Roberts recalled, "still subdued and speaking just above a whisper, he told us he wanted all of Kennedy's staff and Cabinet officers to stay on." Later he returned to tell them about the remarks that he would make when they arrived in Washington. "I'm going to make a short statement in a few minutes and give you copies of it," he said. "Then when I get on the ground, I'll do it over again."[15]

Johnson tried to be sensitive to the Kennedy family as he planned what he would do after arriving in Washington. There was some discussion that he should give a longer address to the nation, perhaps from the Oval Office, as a way to calm fears and project continuity. The office, Johnson was told, was a symbol of the power of the presidency. He needed to assume the trappings of the office in order to convey that he was in charge, to instill confidence. For now, Johnson vetoed the idea. "People will get confidence if we do our job properly," he responded. As some pressed the point, he ended the conversation. "Stop this. Our first concern is Mrs. Kennedy and the family." He was also reluctant to address the nation before arrangements had been made for the funeral. He believed that the nation needed to mourn its slain president before it was asked to accept a new one.[16]

For that reason, Johnson wanted to avoid using any of the official presidential offices or private quarters until after the funeral. He rattled off the groups he wanted assembled for the evening — the entire Kennedy cabinet, representatives of the congressional leadership, and members of the White House staff. Out of deference to the slain president, however, LBJ made it clear that he did "not want to go in the Mansion, or in the Oval Room, or the president's study, or the president's room."[17]

LBJ showed a similar respect for the family when it came to his living arrangements. The Secret Service wanted him to move into the White House that night. "That's the best place to protect you, Mr. President. Communications, security — everything is there," Youngblood said. Johnson was adamant, however, that Mrs. Kennedy not feel pressured to move out. "There will be no hurry involving Mrs. Kennedy. She will have as long as she wants." In a phrase he would use many times during the next few days, he said that moving into the White House "would be presumptuous on my part." He turned to Youngblood and asked, "Can't the Secret Service secure The Elms?" Youngblood nodded. "Yes, sir, Mr. President, we will secure The Elms."[18]

In fact, the Secret Service had already beefed up security at his residence. Teams of agents patrolled the outside grounds. Inside the house, technicians disconnected the three regular phone lines — all of which were listed in the Washington, D.C., phone book — and rewired them through the White House switchboard.

The stress Johnson was under was compounded by reports that there may have been a Soviet connection to the assassination. Shortly after they were in the air, Johnson received a report from General Clifton that Dallas police had arrested a suspect in the president's shooting. This would be the first time that Johnson would hear the name Lee Harvey Oswald. It is not known exactly what Clifton told the president, but at this point the available information was sketchy.

Shortly after the assassination, police discovered the shooter's window perch at the School Book Depository Building.

Eyewitnesses who saw a man in the window with a rifle gave police a description. A few minutes later, the police dispatcher sent out a bulletin for a "white male, approximately thirty, slender build, height five foot ten inches, weight 165 pounds."[19]

Within minutes of the shooting, while the motorcade was still racing to Parkland Hospital, Oswald, twenty-four, had exited the book depository. After the bus he boarded got stuck in traffic, he jumped off and asked a taxi driver to take him to within a few blocks of his rooming house. There he picked up a revolver and a jacket and quickly left.

At 1:15 p.m., Officer J. D. Tippit, a ten-year veteran of the Dallas police force, noticed Oswald walking briskly along Tenth Street. According to witnesses, Tippit pulled up behind him in his patrol car and called him over. Oswald, leaning over the passenger window, answered a few questions. For some reason, Tippit was not satisfied by Oswald's response, because he got out of the car and walked around the front of the car toward Oswald. As he reached the left tire, Oswald pulled out his revolver and shot Tippit, killing him instantly. Oswald then fled on foot to a movie theater, where he entered without paying. Thinking that he looked suspicious, an attendant called the police, who swarmed the theater. At 1:50 p.m., after a brief scuffle, Oswald was arrested and driven to a downtown jail.[20]

Initially, police arrested Oswald for the murder of Officer Tippit, but over the next hour they started piecing together evidence that connected Oswald to the assassination. They learned that he worked in the School Book Depository Building and noticed that he matched the description eyewitnesses had provided of the shooter. By 2:15 p.m. (CST), local FBI officials discovered a thick file on Oswald. The information was potentially explosive, revealing that Oswald had recently written a letter to the Soviet embassy in Washington. At Dallas police headquarters, everyone wondered whether they had caught both the assassin and a Soviet spy.[21]

Alarm bells were also going off in Washington. As soon as he learned that Oswald had been captured and was believed to be the possible assassin, George Ball had his name checked against State Department files to see if they had any information on him. They had plenty. "Within minutes," he recalled, "word came back that he had spent thirty-two months in the Soviet Union as recently as June 1962." They quickly discovered that he had not only lived in Moscow but had applied for Soviet citizenship. Soon afterward, they learned that he was involved in a pro-Castro group called the Fair Play for Cuba Committee.[22]

The details of Oswald's profile shocked Ball. Everyone had assumed that the right wing presented the greatest threat to Kennedy's safety in Dallas. But a communist, and one who once lived in the Soviet Union? If Oswald was acting on orders from either Moscow or Havana, the assassination could be part of a much broader communist offensive. Ball called in two experienced Soviet experts, Ambassador Llewellyn Thompson and Averell Harriman. "Could this be a Soviet move to be followed up by a missile attack?" he asked. Their answer "was a resounding negative," he recalled. Soviet leaders were too rational to sanction the assassination of an American president.

Ball passed the information on to Bundy, but it is unclear how much of it reached LBJ on *Air Force One.* The reports he did receive, however, lessened fears of an international plot. "I had several calls to Washington," Clifton told Manchester. "I talked to Bundy himself. It seemed that there were no indications of trouble around the world.

He told me that Defense was taking its own steps — that McNamara was in full charge there."[23]

Even if Oswald was not acting as part of a Soviet plot, his peculiar background remained worrisome. In the midst of the Cold War, Johnson feared that even the hint of Soviet or Cuban involvement in the assassination would outrage the public and produce calls for war. He remembered the Red Scare in the 1950s, and how demagogues such as Joseph McCarthy tapped into public fear to cripple President Harry Truman's presidency and undermine public trust. Back at the State Department, Ball concluded "there was the danger that Oswald's pretense to Marxist convictions might set off violent anti-Soviet sentiments that could undo all our efforts to develop working arrangements with Moscow." For now, LBJ had lots of questions, but few answers. Why had the State Department allowed Oswald back into the country after he had defected to the Soviet Union? Had somebody screwed up?[24]

The reality would turn out to be less troubling, but no one knew it at the time. Oswald was a self-absorbed loner who had failed miserably at everything he had ever attempted in his life except assassinate the president of the United States. A troubled and belligerent child, Oswald underwent a psychological evaluation at age thirteen. Asked whether he preferred the company of boys or girls, Oswald told the psychiatrist, "I dislike everybody." After dropping out of school at sixteen, he developed a fascination with Marxism, believing capitalism was the cause of his discontent. In a life marked by dramatic turns, the self-avowed Marxist joined the marines the following year. In November 1959 he won an early discharge, claiming he needed to care for his ailing mother. Within weeks, however, he defected to the Soviet Union.

The Soviets only reluctantly allowed him to stay on after he attempted suicide when his tourist visa expired. They worried that if he succeeded in his next attempt, the Soviet government would be blamed for the death of an American citizen. The Soviets sent him to work at a radio and television factory in Minsk, where he met his future wife, Marina Prusakova. Assuming that as a former marine he would be given special treatment, Oswald was disillusioned by the harsh reality of Soviet life.

A chronic malcontent, in 1962 Oswald returned to the United States with his wife and infant daughter in tow. By then his political allegiance had shifted to a "purer" Marxist, Fidel Castro. Still viewing himself as a revolutionary, Oswald moved to New Orleans and set up the Fair Play for Cuba Committee, which contained a total of one member — Oswald. In April 1963, he tried to shoot a right-wing general, Edwin Walker, with the same mail-order rifle that he would use to assassinate Kennedy.

On September 27, 1963, Oswald traveled to Mexico City seeking a visa to enter Cuba. When the Cubans turned him away, he returned to the United States humiliated, directing his anger at the U.S. government. A month before Kennedy's planned trip, he got a job as a stock clerk at the book depository. It appears that only after learning of the Kennedy visit, and studying the published parade route, did Oswald decide to assassinate the president.

Johnson seemed more comfortable confronting the potential international repercussions of the assassination than he did coping with the sensitive emotional moments it created. A few minutes after 3:15 p.m. (CST), LBJ leaned over to Lady Bird and said, "I think we should call the president's mother." Lady Bird agreed. "Have the radioman get Mrs. Rose Kennedy for me, Rufus," Johnson instructed. At first a bad connection blocked the conversation, but the call was quickly rerouted. In the seconds before Mrs. Kennedy came on the line, Liz Carpenter recalled that Johnson "was like a child." He looked at Lady Bird and asked, "What can I say to her?" Once they heard her voice on the other end, LBJ said, "I wish to God there was something that I could do, and I wanted to tell you that we were grieving with you." In a controlled voice, she responded "Yes. Well, thanks a — thank you very much."[25]

Although many of President's Kennedy's aides were having difficulty addressing Johnson as "Mr. President," the deceased president's seventy-three-year-old mother did not.

Johnson quickly lost his composure. According to Carpenter, "He thrust the phone at Mrs. Johnson as though it were a hot potato." "Here's Bird," he said as he handed the phone off to Lady Bird. Mrs. Kennedy thanked Johnson. "I know that you loved Jack, and he loved you." But by this point, Lady Bird was already on the line. "Mrs. Kennedy, we feel like we just had [our hearts cut out]. We're glad that the nation had your son as long as it did."[26]

There were glimmers of good news as

well. At 3:30 p.m., the president requested an update on Governor John Connally's condition. Before Johnson left the hospital a nurse had told Cliff Carter that the governor was not expected to live. While on the plane, however, they had received medical reports that the governor's wounds were not life threatening; he was expected to make a full recovery. Lady Bird asked Nellie, Governor Connally's wife, if the reports were true. "The report he gave was true," Nellie said. "That was the surgeon that had just [got] done operating on him. Yes, John is going to be all right . . . we are almost certain, un-less [something] unforeseen happens." The president got on the line saying, "[I love you,] darling, and I know that . . . that everything's going to be all right . . . isn't it?" She provided the reassurance that he was looking for. "Yes, it is . . . going to be all right." Johnson ended the conversation by telling her to "Give John a hug and a kiss for me."[27]

While Johnson sat in the stateroom laying the foundation for his new administration, the Kennedy camp clustered around the coffin of their slain leader. The Kennedy group reminisced about the past, trying to drown their sorrows in alcohol, but never succeeding in dousing either their profound grief or their resentment toward LBJ. "We all got loaded — Kenny, Larry, Dave, among them," recalled Kilduff. "I was drinking gin and tonic like it was going out of style." He estimated that he drank between "a half and two-thirds of a fifth of gin" on the plane ride back. "I felt nothing — not even light-headed," he said.[28]

The Kennedy team was overcome with grief and guilt. "All the way on the flight I kept thinking of how we had taken the president out in good spirits and now we were bringing him back in a box," Captain James Swindal told Manchester. O'Donnell had to live with the knowledge that he was responsible for planning the final motorcade through downtown Dallas. Although he was following the president's wishes, he helped publicize the route, told the Secret Service not to crowd Kennedy, and gave the final approval to remove the bubble top. According to the FBI, at Parkland Hospital O'Donnell told the Secret Service, "You are not at fault. You can't mix security and politics. We chose politics." Jackie, too, blamed herself — she believed that if she had gone to the hairdresser that morning, the president's aides would have used the bubble top to protect her hair, and possibly saved her husband's life.[29]

The Kennedy people spent much of their time recalling past happy times with JFK. They reminisced about his June trip to Ireland and the Irish songs he loved: "Danny Boy," "The Boys from Wexford," and "Kelly, the Boy from Killane." Already Jackie was thinking about the funeral arrangements. What would be the appropriate way to honor the memory of her husband?[30]

But there was also a tone of bitterness when the Kennedy people talked about LBJ. Kilduff overheard them telling stories about the 1960 Democratic Convention and LBJ's effort to steal the nomination from JFK. "They finally made it," one of them grumbled. Their loss of power seemed to compound their anger toward LBJ. Until Lee Harvey Oswald pulled the trigger and fired off the third bullet just a few hours earlier, they had been able to dismiss Johnson as an annoying distraction. Now Johnson was the president of the United States and their boss.[31]

Johnson claimed to be unaware of any tension on the plane. "If there was friction aboard the plane, I was not aware of it, and neither was my staff," Johnson wrote in his memoirs. "There was confusion and grief and uncertainty, God knows. It was not a pleasant trip for anyone." "I didn't see hostility," Jack Valenti wrote in 1975, confirming Johnson's account. "All I saw was grief — bitter, dry-teared grief."[32]

LBJ, however, offered a more honest assessment in an interview conducted while writing his memoirs. "It was a peculiar situation that they sat back in the back and never would come and join us." Johnson saw their behavior as a byproduct of the alcohol, however, not hostility. "I wouldn't want to say this in the book, but I thought they were just wine heads," he reflected. "They were just drinkers, just one drink after another coming to them trying to drown out their sorrow." He tried to get them to join him, "tried to talk to them about the arrangements," but they were not interested.[33]

Others, however, found the tension on the plane palpable. "We might as well face it," Lawrence O'Brien told Manchester. "There was tenseness on that plane." Some of LBJ's aides commented on the strained atmosphere. "On the plane I had the feeling of being an intruder," recalled Liz Carpenter. "Really, death was the intruder. But I have never felt like such an intruder in my life as I did among the Kennedy people there." Even Lady Bird acknowledged the tenseness, describing the trip to Washington as "silent, strained — each with his own thoughts."[34]

Kilduff also registered the strain between the two camps, and in many ways he was the most reliable eyewitness. In an aircraft packed with partisans — staff members who were loyal to JFK or close to LBJ, Kilduff was unique. He had no personal relationship with Lyndon Johnson. He also lacked strong attachments to JFK and his clan: although he worked in the Kennedy White House, he had joined the administration late, and had recently been told by White House press secretary Pierre Salinger that his services were no longer needed. Dallas might have been his last assignment.[35]

With no emotional attachment to either side, Kilduff was able to offer a fresh, unbiased perspective, and in his view, the tension was real. "Half of the plane was looking backward to what had been and the other half was looking forward," he told Manchester.[36]

O'Donnell, he believed, "was the most bitter." According to Kilduff, O'Donnell was fuming about how some Kennedy aides were able to so quickly switch allegiance to the new president. Much of his hostility was directed at General Clifton, who was busy in the front of the plane relaying messages between Johnson and Washington. At one point, O'Donnell accused Clifton of "deserting the ship." Clifton was puzzled by the comment. "What's eating him?" he asked McHugh. "I'm doing my job." O'Donnell failed to acknowledge that Johnson was now president. "Clifton was professional," reflected Kilduff. "He assumed the role of military aide to the new President and served as his aide."[37]

General McHugh, like O'Donnell, also seemed to be bristling with anger throughout the flight. Reporter Charles Roberts believed that McHugh "never got over the fact that the plane didn't take off when he ordered it to." At one point, McHugh approached the press table, "thumped his finger on my typewriter," and blustered, "I want you to write that members of President Kennedy's staff . . . sat in the rear of the plane with him and Mrs. Kennedy — not up here with them [the Johnsons]."[38]

Throughout the flight, Johnson consistently tried to be sensitive to the needs of the Kennedy people. He instructed Kilduff to ask Mrs. Kennedy if there was anything she wanted. He was also sympathetic to O'Donnell's grief. At one point, Johnson decided that he wanted to talk to O'Donnell about organizing a meeting of the National

Security Council. He sent Bill Moyers to ask O'Donnell to come to see him. Moyers was the perfect man to serve as an intermediary between the two camps. He possessed a quiet, soothing style, and a dignified manner well suited to the difficult task. When Moyers asked O'Donnell to join the president in the stateroom, O'Donnell respectfully refused. "Bill, I don't have the stomach for it and I'm going to stay here with Jackie. I can't leave her." Moyers was sympathetic. "That's fine," he responded. "I don't blame you and the boss understands fully. No problem whatsoever."[39]

Most objective observers on the plane that day gave Johnson high marks for his behavior. Although fully aware of Johnson's vast character flaws, Charles Roberts praised him for his performance on that particular afternoon. "He rose to the occasion as few men could after having such an awesome burden suddenly and unceremoniously thrust upon them," he wrote shortly after the assassination. "To put it more precisely, the hours from 1 P.M. CST, when Kennedy died, to 4:59 P.M. CST, when *Air Force One* touched down at Andrews, were four of Johnson's finest." Roberts complimented LBJ on the consideration he showed Jackie and "all the Kennedy people." He noticed "nothing unseemly at all about his take-over." He said that Johnson's assumption to power, which took place under the most "harrowing conditions," was "careful, correct, considerate and compassionate." Roberts referred to Johnson's actions, both in Dallas and onboard *Air Force One,* as "a masterpiece of cool-headed improvisation."[40]

Kilduff, too, was impressed with the manner in which Johnson conducted himself. "I can't help but feel that he [President Johnson] showed the utmost concern and personal concern for Mrs. Kennedy, all members of the Kennedy family, and the whole Kennedy party that was with us," he told a radio interviewer on the third anniversary of the assassination. "Once he got on the plane, he continued to show that concern. There was no grossness on his part, as has been implied by others in the recent past. He immediately started to issue orders. His reactions were immediate, well thought out, and really, I can't feel that he acted anything other than what we would expect the President of the United States to do."[41]

There is little Johnson could have done to placate the grieving Kennedy clan on *Air Force One.* As Manchester pointed out, once "Johnson had made up his mind to return to the capital in the Presidential plane, there was no way strain could have been avoided between the Kennedy and Johnson people."[42]

JFK had always been Johnson's biggest defender in the White House. He kept the anger and resentment of his staff in check. Now that Kennedy was gone, there was no one to restrain his staff's deep animosity toward the new president. LBJ would learn over the next few days and months what he should have known after almost three years as vice president — RFK, and many of the people around him, were never going to accept him. No act of generosity would win them over; no demonstration of leadership would sway them to follow him. Their profound grief was understandable. Their sense of entitlement was not.

# 12
## "Rufus, Where's My Hat?"

The plane flew from Dallas over Memphis and Knoxville and Roanoke and on to Washington. "Below the clouds were dark and filled with rain," Captain James Swindal recalled. "There was sunshine overhead." Moving at a speed of 560 mph, the flight took two hours and thirteen minutes. The plane could have landed about eight minutes earlier than it did, but Captain Swindal was told to slow down as he neared Washington; the dignitaries who were gathering were planning on a 6:00 p.m. (EST) arrival.[1]

As *Air Force One* made its final approach, military officials instructed the camera crews to turn off their floodlights, so as not to blind the pilot as he made his descent.

The plane touched down at 5:58 p.m. The pilot turned at the end of the runway and taxied toward the terminal building, where a large group of government dignitaries awaited its arrival. As the plane taxied to the reception area, Johnson saw "a cluster of people waiting and watching. There were bright glaring lights pouring out of the black night, a sign that television cameras were waiting to record our arrival."[2]

Dozens of government officials — congressmen, senators, diplomats, cabinet members — along with thousands of citizens were gathered at Andrews Air Force Base to greet the plane. "Many in attendance openly wept, tears running unashamedly down their cheeks," a reporter noted.[3]

The tension between the Kennedy and Johnson camps, so palpable on the ride back to Dallas, was about to play out in the full glare of the world's media.

According to Mac Kilduff, who made the arrangements for the arrival at Andrews, the plan was to use a cargo truck, positioned on top of a forklift, to remove President Kennedy's casket. Military pallbearers would ride the lift up to the back door, gently remove the casket, ride the lift back down to the ground, then carry the casket to a waiting navy ambulance. The ground crew would then roll movable steps up to the back door for the passengers, led by the president and the former and current First Ladies. There would also be steps in place near the front door of the plane in the event LBJ decided to leave the plane that way.

Johnson was unsure precisely how the presidential party would be leaving the plane, or how the casket would be removed. Johnson was adamant, however, that regardless of how they left the plane, he be seen escorting Mrs. Kennedy behind the coffin. He made these orders explicit to Kilduff and he expected them to be carried out. Just as with the swearing in, Johnson wanted the public to see him next to Mrs. Kennedy. For him, the widow was a powerful symbol, a way to send a reassuring message of continuity to the public.

It did not happen that way. As soon as the plane came to a halt, RFK leaped up a set of stairs that had been moved into place and entered through the front door. He pushed his way down the center aisle, walking past Johnson without saying a word. "He didn't look to the left or the right," recalled Liz Carpenter, "and his face looked streaked with tears and absolutely stricken." As he brushed by her, Carpenter heard RFK say, "I want to see Jackie." According to Jack Valenti, he was "murmuring 'excuse me' as he forced his way through the crowded, people-jammed aisleway."[4]

RFK pushed his way to the rear of the

plane, where the rest of the Kennedy camp now clustered around the casket. Johnson had hoped to maneuver closer to Mrs. Kennedy, but the plane was so crowded and cramped that he was pressed against the side of the cabin. "It was literally impossible for him to move any further," Valenti recalled. Johnson "stood trapped in a passageway like any harried commuter hurrying by subway to his job."[5]

Publically, Johnson downplayed the incident, even saying that he did not recall it happening. Privately, he fumed that RFK would board the plane without even acknowledging him. When Johnson's criticisms emerged, RFK's supporters interpreted his pique as another manifestation of his insecurity. Arthur Schlesinger Jr. observed that "a man more secure than Johnson would have sympathized with the terrible urgency carrying him to his murdered brother's wife." Although true, surely Kennedy, who managed to have long conversations with aides during the day, could have offered a respectful nod of recognition to the new president.[6]

As RFK was rushing through the plane, a cargo truck carrying six soldiers was moved into position by the rear door to remove the coffin. According to General Godfrey

McHugh, when Mrs. Kennedy saw the soldiers, she said to him, "I don't want him handled but by his friends. I want you and Ken to carry the casket down to that forklift. I don't want them to come in the plane." Realizing that Mrs. Kennedy wanted the same group of people who had carried the coffin onto the plane to take it off, McHugh ordered the soldiers off the forklift. According to O'Donnell, McHugh grabbed the casket and told the soldiers to wait on the ramp. "We carried it on the plane, we're going to carry it off the plane," he told them.[7]

Both McHugh and O'Donnell maintained that the decision to carry the coffin themselves was spontaneous, inspired by Mrs. Kennedy's last-minute request after the door had been opened and the military pallbearers were already on the platform. "It was a moment of emotion," O'Donnell claimed.

The evidence suggests otherwise. In 1977, Roy Kellerman, who was among those who helped remove the coffin, told a very different story when he met with investigators with the House Select Committee on Assassinations. "Just before the plane was to land," the investigators wrote in their summary of the conversation, "Agent Greer came to the front of the plane and told Mr.

Kellerman that Mrs. Kennedy wanted the Secret Service people who had been with the President in the car to help carry the casket off and drive along to the hospital." Clearly, the Kennedy group developed a strategy ahead of time and handpicked those who would depart with the coffin. LBJ was not a part of their plan.[8]

And so instead of seeing the new president walking solemnly behind the casket with Mrs. Kennedy at his side, a national television audience witnessed a disorganized group of Kennedy aides boarding the lift, and then riding it down with the casket and Mrs. Kennedy. Then it took several minutes for the crew to remove the cargo truck and bring a set of stairs for LBJ to exit. By the time he reached the ground, Mrs. Kennedy had climbed into the ambulance carrying her husband's body and was on her way to Bethesda Medical Center.

Later that evening, Johnson confronted Kilduff about the confusion surrounding the exit from the plane. Kilduff told William Manchester that he tried to pass it off as a misunderstanding. He told LBJ that he had expected that a forklift would be used to remove the body, and then stairs would be brought up for the president and Mrs. Kennedy to walk down together. Instead, there was a truck lift "and [Mrs.] Kennedy had to decide" whether to jump on or not. There was no plot, no conspiracy to prevent LBJ from escorting Mrs. Kennedy.[9]

Despite what he told Johnson, Kilduff privately suspected that O'Donnell had orchestrated the exit to exclude LBJ and "disloyal" Kennedy aides. "Really it was by design," he confessed to Manchester, "because Kenny wanted no part of Lyndon Johnson then." Kilduff pointed out that both he and General Chester Clifton were also excluded from the lift. "This is because I had come in mid-administration, and Kenny felt that Clifton had paid too much attention to the new President on the plane," he said.[10]

Years later, O'Donnell claimed that Johnson never communicated to him that he wanted to accompany Mrs. Kennedy off the plane. "If he had asked, he certainly could have gotten off with the First Lady," he said. O'Donnell was being disingenuous. He understood the power of images and certainly realized the importance of having LBJ leave with the body. A Kennedy aide later confessed that "they felt Johnson wanted to use Kennedy's body for his own purposes."[11]

Johnson *did* want to use Kennedy's body

for his own purposes, but his motives were not selfish. He was the president, and he needed the body of the slain president in order to convey a message of continuity to the nation and to the world. Beyond the symbolic value, LBJ simply wanted to demonstrate his genuine compassion for the widow. "It was almost as if they were angry at Johnson," reflected Charles Roberts. They had no "appreciation of how important continuity was."[12]

As the ambulance carrying the president's body pulled away, an irritated LBJ shouted to Rufus Youngblood, "Rufus, where's my hat?" When he arrived at Parkland Hospital, Johnson had exited the car in such a hurry that he left his white Stetson on the seat. Youngblood was stunned that after everything that had happened that day, Johnson was thinking about his hat. "Then that's where it probably still is, sir." Johnson was annoyed. "Well, get the damn thing!" he shouted. "Call back to Dallas and have one of your men get it!" The flash of anger suggested to Youngblood that Johnson, who had been restrained and subdued, was returning to "normalcy."[13]

A coatless and hatless Lyndon Johnson walked down the steps of *Air Force One* as an honor guard presented arms and a military band played "Hail to the Chief." He recalled the "blinding lights" in his eyes and the cameras following his every move. A disorganized group of government officials surged forward to greet him. Lady Bird walked over to where the congressional leaders were gathered and kissed both Minnesota senator Hubert Humphrey and his wife, Muriel. "We need you both so much," she said. Television cameras caught glimpses of Johnson conferring with Angier Biddle Duke, the State Department's chief of protocol.[14]

The new president then walked over to a battery of TV cameras and lights. Lyndon Johnson was about to introduce himself to the nation. His life had changed dramatically in just a few hours. Overshadowed by a charismatic president and the media-conscious men of the New Frontier, LBJ had toiled in obscurity as vice president. Just a few weeks before the assassination, a popular television show had randomly interviewed 137 people in New York, New Jersey, and Kansas, asking if they knew who Lyndon Johnson was. Forty-four people did not recognize the name.[15]

Now he was about to become the most famous and powerful man in the world.

With helicopter rotors whirling in the background, and Lady Bird standing at his side, a subdued Johnson read the announcement he had prepared on the plane. "This is a sad time for all people. We have suffered a loss that cannot be weighed. For me, it is a deep personal tragedy. I know the world shares the sorrow that Mrs. Kennedy and her family bear. I will do my best. That is all I can do. I ask for your help — and God's."

His arrival and statement were carried live by all the major news networks. Johnson's Texan drawl must have been surprising to a nation grown accustomed to Kennedy's crisp Boston accent. Americans were used to seeing the young, handsome Kennedy with his toothy grin and thick mane of hair. Now he was gone, replaced by a much older, less attractive, and understandably subdued, new leader.

Johnson had to strike a delicate balance in his first official statement to the nation and the world. He needed to convey compassion and sincerity, showing empathy for a nation that was reeling from news of the assassination. His tone needed to be reassuring and soft, projecting strength and resolve, underscoring that he was now in charge and the business of government would continue.

Most observers believed that he pulled off the juggling act brilliantly. *Life* magazine praised his words and his tone. "His eloquence at that moment, so simple as to be stately, defined both a nation's grief and its purpose." LBJ, however, was unhappy with his performance. Struggling to be heard over the background noise, he worried that his tone sounded too strident, too harsh. According to aide Horace Busby, "he believed that it had been a mistake."[16]

Johnson took no questions from the reporters. After reading the statement, he turned and walked to the brown army turboprop helicopter parked next to *Air Force One.* "As I walked to the helicopter, its long blades whirring with impatience, I recalled that someone had once remarked that the Presidency is the loneliest job in the world," he recalled in his autobiography. But his thoughts, he said, were with Mrs. Kennedy. "I knew that my loneliness was only a fraction of the despair weighing so heavily on her heart — that my loneliness could not be compared with hers."[17]

# 13

# "YOU'RE THE MEN I TRUST THE MOST"

Now that he was on the ground in Washington, Johnson started taking charge of the government. Since the shooting earlier that day he had been largely secluded, either in a hospital room in Dallas or on *Air Force One*. LBJ understood the daunting tasks confronting him: he needed to reassure a traumatized nation, comfort a grief-stricken staff, and build bipartisan support for his presidency. Meeting these challenges would draw upon all the skills of persuasion he had developed over many years in politics. It would also demand sensitivity and subtlety that were not part of his emotional makeup.

In the helicopter en route to the White House, LBJ sat on the port, or left, side, in a seat facing forward. As he had requested, George Ball, Robert McNamara, and McGeorge Bundy joined him for the brief trip. Ball and McNamara tussled briefly over who would occupy the seat facing the new president. McNamara won. On the other side were three seats. Ball sat in the first seat, Lady Bird in the second, and Bundy in the third.

Everyone was studying Johnson, reading him for signs of stress and strain during the fifteen-minute trip. They were reassured by his subdued but focused manner. McNamara observed that Johnson was "surprisingly stable," adding "much more so than I would have been in his situation." Ball, however, described him as being in "fantastic shock." He noticed that Johnson "moved erratically, and I saw twitches in his face."[1]

According to Ball, Johnson spent most of the flight talking about the gallantry of Mrs. Kennedy and her willingness to stand next to him for the swearing in. "He had never seen anyone so brave," he told them. McNamara used the opportunity to brief Johnson on how American forces were disposed around the world. He assured the new president that there were no pressing international crises requiring his attention and no evidence of major troop movements or intelligence that would suggest the Soviets were behind the assassination.[2]

Johnson used the occasion to consolidate his relationship with the Kennedy advisers.

Johnson "said nice things about the three of us and said that he wanted us to stand with him," Ball later told William Manchester. The new president said that Kennedy had done something he himself could not have done: "He had gathered the ablest people he had ever seen [in] government, and he wanted us to stay . . . You're the men I trust the most. You must stay with me. I'll need you."[3]

Although both Bundy and McNamara had been close to President Kennedy and were clearly devastated by his death, they were clearheaded in their advice to Johnson. They were able to separate their personal feelings of loss from their responsibility to serve the nation and to assist the new president in a very difficult time. As painful as it must have been, they recommended that Johnson move into the Oval Office as quickly as possible, to prove to the world that he was now in charge. His own advisers had made a similar recommendation, but it probably meant more to him coming from Kennedy's foreign policy team. Perhaps the need to project strength to the rest of the world should outweigh his desire to be deferential to the Kennedys?

As the helicopter approached the South Lawn, those onboard could see the White

House glowing from the television lights that had been set up outside. The helicopter touched down on the South Lawn at 6:17 p.m. As it landed, few reporters were looking at Johnson. They were staring up at the balcony to see if the Kennedy children had gathered to see their father come home.[4]

The new president had work to do, but Lady Bird was exhausted and wanted to go home. "Liz, you go with Lady Bird and help her all you can," LBJ said to Liz Carpenter. The two women separated from the group and headed toward a waiting car.[5]

Johnson, escorted by Bundy and Ball, walked briskly across the lawn just below the Rose Garden. By this point, a handful of aides from another helicopter had landed and were running to catch up. One of the first to reach Johnson was Bill Moyers, who was soon walking directly behind the president. He assumed that Johnson was headed to the Oval Office, but as they approached, Johnson made a sharp turn. "He just veered to the right and hit my shoulder with his right shoulder," Moyers recalled. "I remember two or three people saying, 'Don't you want to go in?' The doors were open, and you could see the president's desk." Johnson, again showing his deference to his slain predecessor, refused the offers. "I'll use my office in the EOB," he said.[6]

As the men crossed the South Lawn on the way to the Executive Office Building, Bundy raised two issues related to the transition. "There are two things I am assuming, Mr. President," he said. "One is that all files created before 2 pm today belong to the president's family, and the other that Mrs. Kennedy will handle the funeral arrangements." He responded, "That's correct."[7]

Bundy then accompanied Johnson to the vice president's office in the EOB across the street from the White House. As he entered, Johnson said hello to his private secretary, Juanita Roberts. A Secret Service agent gave him an update on the measures being taken to provide extra security at his home. Agents had sealed off the area and his phone numbers had been changed and were now wired through the White House. He was told that his children were safe. Lucy had been picked up by the Secret Service and was at home. Lynda was staying at the home of Governor John Connelly in Texas. After the briefing, Agent Lem Johns, who had been with Johnson all day, ordered sandwiches and broth for the president.[8]

Next, President Kennedy's naval aide,

Captain Tazewell Shepard, brought Johnson up to date on the still-evolving funeral arrangements. The tentative plan was for the president's body to be taken to the East Room of the White House after the postmortem, where it would lie in state. The family had not decided when to hold the funeral, although the assumption was that it would take place in three days. The big question was where President Kennedy should be buried — in Arlington National Cemetery or in a family plot in Boston, next to his son Patrick? All of Johnson's decisions had to be worked around the family's plans for the funeral.

Now at his desk, LBJ was ready to get down to the business of running the government. At 6:55 p.m., Johnson held a private ten-minute meeting with Arkansas senator J. William Fulbright, powerful chair of the Senate Foreign Relations Committee, and diplomat W. Averell Harriman. There were pressing questions on Johnson's mind: Did they believe that Oswald was acting as a Soviet agent? Was the assassination part of a larger Soviet plot? Harriman likely repeated to Johnson what he had told George Ball a few hours earlier: Soviet leaders were too rational to ever sanction the assassination of an American president. Afterward, Fulbright told reporters that Johnson appeared "calm and contained."[9]

As soon as the meeting ended, LBJ started placing phone calls. He was a magician on the phone, often juggling more than one call at a time. This was not the time for telephone gymnastics, however. In an effort to forge a sense of unity, Johnson decided to reach out to the three living American presidents and invite them to the White House. The gesture underscored LBJ's intuitive understanding of the public mood and his skillful use of the media. The pictures and news coverage of him meeting with all his living predecessors would not only send a reassuring message of continuity to the nation, it also would demonstrate that the government was consolidating around his leadership.

Johnson's first call went to Harry Truman at 7:05 p.m. They spoke for five minutes. Truman offered his help and promised to come to Washington on Sunday. Herbert Hoover lived in the Waldorf Towers in New York City, but he was recovering from an illness and was unable to take the call. Johnson next phoned Dwight Eisenhower and asked him to visit him in Washington the next morning. He offered to send a government aircraft to pick him up, but Ike said he would use his private plane.

As he was setting up meetings with the former presidents, Johnson remained concerned about the investigation into the assassination. At 7:12 p.m., he reached J. Edgar Hoover, who was home watching television. The two men had known each other for two decades. They lived across the street from each other, and occasionally the Johnsons would invite Hoover over for a drink. Their daughters, Lucy and Lynda, called him Uncle Edgar. Privately, Johnson dismissed Hoover, who lived alone in a house with his male deputy, as a "queer." But he understood that the FBI head could be a good source of information, and he appreciated his public image as a tough cop. Hoover looked forward to having a much better relationship with Johnson than he had with Kennedy. He was particularly eager to ingratiate himself to the new president, hoping to be allowed to stay on in his job beyond the mandatory federal retirement age.[10]

That evening on the phone, Johnson impressed upon Hoover the importance of a complete investigation of the assassination and informed him that he wanted the FBI to head up the inquiry. Hoover called FBI headquarters and sent forty agents to Dallas that night.

A little after 7:30 p.m., the food that Lem Johns had ordered from the White House kitchen arrived. Since the assassination, Johnson had eaten only a small bowl of vegetable soup. He was notorious for devouring large quantities of food in very short periods of time, and tonight would be no exception. According to his official schedule, he devoted four minutes to dinner — from 7:36 to 7:40 p.m.

When he was done, he got up from his desk, walked into the outer room, and greeted a bipartisan congressional delegation. Among those in attendance were Everett Dirksen (R-Illinois), Mike Mansfield (D-Montana), Carl Albert (D-Oklahoma), Hale Boggs (D-Louisiana), George Smathers (D-Florida), Thomas Kuchel (R-California), Charles Halleck (R-Indiana), Hubert Humphrey (D-Minnesota), and Les Arends (R-Illinois). He shook hands with each one, giving them the classic Johnson treatment, leaning in close so that only a few inches separated them.

Johnson had called them together to ask for their help. These men were his friends and colleagues. They had worked together for years on Capitol Hill. Many of the

Democrats in the room had supported LBJ over Kennedy in 1960. He told them that he was speaking to them not as president, but as "friend to friend." Not surprisingly, they offered him their full support and co-operation. "Very intimate and private" was how Hubert Humphrey described the meeting. "We discussed no legislation," he noted in a memo dictated the next day. "The President asked for our help. He spoke to us as one friend to another. And we, each of us in turn, pledged our cooperation, our counsel, our assistance."[11]

LBJ told the assembled lawmakers there were three priorities, and three audiences, they should keep in mind over the next few days and months. First, it was important to send a clear signal to the Soviets that the government was not disintegrating. There must be no sign of weakness that would encourage the Soviets to take advantage of the tragedy. Second, the leadership needed to think about their own legacy and how history would record how they responded in this time of crisis. Finally, it was essential for them to help the American people deal with the crisis. It was important to stress continuity, stability, and order.

Afterward, the congressional leaders predicted that Johnson would move aggressively to enact much of President Kennedy's stalled domestic agenda. These congressional barons had never been impressed with Kennedy's legislative efforts, which many dismissed as indifferent and amateurish. All that would change now that Johnson, perhaps the most skilled legislator of his time, would be overseeing the effort.

Political ambition rarely pauses to mourn. Amid the sorrow and despair, politicians were also trying to grasp the new political realities and position themselves to benefit. As the other members of the congressional delegation filed out of the room, Humphrey stayed behind to have a few words with LBJ. Humphrey saw an opportunity to endear himself to the new president and perhaps win a spot for himself on the Democratic ticket.

It was clear to many Washington insiders that if Johnson were going to win the nomination in 1964, he would have to move to the left and appease the liberal wing of the party. In addition to supporting President Kennedy's domestic program, one of the best ways to convince liberals that he could be trusted would be to pick one to serve as his running mate. Humphrey, an outspoken liberal and civil rights supporter with close ties to organized labor, seemed like an ideal fit. That calculation could not have been far from Humphrey's mind as he maneuvered for private time with the president.

Humphrey ached to be president one day. In 1960, he had run against Kennedy in the Democratic primaries but was forced to withdraw after a decisive loss in West Virginia. Within hours after word reached Washington of Kennedy's death, friends were calling to ask about his plans for 1964. Would he consider running again? Campaigning against Johnson in the primaries was not an attractive option. Becoming vice president, however, was a different story. "I want to become president, and the only way I can is to become vice president," he later told a friend.

Humphrey started his campaign for the vice presidency the day Kennedy died. Many of his friends and colleagues warned him about tying his political future to Johnson. "We said Johnson would cut his balls off," warned one associate. Humphrey, never one to show verbal restraint, poured on the affection. "I think of him as Lyndon, as a dear friend. I assured him of my wholehearted cooperation, of my desire to be of all possible assistance, and asked him to feel free to call upon me," he recalled about their conversation that evening. Johnson put his arm around Humphrey's shoulder and told him that he "desperately" needed his help.[12]

Humphrey no doubt was motivated by a genuine desire to serve the president and to make sure that the business of government would continue. "It is my view that the finest memorial that we could give to President Kennedy would be to carry on, to complete his program, to undertake to fulfill the many dreams and hopes that he had expressed so eloquently and articulately," he wrote in his memorandum describing his thoughts that day. "This I shall try to do to the best of my ability." But Humphrey also saw a tremendous political opportunity: Johnson needed allies to ensure political continuity, and might repay his loyalty by asking him to be his running mate.[13]

Humphrey's campaign to win a place on the ticket in 1964 spilled over into the next day when he went on national television to pledge his fidelity to the new President. Although the Minnesota senator wanted to use the occasion to point out that the transition was smooth, he also reassured the nation about President Johnson. He said that LBJ was not only personally loyal to Kennedy, but his loyalty extended "to program and policy." LBJ, he said, "was not merely a Vice President under the terms of the law," he was also "a devoted friend, associate, companion and political confidant of our late and beloved President Kennedy." He had watched President Johnson "grow," not only on domestic issues, but in world affairs as well. Moreover, he emphasized that Johnson was "an action President. . . . He is restless and demanding," he said, and he would use his considerable legislative experience to help move the Kennedy legislative program forward.[14]

Of course, Humphrey was not the only one with politics on his mind that night. Within hours of returning to Washington, Johnson started laying the foundation for the 1964 presidential race. The political calendar complicated his task. John Tyler, Andrew Johnson, Theodore Roosevelt, and Harry Truman had nearly full terms during which to adjust to the office before having to gear up for election. Johnson had only eleven months, the shortest time span of any vice president trying to win the office in his own right. The 1964 State of the Union address needed to be delivered when Congress reconvened, just forty-seven days after the assassination. There was little time to waste.

Johnson contacted Kennedy intimates to express his sorrow as well as to reach out to potential political allies. Perhaps his conflicts on the plane with Ken O'Donnell and RFK's rude behavior convinced him to initiate steps to prevent a liberal revolt. His earlier fear that RFK had been conspiring to drop him from the ticket in 1964 was now likely replaced by worry that he would try to block his nomination as president in 1964. Would the party view RFK as the rightful keeper of the Kennedy flame? Could the emotional response to Kennedy's death produce a wave of support for RFK to head the ticket?

Johnson began his campaign at 9:06 p.m. with a call to Justice Arthur Goldberg who, despite being on the Supreme Court, remained very well connected within liberal and labor circles. Until his appointment to the Supreme Court in 1962, Goldberg had worked as secretary of labor. He had been impressed with Johnson's work on the President's Committee on Equal Employment Opportunity, and the two men developed a respectful, even friendly, relationship. Johnson started out by flattering him, telling him he had been "such a wonderful friend" that he "just didn't want to leave" the office "without telling you that you're going to have to do some heavy thinkin' for me." He told him he was planning to give a speech before the American people. "I want you to be thinkin' about what I ought to do to try to bring all of these elements together and unite the country," he said.[15]

His next call was to a charter member of the Irish mafia, Dick Maguire, whom Kennedy had appointed as treasurer of the Democratic National Committee. Unlike other Kennedy insiders, Maguire had always treated Johnson with respect. Again, although wanting to express his genuine sympathy, LBJ was also likely searching for allies in the Kennedy camp. "I know what a great personal tragedy this is to you, but it is to me too. And you have been so wonderful to the president, that I want you to know that . . . that I've got to rely on you more than he did." Johnson reassured him of his loyalty to Kennedy — "I've been on your team ever since I got here" — and encouraged Maguire "to be candid and frank" in discussing issues with him.[16]

Speechwriter Ted Sorensen remembered receiving a phone call from Johnson at around 9:30 p.m., shortly after he had finished dinner. Sorenson was more than just a wordsmith; he was one of President

Kennedy's closest friends and most trusted advisers. "Kindly, strongly, generously, he told me how sorry he was, how deeply he felt for me, how well he knew what I had been to President Kennedy for eleven years," Sorenson recalled in his memoirs. LBJ then repeated his standard line that he needed Sorenson even more than JFK had. Johnson asked Sorensen to visit him "in the next day or two." Touched by the gesture, Sorensen said, "Good-bye and thank you, Mr. President." After he hung up the phone he broke down in tears, realizing that "Mr. President" was no longer John F. Kennedy.[17]

Before leaving his office for the night, Johnson wanted to write notes to President Kennedy's children, John Jr. and Caroline. He planned to use official White House presidential stationery and sent Cliff Carter down the hall to get a few pieces from another office. "Go down the hall and you will find a White House secretary," he said. "Ask her for two sheets of White House letterhead and two envelopes." It seemed like a reasonable request. Written on presidential stationery, the notes would probably have more meaning for the children when they were old enough to appreciate the gesture.

When Carter approached the secretary with the request, however, she exploded. "He can't even let the body get cold before he starts using his stationery," she screamed. Reluctantly, she turned over the paper.[18]

Johnson sat at his desk and wrote messages to both children in longhand. "Your father's death has been a great tragedy for the nation, as well as for you, and I wanted you to know how much my thoughts are with you at this time." He placed the notes in their envelopes and sealed them. He planned to deliver them in person the next day.

Before leaving his office, Johnson called Horace Busby, his favorite speechwriter, who was at an office on Connecticut Avenue in downtown Washington. "I'm going to be leaving here soon," he said in a matter-of-fact tone. "I'll come by and pick you up. We will call when I leave, and we will come by and pick you up — you wait at the curb." Busby suggested that such a move would attract too much attention and offered to drive to The Elms in his own car. "What's the matter," LBJ asked him. "Are you running from the press?"[19]

# 14
# "IT'S GETTING LATE, MR. PRESIDENT"

After landing at the White House, Lady Bird and press aide Liz Carpenter climbed into the back seat of a government car and were driven directly to the Elms. Finally away from the center of activity, Lady Bird had the chance to ponder how the day's tragic events were going to change her life. "I thought — I will have to sell our house, give up control of my business, see about getting Lynda Bird to come and live in Washington with us and go to school somewhere up here (and that will be a selling job!)" she wrote in her diary. "There are all the million and one things to be done — just the simple things that are part of going on living, if one is among those who are going to go on living. Lyndon will be wrestling with the very big business of making the country go on living."[1]

Lady Bird arrived at the Elms at 6:40 p.m. A crowd of reporters had gathered outside the entrance. The gilded, black wrought-iron gates that protected the entrance were usually left open, but on this night they were sealed and patrolled by the Secret Service. As the car carrying the First Lady approached, the gates swung open. They drove up the curved driveway and parked near the two giant elm trees that flanked the entrance to the house.

As she exited the car, a Secret Service agent filled her in on what was going on. "Your phone has been phased out and the White House numbers are installed in your house," he informed her. "And Lucy has been taken from school and is at the house now." As she approached the house, Lucy was standing on the steps; the two embraced and walked inside together.

The Elms was designed for entertainment. Double doors opened into a foyer with a coat closet on the right and a powder room on the left. Straight ahead was a large entrance hall with a black and white marble floor. The hall led to the terrace room, which the Johnsons used as their living room. It was a spacious, ornate room. The walls and floor were made from 150-year-old oak that came from a château in Versailles; there was a fireplace, and a set of French doors and windows opened onto a flagstone terrace.[2]

Here, Lady Bird offered her daughter some comforting words. Calling her by her pet name, Lulu, she provided needed reassurance. "Your daddy's all right. He'll be home soon. All this will change our lives, of course. You must give it real thought. But it needn't — it doesn't change you, or the rest of us."[3]

After talking to Lucy, the new First Lady made plans for dinner. As far as she knew, Lyndon had eaten little more than soup and crackers since breakfast. "He'll probably have people with him and he hasn't had anything to eat yet." She walked past the dining room to the pantry, which contained a commercial-size double oven with six burners. Since Lyndon often invited colleagues home after work, and they entertained frequently, the Johnsons had a small kitchen staff who prepared many of their meals. Lady Bird asked them to start making some fried chicken for Lyndon. Since his heart attack, she had tried to cut down on the amount of fried food he ate, but she felt tonight could be an exception.[4]

After getting the staff organized, Lady Bird realized she had not changed her clothes all day — she was still in the same outfit she had worn for the chamber of commerce breakfast in Fort Worth. At 7:15 she went up to her room, put on a green robe, and lay down on the bed for a few minutes. She turned on the TV and watched the news. She called her daughter Lynda Bird at the University of Texas to deliver the same reassuring words she had offered Lucy a few minutes earlier.

At 9:24 p.m. the Secret Service informed Lady Bird that LBJ had left his office and was on his way home. A few minutes later she received word that he was pulling up to the gates. Still dressed in her green robe, she went downstairs to greet him at the door. They embraced and spoke quietly for a few minutes. "I've got some fried chicken for you," she said. "Darling," he replied, "I should have called you from the office. I had something to eat there." Lucy was also standing in the entrance to greet her father. It was the first time she had seen him since the tragedy in Dallas earlier that day. "He looked like he'd been run over by a truck," she reflected in an oral history, "and yet very strong." He was a paradox, she explained. "He looked like part of him had been gutted and another part of him was just as strong and sturdy as an Olympic champion."[5]

That night, a crowd of friends had gathered at the house. Horace Busby counted sixteen people. Among them was Dr. Willis Hurst, the Emory University heart specialist who had saved LBJ's life back in 1955. Hurst scanned the president, looking for possible signs of fatigue. He found none. "Johnson was more controlled than calm," Busby observed. "His words of greeting were barely audible."[6]

Johnson stood, facing the large portrait of Speaker Sam Rayburn that hung on the wall just above the television. Rayburn, who had died two years earlier, had been a mentor to Johnson. Moyers observed that "Johnson was drinking a glass of carbonated orange soda. He raised his glass and said, as if there was nobody else around, 'Oh, Mister Sam, I wish you were here now. How I need you.' "[7]

Many friends had gathered at the Elms to show their support for LBJ. It must have been apparent, however, that Johnson wanted privacy, because most filtered out and went home shortly after he arrived. Joining him now were Busby and his wife, Valenti, Moyers, Hurst, and Carter. Very little was said. Johnson settled back down in a special chair to support his lower back and asked Busby to turn on the television set.

For the past eight hours, most Americans had stopped what they were doing and sat glued in front of their television sets collecting bits and pieces of information about the shooting, the alleged assassin, and the impact of Kennedy's death on the nation. With the exception of the brief news report he watched after boarding *Air Force One* in Dallas, Johnson had been largely cut off from this national discussion. So consumed had he been with laying plans for the transition that he had had little time to discover the details of what actually took place in Dallas or to tap in to how it was all playing out on television. "I guess I am the only person in the United States who doesn't know what has happened today," he said.[8]

Johnson wanted some hard news. Busby tried the major stations, but most were showing commentators discussing the significance of the day's events, or documentary-style footage of key moments in President Kennedy's life — images of the 1960 convention and clips of his more famous speeches. When images of the president playing with his children appeared on the screen, Johnson had to stop watching. "No, no," he said. "Turn it off, turn it off. It's all too fresh." Instead of turning the television off, someone switched channels and lowered the volume.[9]

It was more than an hour before the television, which remained playing in the background, broadcast a news story about the day's events. Johnson watched "intently" as the reporter described the spot where Kennedy was hit, and how the rifleman had been perched in a window on the sixth floor of the School Book Depository Building. The rest of the nation knew most of these details, but Johnson was probably learning about them for the first time.

Johnson also wanted an update about Connally. He placed a call to Parkland Hospital to talk with Nellie Connally, listening quietly as she described her husband's near-fatal wounds. A single bullet had ripped through his back and exited through his chest, shattering a rib and puncturing a lung, before splintering bones in his wrist. But he was lucky: doctors were able to stop the bleeding and repair most of the damage. They expected the governor to make a full recovery. Relieved that his friend was going to survive, LBJ said in a soft voice, "Take care of Johnny. I need him now."[10]

As he hung up the phone, a news flash indicated that the Dallas police were about to issue an indictment against Lee Harvey Oswald. According to the news report, the indictment was going to claim that Oswald might have acted as part of a communist conspiracy. Although Dallas police were confident they had apprehended the man who shot Kennedy, there were still many unanswered questions about Oswald's motives, and about whether other people or groups might have conspired with him. Oswald's peculiar background — his professed Marxism and connections to the Soviet Union and Cuba — raised legitimate questions about whether he was part of a larger conspiracy. Johnson, however, worried about making such an inflammatory charge based on so little evidence. That was not what the nation needed right now. "We must not start making accusations without evidence," he said. "It could tear this country apart."[11]

Johnson wanted to know if the news reports were correct, and if they were, to take steps to make sure the reference to a "communist conspiracy" was not included in the formal indictment. He asked Busby to call the attorney general of Texas, Waggoner Carr. "I seem to remember that there is some law in Texas permitting the Texas attorney general to take over in a situation like this." Johnson was right: Carr had the authority to set up a court of inquiry and take over the investigation from the Dallas police. Because the assassination of a president was considered a local crime, the president could not simply instruct RFK or the FBI to seize control of the case. Fortunately, Johnson understood local laws and customs and knew how to navigate around the maze of conflicting bureaucracies.[12]

While trying to maintain control over the handling of Oswald's indictment, LBJ remembered to pay his debt of loyalty to Youngblood. Johnson asked to talk with James Rowley, the director of the Secret Service, who was sitting in an adjacent room. "Jim," he said, "I don't know how your shop operates, but Youngblood deserves something — a decoration, a promotion or whatever you do. He was great. If I'd been in his spot, I don't think I'd have had the nerve to knock the Vice President to the floor." Youngblood would stay at the residence until after midnight, then go home for a few hours of sleep before starting his first full day protecting the president.[13]

Busby, who had known Lyndon Johnson for nearly sixteen years as a congressman, a senator, and vice president, noticed both familiar and unfamiliar behavior on this first night of his presidency. "His composure and

coolheadedness were precisely what I antici-
pated. His mellowness and gentleness were
not." Johnson was a man of energy and
ambition who seemed frustrated when there
was not enough activity to keep him occupied. During those moments, he was
capable of bouts of self-pity and personal
cruelty. In many ways, the presidency was
the one job for which he was qualified. It
was the only position big enough, and
demanding enough, to focus his energy and
keep his demons in check. "Short of that,"
Busby observed, "he was always a man making important the unimportant to occupy
his vast energies and abilities. That night, he
was in every subtle sense The President."[14]

Johnson knew that he had to get some sleep,
but his mind was still racing, turning over
the problems that would confront him the
next morning. Before he closed his eyes for
the night, LBJ would build the scaffolding
of his presidency, revealing how he would
transcend the cautious politics of the Kennedy era and place his own unique stamp
on the presidency.

Johnson went upstairs to his bedroom accompanied by Dr. Hurst. The room was
decorated with mural-size paintings of
scenes from Texas. The two men stood next

to LBJ's super-sized king bed, and Hurst asked Johnson if he wanted to take a sedative to help him sleep. Johnson, still worried that some new crisis could develop during the night, declined the offer.[15]

Downstairs, Horace Busby was about to leave when one of the servants came down and said that Johnson wanted to see him.

It was not uncommon for Johnson to have aides sit with him at night. They used to call it "hand holding" or "gentling down." An aide would often pull up a chair next to the bed while Johnson ruminated about issues that were on his mind. The sessions sometimes lasted hours before LBJ eventually nodded off. Lady Bird did her best to block out the conversations, but with limited success. "The president," Busby noted, "was never a heavy sleeper, but pity poor Lady Bird — hands over eyes and arms over ears."[16]

Johnson had a lot on his mind. He had woken up that morning assuming that he would finish two terms as a loyal vice president and then probably retire quietly to his ranch in Texas. Now he was president, and under the most tragic circumstances. A host of questions swirled around his head: Would the nation accept him as a legitimate leader? Would the Kennedy cabinet stay on the job? Would the Soviets try to take advantage to further their strategic advantage in the Cold War? How would he manage the delicate task of fulfilling Kennedy's agenda while also making his own mark on the office?

Busby entered the room and sat in a chair next to the bed. While Lady Bird tried to sleep, Johnson sat on the edge of the bed. There were long silences, but mostly LBJ talked about what he knew best — getting legislation through Congress. He had been sworn in as president a few hours earlier, but already he was laying out the agenda for his administration. He was like a race horse finally let out of its stall. After three years of pent-up frustration sitting on the sidelines watching Kennedy's aides spin their wheels getting nowhere with Congress, Johnson was finally breaking loose.

LBJ had always believed that Kennedy was more style than substance. By the fall of 1963, JFK's legislative program was stalled in Congress. Kennedy had submitted a tax reduction bill calling for $13.5 billion in cuts. Congress had already whittled that down to $11 billion, and neither the House nor the Senate was in a hurry to pass the measure. His civil rights bill was also tied up in House committees and facing the prospect of a Senate filibuster.

As Johnson ran down the list of bills he planned to start working on, he came to a surprising realization: "You know," he told Busby, "almost all the issues now are just about the same as they were when I came here in Congress nearly thirty years ago." This was more than the Kennedy program he was fighting for; it would be his legacy, his life's work. He had the chance to break the logjam that had blocked progress on a host of issues left over from the New Deal.[17]

While Johnson was focused on legislation, Busby pointed out that their lives were about to change. Johnson agreed. "I guess we won't be going home for a while," he said with an air of sadness. Lady Bird, reading in bed next to him, chimed in. "Well, at least it's only for nine months," she said. At this point, Lady Bird was assuming that LBJ would simply finish out Kennedy's term in office and that the party would nominate a new candidate at its convention that summer. Realizing that it would take until January to finish out the term, she corrected herself. "No, I guess it will be for fourteen months." Busby pointed out the flawed math. "Mrs. Johnson, it won't be nine months — it is more likely to be nine years."[18]

Shocked, Lady Bird stared at Busby. "No," she said forcefully. Lyndon reached over and gave her a reassuring pat on the arm. "I'm afraid Buzz is right. At least, it may be for five years."[19]

Busby left the room to go home, but Johnson wasn't ready to go to sleep. He used the house phone to call Valenti, Moyers, and Carter. He had already asked the three advisers to spend the night. They had gone to their rooms a few minutes earlier and were starting to undress. "Come on to my room," he said. "I want to talk to you." When they entered the room and saw Mrs. Johnson huddled under the covers, they retreated. But Johnson waved them in. "We won't bother Mrs. Johnson," he said. "There is so much to do, so much to talk about. Sit with me for a while." LBJ disappeared into the bathroom and emerged wearing striped pajamas and slippers.[20] Sitting upright with his back resting against the headboard, he talked about the day's events and his plans for the future. But first there were also some practical matters to be settled. Moyers lived in Washington, but both Carter and Valenti were based in Texas. Carter had packed for an overnight trip to Austin and had no clothes to wear.

"I'll just have the girls bring you in some shorts, undershirts, socks, and [they] can buy some new shirts."[21]

The three men who happened to be with Johnson in Dallas that day now would play key roles in his administration. While LBJ spent most of the day reassuring top Kennedy aides that he wanted them to stay, that evening he also started laying the groundwork for an eventual staff turnover. He had been around Washington long enough to know that a president needed to surround himself with loyal people. He was not ready to acknowledge the transition, but he initiated the process that night from his bed. He told Valenti that he wanted him to take a two-year leave from his advertising firm in Houston and work in the White House. He asked Moyers to step down from his Peace Corps job and join his staff. He instructed Carter to move from his White House staff position to the Democratic National Committee in order to represent his interests.

His aides were exhausted after a long and difficult day, but Johnson was full of energy. He talked about the meetings he had scheduled for the next day, and about the foreign leaders who would be coming to Washington for the funeral. "The important things now, are a Cabinet meeting, a Security Council

meeting, a White House staff meeting —
maybe we ought to call those boys together
at nine tomorrow morning, before the
cabinet meeting," Carter recalled him saying. As he was speaking, the television was
playing quietly in the background. LBJ
heard the commentator announce, "We
bring you some biographical film clips of
the new President of the United States —
Lyndon Baines Johnson."[22]

Mrs. Johnson, who had grown accustomed
to these late-night discussions, tossed and
turned for a few minutes before excusing
herself. "Good night, all," she said as she
left the room in search of a quiet place to
sleep.

At this point, Johnson was on a roll. For
the second time that evening, he laid out
his legislative agenda. "I'm going to get
Kennedy's tax cut out of the Senate Finance
Committee, and we're going to get this
economy humming again. Then I'm going
to pass Kennedy's civil rights bill, which
has been hung up too long in the Congress.
And I'm going to pass it without changing
a single comma or a word. After that we'll
pass legislation that allows everyone anywhere in this country to vote, with all the
barriers down. And that's not all." According to Valenti, LBJ continued listing the

priorities: "We're going to get a law that says every boy and girl in this country, no matter how poor, or the color of their skin, or the region they come from, is going to be able to get all the education they can take by loan, scholarship, or grant, right from the federal government."[23]

It seemed that images on the television screen prompted some new agenda idea. When a commentator made an observation about Harry Truman, LBJ blurted out, "By God, I intend to pass Harry Truman's medical insurance bill. He didn't do it, but we'll make it into law," Valenti recalled him saying. "Never again will a little old lady who's sick as a dog be turned away from a hospital because she doesn't have any money to pay for her treatment."[24]

Valenti realized that he was part of a great "historic moment." "Before he was president for a full day, LBJ laid out for the three of us in his bedroom what later became the design for the Great Society," he observed.[25] "Now that he was in command he was committed," he wrote, "to the shattering of the political and social structure, for it would take no less than that to reintroduce the poor, the aged, the blacks, those denied an education, to a new opportunity which, as LBJ saw it, was absolutely essential to an equitable America."[26]

There were dozens of details that Johnson needed to tend to before he could entertain visions of his Great Society. LBJ shifted the conversation from the subject of his lofty long-term goals back to the immediate challenges confronting him. There was a discussion about whether he should address the nation before the funeral. If so, should he give the address from the Oval Office or before a joint session of Congress? Humphrey had already urged him to wait and make his first address before Congress. He knew that Johnson was not a skilled speaker. While television had enhanced his predecessor's qualities, it detracted from Johnson's. His talents were better suited to back-room negotiating than to giving inspiring public speeches. "I was determined that his first speech be given where he was at home and before the live audience," Humphrey noted. "He would be credible if he could forget about cameras and just deliver his address to the joint session."[27]

Moyers disagreed with Humphrey's recommendation, and suggested that rather than wait to deliver a formal address, LBJ should hold a press conference over the weekend to reassure the nation as soon as possible. But LBJ was reluctant. He was still upset about his performance at Andrews Air Force Base and not eager to go before the cameras anytime soon. And he continued to believe the American people needed an appropriate amount of time to say goodbye to JFK.

Beneath Johnson's stated reasons for avoiding the press conference lay an ongoing anxiety that if he moved too quickly and too publicly to consolidate his position, RFK would create a public rift that would undermine his presidency. "What can I do?" he asked Orville Freeman, secretary of agriculture, on Saturday afternoon. "I do not want to get into a fight with the family and the aura of Kennedy is important to all of us." For now, he wanted to wait. He asked Valenti to solicit the views of congressional leaders before he made a final decision about when first to speak to the nation.

Realizing that he had another long day ahead of him, his advisers recommended that Johnson get some sleep. "It's getting late, Mr. President," Cliff Carter told him. Johnson looked at the little clock next to his bed. It was 3:09 a.m. "We'll be leaving here at 8:00 in the morning," LBJ said.

# 15

# "I REMEMBER THE WORD THAT HE USED — OBSCENE"

While Johnson, in his pajamas, sketched out an ambitious agenda for his presidency, the grief-stricken members of the Kennedy clan gathered in a private suite on the seventeenth floor at Bethesda Naval Hospital. In these hours, sharing both their heartbreak and their contempt for Johnson, the Kennedy group created their own narrative of the day's events. It would justify their actions and reinforce their belief that Johnson was unsuited to fill the void created by JFK's death. During this time, the Kennedy clan's complaints and suspicions about the new president hardened into an indictment. Confusion, misunderstanding, and suspicion had defined much of the interaction between the Johnson and Kennedy camps that day, but by late Friday night ambiguity had disappeared, and so, too, did any hint of generosity.

Once at Bethesda, the Kennedy clan waited for hours as doctors performed an autopsy on JFK's body and then morticians struggled to camouflage the president's head wound. The doctors were having a hard time figuring out the trajectories of the bullets, and the morticians had difficulty reconstructing the president's shattered head. At the time, no decision had been made about whether there would be an open casket, so the morticians tried to be as precise as possible.

Godfrey McHugh stayed with the body for the entire autopsy. "His body was totally nude, yellow, yellow, yellow, like he had been painted yellow." The doctors told him that this was a result of the Addison's disease. He said later that RFK called every hour trying to push the process along. "Why does it take so long? Mrs. Kennedy is here . . . she's terribly emotionally upset and she can't stand it."[1]

The long delay gave those waiting on the seventeenth floor plenty of time to reminisce and share stories of happier times. Family and friends now joined the original group that had been in Dallas. Jackie described in graphic detail every aspect of the shooting and the painful minutes that followed. "I was so startled and shocked she could repeat in such detail how it happened," recalled Robert Kennedy's wife, Ethel. Her personal physician, Dr. John Walsh, thought it would be good for her to talk about the day. "It's the best way," he said. "Let her get rid of it if she can." A few hours later, fearing that she would collapse from exhaustion, Dr. Walsh injected her with a powerful sedative. It had no impact. It was as if he had injected her with Coca-Cola.[2]

In an instant, her world had changed. She worried about what it would be like to raise her children without a father. "Bobby is going to teach John," she said. "He's a little boy without a father, he's a boyish boy, he'll need a man." She knew that she would have to vacate the White House now that her husband was dead. Her plan was to move back into the Georgetown house they occupied while Jack was in the Senate. "That was the first thing I thought that night — where will I go? I wanted my old house back." Robert McNamara offered to buy back the house for her, but already she was having second thoughts. "I thought — how can I go back there to that bedroom[?]"[3]

While she was waiting for the autopsy and

embalming at Bethesda Naval Hospital, Mrs. Kennedy called a family friend, artist William Walton. She asked him to consult a book of sketches showing Lincoln's lying in state at the White House. She wanted her husband's viewing and funeral modeled after Lincoln's. Historian and Kennedy aide Arthur Schlesinger Jr. and speechwriter Richard Goodwin rushed to the Library of Congress and spent the night researching other details of the Lincoln rites.

While Jackie occupied herself with planning a state funeral worthy of her husband, other members of the Kennedy group focused their bitterness on Lyndon Johnson. Even as the ambulance drove from Andrews Air Force Base to the Bethesda Naval Hospital, McHugh began regaling RFK with stories about Johnson's behavior that day. "McHugh said that Lyndon Johnson had been — and I remember the word that he used — obscene," RFK said later, recalling the conversation. "There wasn't any other word to use and it was the worst performance he'd ever witnessed." Although Johnson had gone out of his way to reassure every Kennedy staff member he encountered of his desire to have them stay on in his administration, RFK was speculating about the changes he would make. "A lot of heads are going to roll but I wonder who will be first," he said, thinking out loud. "I'll bet Kenny will be one of the first."[4]

Once they arrived at the hospital, it was O'Donnell's turn to vent his spleen with RFK. O'Donnell plied RFK with horror stories about Johnson's behavior — about how he insisted on taking President Kennedy's plane instead of his own, and how insensitive he was to Jackie, forcing her to sit on a hot plane in the city where her husband had just been murdered. To top it off, LBJ then insisted that Jackie stand with him for the oath.

RFK fed O'Donnell's rage. Although there is considerable evidence to suggest that RFK supported Johnson's decision to take the oath in Dallas, that was not the story he told O'Donnell that night. "I was too surprised to say anything about it," Bobby said of Johnson's suggestion that he take the oath in Dallas. "I said to myself, what's the rush? Couldn't he wait until he got the President's body out of there and back to Washington?"[5]

For RFK, already inclined to view Johnson's actions in the worst possible light, the stories he heard that evening from McHugh and O'Donnell confirmed his fears about

320

the man who now occupied his brother's chair. In his effort to communicate a message of continuity to the nation and the world, Johnson had every reason to take the oath in Dallas, and to ask the former First Lady to stand next to him. But Kennedy viewed those actions through a very different lens. This was the power-hungry LBJ who somehow disrespected his brother's memory by insisting on taking the oath so quickly, and who exploited a grieving widow for his selfish political purposes. Later that spring, speaking to an aide, RFK listed a series of grievances he had accumulated against Johnson in the first few days after the assassination. First among them, he said, was "the treatment of Jackie on the plane trip back and all of that business."[6]

Although Robert Kennedy's fury at Johnson was unnecessary, it was at least partially understandable. RFK had spent much of his adult life working to advance his brother's political career. In 1960, he and his brother had realized the family ambition of placing a Kennedy in the White House. Now, in an instant, it was gone. He must have thought back to the 1960 Democratic Convention, when he failed both to convince his brother to drop Johnson and to nudge LBJ to reject the offer. If only his brother had taken his advice. Now RFK faced the worst of all possible situations: his brother was dead, and a man unworthy to succeed him was president.

Years later, Lawrence O'Brien, whose relationship with O'Donnell would sour because of O'Brien's decision to stay on and work in the new Johnson administration, reflected that "it was a gut reaction to be negative toward or antagonistic to Lyndon Johnson. This terrible thing, this man has replaced him, and there's something awfully unfair about what happened." The Constitution made Johnson president, but the "fact that he succeeded Jack Kennedy was an irritant to some Kennedy people," he observed. "Somehow or other there was some degree of responsibility on Johnson's part, as irrational as that might seem."[7]

Indeed, many Kennedy loyalists convinced themselves that Johnson had pressured JFK into going to Dallas and therefore was at least partly responsible for his death. In their minds, Kennedy reluctantly traveled to Dallas to straighten out a nasty political feud that LBJ should have handled on his own. The reality was much different, but given the intensity of their disdain for Johnson, truth gave way to myth.[8]

■ ■ ■ ■

Finally, at 3:30 a.m. morticians finished their painstaking work on the president's head. Kennedy's valet, George Thomas, brought clothes to the hospital. "He had four summer suits and four winter suits, and two good pairs of brown shoes and two good black pairs," Dave Powers told William Manchester. They agreed on a blue-gray suit and a blue tie. They placed a white handkerchief in his pocket.[9]

At 3:56 a.m., the coffin was loaded into a hearse for the thirty-five-minute drive back to the White House.

# 16
## "It Was a Gray Day, Fitting the Occasion"

On Saturday, November 23, reporters camped outside the Elms noticed the lights in the house were on before dawn. Johnson was up at 7:00 a.m., less than four hours after he went to sleep. His houseguests — Jack Valenti, Bill Moyers, and Cliff Carter — also rose early, ready for their first full day working for the president.

"It was a gray day, fitting the occasion," Lady Bird recalled. A cold front had moved in, replacing the unseasonable warmth with a cold wind and driving rain. LBJ ate breakfast in bed with Lady Bird before placing a call to Homer Thornberry, asking him to come over to the Elms and drive with him to the White House.[1]

According to the Secret Service log, Johnson left his residence at 8:40 a.m., accompanied by Thornberry, Moyers, Valenti, and Carter, and escorted by a handful of Secret Service agents and motorcycle policemen. The presidential entourage arrived at the White House fifteen minutes later.[2]

LBJ's first stop was the Oval Office, which he found in disarray. For the second time in two days, workmen were moving furniture out of the office. Mrs. Kennedy had used the Texas trip to redecorate the office. On Thursday, shortly after the president left Washington, workers had removed all the furniture, including the desk carved from the HMS *Resolute* and the rocking chair, and installed a new red carpet and white curtains with red trim. They took down the naval prints that hung on the walls to make room for a fresh coat of paint. They began moving the furniture back in the next day and didn't stop, even on Friday afternoon, after word reached Washington that the president was dead.

When she returned to the White House early on Saturday morning, Mrs. Kennedy asked a photographer to take pictures of the office as it would have appeared when her husband returned from Dallas. After the photographs were taken, the furniture was moved out again, this time permanently, to allow Johnson to decorate the office to his taste. Secretary of Agriculture Orville Freeman, who peeked into the Oval Office that morning, saw workers busy packing

Kennedy's possessions. "The desk, always cluttered with pictures and pieces of ivory and all kinds of gadgets . . . was now clean. . . . The ships that he loved and were around the room were piled in one corner."[3]

Overnight, Johnson had apparently given more thought to the recommendation of President Kennedy's foreign policy team that he occupy the Oval Office as soon as possible. When he found Evelyn Lincoln packing up Kennedy's personal belongings, he repeated his now standard line, "I need you more than you need me." He then said that he wanted to send a reassuring message to allies and enemies that the government was functioning. "I have an appointment at 9:30 a.m. Can I have my girls in your office by 9:30?" Although surprised that he was giving her less than one hour to move all of her belongings, she instinctively responded, "Yes, Mr. President." Johnson then asked if it would be possible to get Bill Moyers moved into Ken O'Donnell's office. "I don't know, Mr. President," she said, pointing out that she could not speak for O'Donnell.

Lincoln left the Oval Office and returned to her own, where she ran into the attorney general. "Do you know he asked me to be out by 9:30?" she said to him. RFK was shocked. President Kennedy's rocking chair was stacked upside down in the hallway. His body was lying in the East Room. Was it really necessary for Johnson to move so quickly, RFK wondered?

A few minutes later, RFK confronted LBJ. It was their first face-to-face encounter since the assassination and their first conversation since the swearing in. Both men were deeply suspicious of each other. Johnson was convinced that Kennedy was looking for a reason to deny him the office. "During all of that period," Johnson reflected, "I think [Bobby] seriously considered whether he would let me be president, whether he should really take the position [that] the vice president didn't automatically move in. I thought that was on his mind every time I saw him in the first few days."[4]

There was no precedent for the situation in which LBJ and RFK found themselves. No president had ever taken over the office and inherited his predecessor's brother as a member of the cabinet. It was a highly uncomfortable situation. It would have been understandable, even appropriate, for Robert Kennedy to resign his position, pleading grief. Certainly, RFK should have made that offer. Johnson, who had gone out of his way to keep Kennedy people in their posts, could not have singled Robert out and asked him to resign. Given RFK's antipathy toward Johnson, it is very difficult to see how he could serve under him.

But RFK had no intention of resigning. He now believed his mission was to make sure that his brother's policies were carried out. He needed to stay, precisely because he did not trust Johnson. He wanted to stay close to make sure there was no deviation from President's Kennedy's goals. RFK's mission was not to serve a new president, but to protect the reputation of his dead brother.[5]

The conversation between the two men that morning was formal and brief. Johnson recited his line about needing him more than his brother had. Kennedy had heard it recited from a dozen people already. He did not really want to talk with Johnson about his role in the new administration. "I said I don't want to discuss it," RFK told William Manchester, "and . . . that it was going to take us a period of time to move out of here, and I think, maybe, can't you wait?" An apologetic Johnson responded, "Well, of course." Then he explained to Kennedy that he "didn't want to move in" so quickly, and that he was simply following the advice of both the secretary of state, Dean Rusk, and the secretary of defense, Robert McNamara.[6]

In RFK's mind, Johnson's desire to occupy the Oval Office less than twenty-four hours after the assassination was further proof of LBJ's insensitivity, his naked lust for power, and his disrespect for the slain president's memory. What he did not know at the time was that Johnson's actions had been predicated on a misunderstanding about when the Oval Office would be ready.

When McGeorge Bundy made the recommendation the previous day that Johnson move into the Oval Office, he assumed that workers would remove most of JFK's belongings by Saturday morning. When Bundy arrived at the West Wing early that morning, he encountered both Robert Kennedy and Evelyn Lincoln. They told him that moving the president's furniture was taking longer than expected, and they hoped that Johnson would give them more time.[7]

Bundy then went to Johnson's office at 8:00 a.m. and left the following message: "When you and I talked last night about when the President's office in the West Wing would be ready, I thought possibly it would be immediately. However, I find they are working on President Kennedy's papers and his personal belongings and my suggestion would be that — if you could work here in the Executive Office Building today and tomorrow, everything will be ready and clear by Monday morning."[8]

Because LBJ went directly to the Oval Office on Saturday morning, he did not get Bundy's note until after his meeting with Lincoln. The mix-up over Johnson's desire to use the Oval Office was an example of how missed signals — unavoidable amid the chaotic changes — intensified already savage animosities.

Johnson was clearly worried that RFK might to try to sabotage his presidency, but other potential problems were swirling around him. By Saturday morning, major newspapers and commentators were discussing the political implications of the assassination. Some speculated that Kennedy's death would unite the various factions of the Democratic Party and build public support for the martyred president's agenda. One congressman suggested there would be "a decided tendency to unite in support of a martyred President — to build a legislative monument . . . to his memory." But would Johnson be the candidate the party would rally around? Most party insiders assumed he would be the nominee in

1964, but some speculated about the possibility of an RFK candidacy. "If the great national wave of sadness and sympathy is still perceptible a year from now," opined the *New York Times,* "it is the Attorney General rather than the President to whom it is more likely to attach."[9]

Regardless of whom the Democrats nominated, most observers believed that, politically, Republicans would benefit most from Kennedy's death. The "hushed, almost ashamed" assessment was clear, the *New York Times* wrote. "The death of the President gave new life to Republican hopes." Assuming that LBJ was the nominee, the editors speculated that any gains he would make in the South would be more than offset by losses in other states, especially California. "President Johnson is regarded widely in California as an arch-conservative who, while in the Senate, tried to scuttle civil rights legislation," noted one Republican quoted in the *Times* article. Given the narrowness of the Democratic victory in the 1960 presidential race, the newspaper concluded that the potential Republican gains in the North would tip the balance in their favor in 1964.[10]

The press also raised concerns about whether Johnson's style and experience would be of much help to him now that he was president. The "unknown factor," wrote the *Washington Post,* was "What kind of a President will Lyndon Johnson be?" No one knew. Some commentators believed that Johnson would use his legendary parliamentary skills to force Congress to act on a host of backlogged legislation. The *New York Times* pointed out, however, that LBJ might believe that his old tactics were inappropriate now that he was president, and "if he chose to employ them he would soon find they lacked their old effectiveness." For that reason, the jury was out on whether Johnson's would be an effective chief executive. As the *Times* noted, LBJ's "leadership qualities as President were not universally taken for granted."[11]

Johnson had already arranged a series of meetings that morning with the key members of Kennedy's foreign policy team. The meetings not only highlighted LBJ's ongoing concern about the international implications of the assassination, they provided him with the opportunity to deliver his key message: he shared his predecessor's goals and he needed JFK's advisers to stay at their posts. Johnson again revealed his savvy use of the media. He made sure that photographers were positioned to record the discussions; he thus could communicate to the nation and the world the larger message that the government was consolidating around his leadership.

At 9:15 a.m., Bundy escorted the president to the west basement and the top-secret, windowless Situation Room. There he was briefed by CIA director John McCone. Since he had already given Bundy his standard speech about wanting him to stay on as National Security Council director, Johnson now focused his attention on McCone. LBJ opened the discussion by recalling his long personal relationship with McCone and his respect for the agency. As McCone recorded in a private memo a few days later, Johnson said that "he and I had seen eye to eye" on a number of major issues and that "he had complete confidence in me and expressed the wish that I continue in the future exactly as I have in the past."[12]

The purpose of the briefing was to bring the new president up to date on any foreign policy problems that required his immediate attention and to establish procedures for how he would be briefed in the future. McCone explained how the "President's Checklist" worked. McCone noted that

Johnson was "not familiar" with the practice started in the Kennedy administration. Every morning the CIA prepared a document, later called the "President's Daily Brief," with the latest intelligence information from around the world. They agreed that McCone would personally brief Johnson in the morning "for the next few days," and senior CIA officials would do the same for LBJ's staff. "The President asked that any matters of urgent importance be brought to his attention at any time, day or night."[13]

At 9:28 a.m., newsmen saw Johnson walking briskly across the street and down the alley to the Executive Office Building, accompanied by Moyers and Thornberry. Secretary of State Dean Rusk awaited them in his office. According to the official diary, the purpose of the session was to establish "continuity in foreign policies — importance of Secy. Rusk remaining." To help underscore the message of continuity, Johnson allowed photographers into the room to take pictures at the beginning of the meeting.[14]

In keeping with the stated purpose, Johnson assured the secretary of his intention to carry on President Kennedy's foreign policy. "We all needed to pitch in and keep the country going during this moment of great tragedy," LBJ told him. Rusk understood that it was customary for cabinet officers to tender their resignations to a new president. "I offered to resign, but Johnson urged me to stay on, saying that it was my duty to do so. Under those circumstances," Rusk recalled, "I could not refuse the president."[15]

No notes were taken during the meeting, but it is likely that the two men talked about Vietnam. Years later, Johnson recalled that he started working on Vietnam "the day after we got back to Washington after Dallas." In those first few days of his administration, "Vietnam was on top of the agenda."

By the time Johnson became president, the United States was already heavily invested in supporting the South Vietnamese government's struggle against the communist North. For most of his administration, Kennedy had managed to keep the issue on the back burner, but by November 1963, the deteriorating situation on the ground forced it to the front of the agenda. In the first twenty-four hours after the assassination, Johnson sketched out his vision of a Great Society, but he also was forced to contend with the issue that would ultimately

335

doom his presidency.

Between 1955 and 1961, the United States had provided over $1 billion in economic and military assistance to South Vietnam. The American effort, however, depended on the success of South Vietnam's premier, Ngo Dinh Diem, who ruthlessly suppressed dissenters, including powerful Buddhist groups. Between 1961 and 1963, Kennedy increased economic aid and also expanded the number of American military advisers to 1,600. The infusion of American support did little to stabilize the Diem regime. The North Vietnamese–supplied Vietcong established control over large portions of the countryside.

In the fall of 1963, confronted by the possibility of a massive revolt against the Diem government, Kennedy had reconsidered his support. When South Vietnamese generals approached Washington with plans for a coup, Kennedy reluctantly agreed. On November 1, 1963, the generals seized key military and communications installations and demanded Diem's resignation. Later that day, Diem was captured and, despite American assurances of safe passage, murdered. Kennedy had resisted pressure to commit American troops, but the heavy investment of money and military "advisers" had done little to slow the communist gains.

By the time Kennedy left for Dallas, American policy in Vietnam was at a crossroads. On November 21, he told an aide that he wanted "an in-depth study of every possible option we've got in Vietnam, including how to get out of there." To discuss the deteriorating situation, JFK had scheduled a meeting with Henry Cabot Lodge, the U.S. ambassador to the Republic of Vietnam. The meeting was set for after Kennedy's return from Dallas.[16]

Johnson inherited a crumbling situation in Southeast Asia with no clear path for the future. He lacked Kennedy's nuanced understanding of the world, and his willingness to challenge the conventional wisdom. Kennedy had sent Johnson to Vietnam in 1961 to allay Diem's fears that the United States was abandoning him. With typical exuberance, Johnson had announced that Diem was the "Winston Churchill of Southeast Asia." Since that trip, he had devoted very little time to Vietnam. "I suspect he felt that Vietnam would yield to reason and informed judgment," observed Jack Valenti.[17]

The situation in Vietnam would confront LBJ with critical choices in the first months of his presidency: How could Washington pressure the new government to institute reforms? Did the coup weaken the military effort, and if so, should the United States consider increasing its military presence in the country? In all of his initial meetings on the subject, Johnson expressed frustration with the war effort, skepticism about general U.S. policy in Vietnam, and a strong reluctance to expand the war effort unless the South Vietnamese government enacted significant social reforms. A few days later, even after listening to Ambassador Henry Cabot Lodge give what McCone described as an "optimistic," "hopeful" report, Johnson expressed "misgivings" about the American effort in Southeast Asia. He made it clear that he had never favored the overthrow of Diem, and he rejected the idea that "we had to reform every Asian into our own image."[18]

Johnson found himself trapped in the same dilemma that had frustrated Kennedy: he had no strategy for winning the war and he feared the consequences of "losing" Vietnam to the communists. Years later LBJ, reflected that he did not want to be "the first American President to put my tail between my legs and run," but he also "didn't want to increase our commitments" and "didn't want to escalate them."[19]

Tragically, Johnson would soon abandon his early skepticism and launch a major land war in Asia.

Johnson still had to deal with the aftermath of President Kennedy's death. There were unanswered questions about the assassin, his motives, and whether other individuals or groups might have been involved. Americans were waking up to news stories about Lee Harvey Oswald, who was professing his innocence, declaring "I did not kill the president. I did not kill anyone. I don't know what this is all about." But already the FBI claimed to have pictures of Oswald posing with the rifle they believed he used to murder the president. Dallas police captain Will Fritz, head of the homicide division, said, "I think the case is cinched."[20]

At 10:01 a.m., J. Edgar Hoover called to give LBJ an update about the investigation in Dallas.[21] "I just wanted to let you know of a development which I think is very important in connection with this case," Hoover announced in his staccato voice. It appears that Hoover was trying to disparage the efforts of the Dallas police, telling Johnson "the evidence that they have at the present time is not very, very strong." He reassured Johnson, however, that the FBI was gathering evidence that would prove Oswald's guilt. The FBI lab was testing the gun and bullets, and they were able to prove that Oswald, using the alias "A. Hidell" had purchased the gun from a sporting goods store in Chicago. Hoover expressed shock that such a cheap gun could be responsible for such a deadly act. "But the important thing is that this gun was bought in Chicago on a money order — cost $21 — and it seems almost impossible to think that for $21 you could kill the president of the United States." The actual price was $21.45. Oswald paid $12.78 for the rifle, $7.17 for the telescopic lens, and $1.50 for postage and handling.[22]

Johnson was clearly still worried about the possible Soviet connection, and he pumped Hoover for information. "Have you established any more about the visit to the Soviet embassy in Mexico in September?" he asked. Hoover had no new information to offer, but he revealed that the FBI routinely read all of the mail sent to the Soviet embassy in Washington. They had intercepted a letter from Oswald complaining that the FBI was harassing his wife. There was nothing incriminating in the letter, however. "The case as it stands now isn't strong enough to be able to get a conviction," Hoover informed Johnson.[23]

The conversation revealed how little Johnson knew about what had taken place in Dallas. For example, Johnson assumed that Oswald used the same gun to kill Officer Tibbett. "That is an entirely different gun," Hoover told him. "You think he might have two?" Johnson asked. Hoover said that Oswald used a revolver to shoot the officer. Johnson requested that Hoover provide him with a written synopsis and keep him informed of any new developments.

The discussion also exposed the self-important and self-serving Hoover at his worst. Instead of admitting to Johnson that he did not know the answers to some of his questions, he simply fabricated information. He told Johnson that detectives found one full bullet on the president's stretcher at Parkland. "It had apparently fallen out when they massaged his heart." In fact, the bullet he referred to was found on a stretcher used to carry Governor John Connally into the hospital. Later in the conversation, he claimed that Oswald fired the shots from the fifth floor, disposed of the gun on the sixth floor, and then fled to a movie theater "where he had the gun battle with the police officer." Oswald fired the shots from the sixth floor, not the fifth, and there was no "gun battle" at the movie theater.[24]

Johnson was not so busy with the affairs of state that he could not devote some time to his reelection. According to his official schedule, at 10:17 a.m. he placed a call to George Meany, the powerful head of the AFL-CIO (American Federation of Labor and Congress of Industrial Organizations), to assure him that he supported key components of the labor agenda. In addition to contacting Meany, LBJ sent him a telegram inviting him to the private viewing of the president's body. While Johnson reached out to Meany, he asked Hubert Humphrey to call other leaders of the labor movement.[25]

Shortly after he finished this phone call, Johnson switched gears again. At 10:21, he sat down for a formal, fifty-minute meeting with Robert McNamara. No one epitomized the Kennedy style more than McNamara. A Republican who had earned a reputation as a numbers-crunching whiz kid, he had been named the president of Ford Motor Company just seven weeks before JFK called to ask him to head the Pentagon. He awed Washington with his precision and skilled management of the unwieldy Defense Department. "I had no patience with the notion that the Pentagon could not be managed," McNamara reflected.

McNamara was crucial to LBJ's goal of keeping the Kennedy foreign policy team intact. LBJ told McNamara that he and the secretary of state were the two most visible leaders of America's role in the world. According to his briefing notes for the meeting, Johnson said, "You are the most qualified man that I know or that I ever heard of to handle the Defense Department." He made it clear that "it is vital that this country close ranks and march forward with unbroken continuity. We must have both strength and the appearance of strength. There must be no move that would even remotely lead others to think that our policies of strength are changing. I am counting heavily on you." Once again, Johnson allowed a small group of reporters to capture the final minutes of his meeting with McNamara.

Later that evening, Johnson told his dinner party guests that he had "told McNamara he wanted him to stay on, and if he heard any rumors about his leaving, he'd send a policeman out to get him."[26]

As LBJ was meeting with McNamara, a line

of black limousines formed outside, dropping off dignitaries beneath the north portico for the private viewing of President Kennedy's body in the East Room of the White House.

# 17
# "Honey, You Stay As Long As You Want"

As Lyndon Johnson's first twenty-four hours as president were coming to an end, a clear pattern was emerging. Drawing on his long years of service in politics, Johnson skillfully seized the reins of government. He balanced the need to reassure Americans and the world that he was in charge with a desire to be respectful of the Kennedy family and sensitive to a nation in mourning. There were no instant polls of the public mood to guide his actions in those first few hours. Johnson was navigating on instinct. Although he had never been comfortable with television, he revealed a shrewd understanding of its power and used it effectively to communicate with the nation.

The transfer of power, however, was not without its problems. LBJ's misunderstandings with Kenneth O'Donnell at Parkland Hospital, combined with his decision to take the oath in Dallas, accentuated old tensions between the Kennedy and Johnson camps. There was probably little LBJ could have done to secure Robert Kennedy's support, but he made matters worse by refusing to accept responsibility for his decision to remain in Dallas until after the oath had been administered. The rude reception he received from RFK when *Air Force One* landed in Washington highlighted the growing conflict between the two men.

Over the next few hours, Johnson would continue juggling his many responsibilities: offering support to a grieving widow, sending messages of strength and assurance to the nation, and monitoring the latest reports on the investigation into Kennedy's murder. A cloud of anguish and anger hung over the White House on the morning of Saturday, November 23, as Kennedy loyalists both mourned their fallen leader and confronted the difficult reality that Lyndon Johnson was now president.

The Kennedy family had arrived back at the White House with JFK's body at 4:35 a.m. Workers had spent most of the night and the early morning preparing the East Room for the viewing. Arthur Schlesinger Jr., writing that day in his journal, described the scene as Kennedy returned to the White

House for the last time. "The casket was carried into the East Room and deposited on a stand. It was wrapped in a flag. Jackie followed, accompanied by Bobby . . . A priest said a few words. Then Bobby whispered to Jackie. Then she walked away. The rest of us followed."

Jackie went up to her room, but Bobby returned to the East Room and asked Schlesinger to view the body and make a recommendation about whether to have an open casket. "And so I went in, with the candles fitfully burning, three priests on their knees praying in the background, and took a last look at my beloved President, my beloved friend," Schlesinger wrote. "For a moment, I was shattered. But it was not a good job, probably it could not have been with half his head blasted away. It was too waxen, too made up. It did not really look like him." Schlesinger reported back to Bobby, who made the decision to have a closed coffin.[1]

Mrs. Kennedy had slept for a few hours with the help of a powerful tranquilizer. Early on Saturday she was overseeing final preparations for the day. She collected a few items to be placed in the coffin. There were some of President Kennedy's cherished items — gold cufflinks she had given him

on their first anniversary, a PT boat tiepin
— to be placed in the coffin. She helped
Caroline and John Jr., who would turn three
years old on the day his father was to be
buried, write scribbles; and she composed
her own long letter that began, "My darling
Jack." She and Bobby carried the items
down to the East Room and placed them in
the coffin. Jackie kissed her husband, cut off
two locks of his hair, and placed them in
small ceramic frames. She kept one and
gave the other to Bobby.[2]

At 10:00 a.m., about seventy-five family
members and close friends attended what
many believed was the first Catholic mass
ever held in the White House. RFK had
already stepped into the role of paterfamil-
ias. "The whole family was like a bunch of
shipwreck survivors," said JFK friend Lem
Billings. "I don't think they could have
made it at all without Bobby. He seemed to
be everywhere. He always had an arm
around a friend or family member and was
telling them it was okay, that it was time to
move ahead."[3]

The grieving Kennedy family wanted this
mass to be strictly a private family affair.
Once the mass ended, Kennedy's body
would remain in the East Room for the next
twenty-four hours. Official Washington —

former presidents, members of Congress, the executive branch, and the Supreme Court, along with other dignitaries and diplomats — would have the opportunity to pay their respects. On Sunday, the president's body would be moved to the Capitol Rotunda to lie in state before the funeral on Monday.

At around 10:20 a.m., Lady Bird went to LBJ's office to walk with him to the White House for the eleven o'clock viewing. The president and First Lady were scheduled to head the procession of government leaders viewing the body. Lady Bird was soon joined by a group of congressional leaders who had arranged to accompany him as well.

Johnson entered the East Room followed by former Presidents Dwight D. Eisenhower and Harry Truman, who had arrived earlier that morning, and the chief justice of the Supreme Court, Earl Warren. Lady Bird noted "that an aura of quiet prevailed." As Mrs. Kennedy had requested, the East Room looked exactly the way it had in 1865. It was decorated entirely in black. The bulbs in the great chandeliers were dimmed. The president rested in a closed, flag-draped casket, which rested on a catafalque. Flickering candles stood at each corner. Hubert Humphrey described it as "a very solemn occasion. The entire atmosphere was one of deep silence, profound respect, and great sorrow."[4]

Mrs. Kennedy had demanded one significant change in the military honor guard that watched over the president. According to General Godfrey McHugh, traditionally the military guards were posted "watching the outside, turning their backs on each corner of the casket to prevent enemies from coming and robbing the casket." Earlier that morning, Mrs. Kennedy said to McHugh, "Godfrey, I want you to order them to face the casket." McHugh explained that would be contrary to standard military practice, but she cut him off. "I don't want it done that way," she insisted. "I don't want them to turn their backs on the President." McHugh passed the request on to the navy lieutenant in charge of the detail and he ordered the change.[5]

The atmosphere in the room was somber. Lady Bird recorded that LBJ, wearing a charcoal black suit, "walked slowly past the President's body in the East Room." Former presidents Truman and Eisenhower followed behind, along with members of the cabinet and the Supreme Court, federal judges, members of Congress, governors, and diplomats. Some members of the cabinet, Lady Bird noted, had been "half way round the world" when they received the news. "They were here now, standing shocked and sad-faced, filing past as all of us had filed past, like automatons."[6]

After viewing the body, Lady Bird and President Johnson went to the family quarters of the White House to talk with Mrs. Kennedy. They stayed for about twenty minutes. Mrs. Kennedy offered to move out of the White House as soon as possible, but Johnson refused the offer. "Honey, you stay as long as you want. I have a nice comfortable house and I'm in no hurry. You have tragedy and many problems."[7]

Mrs. Kennedy accepted LBJ's offer. She remained in the Executive Mansion until December 7, when she moved into the Washington home of diplomat Averell Harriman. A few weeks later, she moved again to a house in the Georgetown section of Washington. Even after they moved out, however, the Kennedys continued to use the White House. Caroline's first-grade class had been meeting on the third floor of the mansion. Not wanting to disrupt the class, Mrs. Kennedy asked Johnson if they could

351

continue to meet until their Christmas break. LBJ readily agreed.

While being gracious to Jackie, Johnson was still thinking about the media and his public role. After speaking with Mrs. Kennedy, Johnson walked back to his office in the Executive Office Building accompanied by President Eisenhower. He made sure that photographers were present to record the moment. His meeting with Ike was scheduled for later in the afternoon, but Johnson wanted the world to see him conferring with the former supreme commander of NATO, the man that JFK had replaced in office. He knew it would send a reassuring signal to allies, a warning to potential enemies, and a comforting bipartisan message to many Americans.

At 12:20 p.m., LBJ and Lady Bird departed for a private service for President Kennedy at Saint John's Episcopal Church, just a few steps from the White House. Lady Bird described it as "a sort of a very 'high church,' a stern, rigid church, but most fitting for the day." Every president since James Madison had worshiped at this church, which is why it was dubbed the "church of the presidents." Only LBJ, the First Lady, and a few members of his staff were present. A Secret Service agent escorted them across the street. As organ music played in the background, they were introduced to the Reverend Harper, who led them down to a pew in the second row. "O, God, bless Thy servant Lyndon and all others in authority so they may do Thy will," Harper preached. It was a simple service lasting ten minutes.[8]

At 12:35 p.m., LBJ returned to his office in the Executive Office Building for the meeting with Eisenhower. The two men had worked together when Johnson was majority leader and Ike was president. It was clear from the talking points that aide Horace Busby prepared for him that Johnson wanted to stress the importance of continuity. It was necessary, Busby wrote, for the world to understand that the "U.S. Government is stable, functioning, effective," and that the assassination "doesn't presage civil disorder." Clearly, the White House was worried about news reports highlighting Lee Harvey Oswald's ties to the Soviets and Cubans. Busby pointed out that it was important "not to inflame opinion because of known background of the slaying suspect." Party politics, he observed, "must be laid aside in favor of demonstrations of unity" and "speed" in passing Kennedy's legislative agenda.[9]

Eisenhower later told William Manchester that Johnson seemed nervous and fidgety during the meeting. "He was, as he always is, nervous — walking around, and telephoning everyone. He loves to phone and he was phoning all the time. I would mention someone in the conversation and he would snatch up the telephone and call the person." While Ike sat, LBJ talked on the phone with Humphrey and Oklahoma congressman Carl Albert about the possibility of addressing a joint session of Congress the day after the Kennedy funeral. He also placed a call to Frederick Kappel, president of the Business Council, asking for the "united support of every segment of the country."[10]

In between phone calls, Johnson asked Ike for advice on a host of issues, both domestic and foreign. To Eisenhower, Johnson seemed primarily interested in fulfilling the Kennedy agenda, not proposing new initiatives. "As far as I could see at that time, Lyndon Johnson's only intention was to find out what was going on and to carry policy through," Ike reflected. "He suggested nothing new or different. He wanted to talk about Laos, Cuba, and so forth. He seemed to be less informed about foreign policy than about domestic policy."[11]

The meeting between Eisenhower and LBJ was briefly interrupted when CIA chief John McCone entered the office to give LBJ the latest update on the Oswald investigation. McCone reported that Mexican officials were holding a Cuban embassy official who had met with Oswald when he visited Mexico City two months earlier on September 27. He was being interrogated about possible connections to Oswald.[12]

It is unclear how much detail McCone shared with Johnson at that time, but by Saturday afternoon some senior analysts in the CIA were suspecting a possible Soviet plot to kill Kennedy. "Putting it baldly," a senior CIA official wrote in a memo on November 23, "was Oswald, wittingly or unwittingly, part of a plot to murder President Kennedy in Dallas as an attempt to further exacerbate sectional strife and render the U.S. government less capable of dealing with Soviet initiatives over the next year?"[13]

The news about Oswald's meetings with Cuban officials were deeply troubling. If the information was correct, and if it became public, how would the nation react? Would Americans demand retaliation? For now, Johnson asked to be kept informed of any developments.[14]

■ ■ ■ ■

Johnson also discussed with Eisenhower how to handle the issue of staff resignations. The new president faced a delicate situation: he needed to keep the Kennedy people in order to show continuity, but he also understood that eventually he had to surround himself with aides who were loyal to him.

Despite Johnson's strong urging that the Kennedy staff members stay on the job, it was still unclear how many would accept his offer. Most did not know what to make of the new president — and what little they did know was not particularly attractive. "Few of us were well-acquainted with our new leader," George Ball observed. "As Vice President, he had been an unhappy, brooding, sometimes irascible man." People had tried to avoid him, and no one wanted to cross Lyndon Johnson for fear of one of his emotional eruptions. Could those who were so closely identified with JFK, Ball wondered, "happily function under a Texan who had made his way by slicing through the political sagebrush with a machete and was burdened by the baggage of regional attitudes and prejudices?" How "many of us would stay once we had tested the new leader and he had tested us?" Ball asked. "No one could say."[15]

Schlesinger had turned in his letter of resignation that morning. Johnson glanced at it before handing it over to McGeorge Bundy. "Please take this letter back and have him withdraw it." He said that he did not want any letters of resignation. Eisenhower suggested that Johnson reconsider his decision. "Take 'em all," Ike said. "You must be your own self and establish yourself, and you must take them all and decide in 3 or 4 days which ones you are going to accept." He advised LBJ to preserve his range of freedom by asking everyone to submit their resignations. Johnson could then announce that he was not accepting them "for the time being," while leaving open the option of doing so at a future date. Johnson rejected the recommendation. Years later, he regretted not taking Eisenhower's advice.[16]

The men who made up the Kennedy administration were not monolithic in their response to the assassination or their views of Johnson. According to Schlesinger, by Saturday morning the Kennedy people were already dividing into rival camps. The "realist" group, which included Bundy, Larry

O'Brien, and Robert McNamara, understood they needed Johnson to fulfill Kennedy's legacy. While JFK had managed few legislative victories, they believed his administration had nudged the country in the right direction, setting the stage for bolder initiatives later. Whether they liked Johnson, or trusted him, was irrelevant: he was the only game in town. Bundy stayed on for two more years as Johnson's national security adviser. McNamara would remain as defense secretary for five years, and emerge as the architect of LBJ's failed Vietnam policy. O'Brien continued to serve as a congressional liaison until 1965, when LBJ appointed him postmaster general.

The "sentimentalists," who included Schlesinger, RFK, and O'Donnell, could never make the transition. They were too devastated by the death of their leader and friend, and too distrustful of Johnson to continue working in the White House. "My heart is not in it," Schlesinger wrote in his diary the day after the assassination. The stories, many of them exaggerated, about Johnson's callousness in the hours after the assassination, confirmed their suspicions that he was not worthy to fill the chair once occupied by the regal JFK. Schlesinger was the first to leave, in January

1964. Robert Kennedy remained as attorney general until September 1964, when he left to run a successful campaign for a New York senate seat. O'Donnell remained on the White House staff until after the 1964 election.[17]

The sentimentalists complained that Johnson was moving too quickly to replace JFK, and they wasted no time in plotting to get him out of the White House. That morning, Schlesinger spoke with Democratic Party chairman John Bailey about whether "it might be technically feasible to beat Johnson at Atlantic City," the site of the party's 1964 convention. Bailey said it was possible, but the effort would damage the party and allow the Republicans to carry the election.[18]

There were a few close Kennedy associates who fell into neither camp. Speechwriter Ted Sorensen felt no animus toward LBJ; he was simply too devastated to continue working in the White House. Johnson, Sorenson reflected, "could not have been more gracious. Not known for his soft and tactful manner, particularly when he was engaged in the power of persuasion, Johnson was the picture of tact in his relations with me during the three months I remained at the White House." Sorenson left the administration at the end of January 1964.[19]

Even some of the sentimentalists offered grudging praise for the new president. "Johnson has behaved, in the main, with great consideration," Schlesinger wrote in his journal. The liberal historian admitted that on many issues, LBJ would be better than Kennedy. "My guess is that he will be pretty good on issues, and that in some respects he will be more liberal than JFK."[20]

For most sentimentalists, however, no act of kindness or generosity could have convinced them to accept LBJ as president. For now, consumed with sadness and grief, they devoted their energy to healing their emotional wounds, supporting each other, and providing comfort to the president's widow. But they never abandoned their hopes of one day recapturing the White House for another Kennedy.

Within a twenty-four-hour period, Lyndon Johnson's world was turned upside down, and the American political world was shaken to its core. At 12:29 p.m. (CST) on Friday afternoon, Lyndon Johnson had been convinced that his long and distinguished political career was coming to an end. He felt ignored, underutilized, and unappreciated. By the same time on Saturday, he was operating in high gear, establishing his authority as president of the United States. He found himself at the center of the action, juggling a dozen details, holding private meetings with ex-presidents, issuing orders, and laying plans for the future. A day earlier, no one had noticed him when he walked into a room, and around the White House many Kennedy aides called him by his first name. Now when he entered a room, people stood at attention, and even lifelong friends referred to him as "Mr. President."

LBJ hated the way he became president, but he loved the power and the attention that it afforded him. He would go on to become one of America's most controversial chief executives, responsible for a tide of social legislation that would transform the lives of millions of Americans. But he would also send hundreds of thousands of U.S. troops to fight in Southeast Asia. At home, race riots and student protests would shatter his dreams of building an enduring liberal coalition. The combined weight of violence at home and an unpopular war abroad would doom his presidency and tear apart the Democratic coalition. In those first few hours of his administration, Johnson offered a glimpse into the qualities of both greatness and tragedy that would define his presidency.

# CONCLUSION:
## IN KENNEDY'S SHADOW

The journalist Tom Wicker, columnist for the *New York Times,* sat in his stuffy, cramped room at the Baker Hotel in Dallas on Saturday morning trying to come to terms with what had transpired in the past twenty-four hours and speculating on what it would mean for America's future. "Perhaps only at the death of a President does it come fully clear how nearly the national life — the basic expression of what John F. Kennedy loved to call 'the great republic' — has become centralized and symbolized in the White House and the man who lives there," he wrote. "What is most certain today, as Lyndon Johnson ends his first twenty-four hours as President, is that there will be little change, yet there will be great change."[1]

The early verdicts on Johnson's handling of the transition were uniformly positive. On Tuesday, when Wall Street opened for business for the first time since the assassination, stocks skyrocketed 32.03 points to 743.52. The increase topped the previous single-day record of 28.40, set on October 30, 1929. The *New York Daily News* headline screamed:[2]

## STOCKS ZOOM; MARKET HAILS
## OUR NEW CHIEF

Johnson stepped gracefully into his new role. Friends and colleagues noted how much LBJ had changed in those first few hours. On Saturday afternoon, Secretary of Agriculture Orville Freeman commented on seeing "a different Lyndon Johnson than from the past 3 years. Actually the frustration seemed gone, he seemed relaxed, the power, the confidence, the assurance of Majority Leader Lyndon Johnson seemed to be there." An aide observed that LBJ moved with the "natural grace of the gentleman he is, but also with a sense of responsibility." Others told reporters that they sensed "a new strain of dignity," which they speculated came from his awareness that he was now under intense media scrutiny.[3]

Objective reporters noted a measurable change in the way Johnson carried himself in the days following the assassination. He was a man used to employing intimidation to get what he wanted and to bend people to his will, but in these critical hours Johnson revealed a rare sensitivity. "Johnson has not always been famous for tact," observed Steward Alsop, "which makes his role during the transition all the more remarkable." The journalist John Steele observed that as president, Johnson offered "a striking contrast with the fidgety, irascible, short-tempered, vain man we sat with only a few weeks ago in his Capitol Hill vice presidential office."[4]

LBJ's main goal in his first twenty-four hours as president was to comfort a shocked and grieving nation and thus reassure the American people that their government was still functioning. By all accounts, he succeeded in large part due to his masterful handling of the media. Television news came into its own on November 22, 1963. Throughout the day, Johnson carefully choreographed the images that America saw of him. He allowed a photographer to record the swearing in on *Air Force One,* and he insisted that the press be granted access to his arrival at Andrews Air Force Base later that evening. On Saturday, he made sure a photographer snapped pictures of his meetings with key members of the Kennedy cabinet. Johnson's skillful use of symbolic images demonstrated to a nervous public that while Kennedy was dead, the American presidency remained intact.

Johnson's performance during the hours and days immediately following the assassination earned him high praise from the media. The *Wall Street Journal* noted that LBJ "has done much to command respect and encourage confidence. People have been impressed as much, perhaps, by the President's demeanor as by his words and acts." Veteran journalist Walter Lippmann wrote that the assassination "taught us how right President Kennedy was when he chose Lyndon Johnson as his running mate. His choice was not only the smartest kind of politics, it was most discerning and wise." The *Cleveland Ohio Plain Dealer* editorialized, "The manner in which Mr. Johnson has stepped into the breach created by the assassination of John F. Kennedy has been such as to inspire the confidence of the world in the continuity and stability of the American form of government."[5]

Johnson spent the first days of his presidency emphasizing the theme of continuity, telling everyone who would listen that he planned to carry on the policies of his slain predecessor. But as his bedroom ruminations on Saturday night revealed, Johnson was not going to be content with simply completing Kennedy's agenda. He was dreaming of his own "Great Society," an ambitious expansion of federal power not seen since the early days of the New Deal.

Always the political tactician, Johnson realized that the outpouring of grief following Kennedy's death provided him with a powerful tool to build political support for an expansive liberal agenda. As columnist Stewart Aslop pointed out, LBJ's "single greatest asset is the memory of his predecessor." Over the course of the next few years, Johnson employed the Kennedy myth and memory to realize his vision of a Great Society. "Everything I had ever learned in the history books taught me that martyrs have to die for causes. John Kennedy had died. But his 'cause' was not really clear. That was my job. I had to take the dead man's program and turn it into a martyr's cause. That way Kennedy would live on forever and so would I."[6]

Johnson wasted little time turning JFK's death into a rallying cry to pass the slain leader's stalled legislative agenda. On November 27, two days after the nation buried Kennedy, Johnson addressed a joint session of Congress, declaring his intention to push for the completion of the Kennedy legislative agenda. "No memorial oration or eulogy could more eloquently honor President Kennedy's memory than the earliest possible passage of the civil rights bill for which he fought so long," he said. Action was necessary, he told congressional leaders, "to honor the President's memory" and "to continue his work." The twenty-four-minute speech was interrupted thirty-two times by applause. When he finished, congressional leaders gave him a two-minute standing ovation.[7]

Johnson was not content merely to pass Kennedy's agenda. He sought to create a program that would bear his personal brand. In January 1964, in his first State of the Union address, Johnson declared "unconditional war on poverty in America," and followed up with a legislative proposal, which Congress passed in the summer of 1964. Using the skills he had learned from years on the Hill, Johnson also assumed personal control over the fight to pass Kennedy's civil rights bill. The bill that Johnson eventually pushed through Congress was stronger than the one Kennedy initially submitted. The *Congressional Quarterly* hailed it as "the most sweeping civil rights measure to clear either house of Congress in the 20th century."[8]

As expected, LBJ won his party's nomination in 1964. After dangling the vice presidency in front of him for months, he finally selected Hubert Humphrey as his running mate. Campaigning as the heir to the JFK legacy, Johnson crushed Arizona senator Barry Goldwater in the general election, scoring massive majorities in the House and Senate.

Kennedy's tragic death, and Johnson's skillful management of the transition of power in the twenty-four hours that followed it, helped set the stage for the great legislative achievements of the Great Society. In the first six months of 1965, the administration submitted eighty-seven bills to Congress and saw eighty-four of them become law. Congress passed consumer protection acts and provided aid for mass transit, urban development, and slum clearance. Not surprisingly, many observers viewed the Great Society as a "Second New Deal" and hailed LBJ as the new FDR.

LBJ rescued two staples of the Democratic agenda held hostage by congressional conservatives since the days of Harry Truman: medical insurance for the elderly and education funding for the young. The president also managed to quiet opponents of federal aid to education and convince Congress to pass his Elementary and Secondary Education Act of 1965. On August 6, 1965, Johnson signed the Voting Rights Act, which guaranteed African Americans access to the franchise. "They came in darkness and chains," he said at the signing ceremony. "Today we strike away the last major shackles of those fierce and ancient bonds."

Within a few years, however, the bright, early promise of the Johnson presidency would be overshadowed by an unpopular war, racial riots, and student protests. During the opening act of the Johnson administration, the press seemed to believe it was part of their patriotic duty to write flattering, uncritical reviews about LBJ; by 1968 it was difficult to find a positive story about him. The public, who rallied around LBJ and his agenda in the early days, providing him with an unprecedented mandate in 1964, soon turned sour.

Many of the less attractive qualities that Johnson revealed in the twenty-four hours following the assassination — his insecurity, his paranoia, his willingness to deceive — would grow over time and eventually eclipse the bright hopes of his administration. Johnson was haunted by the tragic circumstances that forged his presidency. "I always felt bad for Harry Truman and the way he got the presidency," LBJ once said. "But at least his man wasn't murdered." In the wake of the horrible tragedy that unfolded in his home state, Johnson feared that the American people, and many members of the Kennedy staff, would not accept him. "I took the oath," Johnson told Doris Kearns Goodwin. "I became President. But for millions of Americans I was still illegitimate, a naked man with no presidential covering, a pretender to the throne, an illegal usurper."[9]

LBJ's fear that the nation would not accept him as the legitimate heir to the presidency convinced him that he needed someone close to the slain president, either Kenneth O'Donnell or RFK, to endorse every decision he made on that fateful day. He proved himself willing to manipulate both men in order to obtain the political cover he desired — or he simply lied and manufactured their compliance. He claimed that O'Donnell specifically ordered him to board *Air Force One,* when that decision was most likely made by the Secret Service. He insisted that O'Donnell was the first person to tell him that JFK was dead, when the evidence shows that Emory Roberts delivered the news. Later he manipulated a grieving RFK into agreeing that he should take the oath in Dallas. After getting RFK to endorse his decision to take the oath in Dallas, he told everyone on the plane that the swearing in was the attorney general's idea.

The pattern of deception so evident in the early hours of LBJ's administration would eventually erode the moral authority of his presidency. Johnson's penchant for bending the facts to suit his purposes raised doubts about his integrity and created a credibility gap that eventually undermined public trust in his administration. Ironically, the pervasive television coverage that at first helped establish Johnson's credibility would later play a key role in destroying it.

Johnson told so many small lies, and some big ones, that many people started to question everything he said. Early in his presidency, Johnson told reporters that his great-great-grandfather died defending the Alamo. When a journalist informed him that none of his relatives had ever fought at the Alamo, Johnson exclaimed, "God damn it, why must all those journalists be such sticklers for detail?"

Many of the lies he told were more serious. In April 1965, Johnson sent the marines to quell an insurrection in the Dominican Republic. When reporters suggested that the president had overreacted to a situation that offered no threat to American security, Johnson responded by exaggerating the magnitude of the crisis. He told stories — all proven false — of fifteen hundred innocent people murdered and beheaded, and of the American ambassador being forced to seek cover from stray bullets spraying the U.S. embassy. Almost nothing Johnson said about the crisis was true, prompting renewed questions about his honesty. "How do you know when Johnson is telling the truth?" a skeptic asked. "When he scratches his head, rubs his chin or knits his brow, he's telling the truth. When he begins to move his lips, he's lying."

Johnson repeated this pattern when he justified his decision to expand the Vietnam War. Privately, Johnson anguished over the war, often questioning whether the United States could win a military struggle in Southeast Asia, but he never shared his private doubts with the public. Instead, while planning for war, Johnson talked about peace, deliberately misleading Congress and the American people about his planned escalation of the conflict. While confidently predicting victory in pubic, privately he feared defeat. Johnson fundamentally altered the nature of the war and dramatically enlarged America's commitment to it. When challenged, he claimed that he was simply following the policies set by his predecessor.

Over the next two years, press reports contradicted the optimistic military pronouncements from the White House, gradually chipping away at Johnson's credibility. The crowning blow came on January 31, 1968, the day of the Vietnamese lunar new year, called Tet: the Vietcong invaded the U.S. embassy compound in Saigon and waged bloody battles in the capitals of most of South Vietnam's provinces. Televised footage of marines defending the grounds of the American embassy in Saigon shocked a nation that had been told the enemy was nearly defeated and the war almost won.

The Tet Offensive dealt Johnson's credibility a crushing blow. On February 27, television anchorman Walter Cronkite, echoing many Americans, declared that the United States was "mired in stalemate." At that moment, Johnson turned to an aide and said, "It's all over." Johnson knew that if he had lost Cronkite, he had lost "Mr. Average Citizen." He was right: public support for Johnson, and his Vietnam policy, dropped dramatically after the Tet Offensive.

The tortured relationship between Johnson and RFK, which predated the assassination, took on greater meaning after JFK's death. The tension between the Johnson and Kennedy camps, so apparent on the plane ride back to Washington after the shooting, intensified into open warfare in the years that followed. RFK's contempt for Johnson transformed into rage, while LBJ's fear of Kennedy turned into full-blown paranoia. "Lyndon Johnson had come on stage before a black curtain," Liz Carpenter told William Manchester, "and the Kennedys made no move to lift the darkness for him, or for the country." Over time, the personal differences between the two men would divide the nation, forge a major fissure in the New Deal Coalition, and produce a civil war within the Democratic Party.[10]

LBJ's actions in the hours following Kennedy's assassination were framed by fear — not only fear that he might also be the target of an assassin's bullet, but dread that a defiant and vengeful RFK would try to deny him the presidency. Although Johnson knew within minutes of arriving at Parkland Hospital that JFK had suffered a traumatic head wound, he rejected the advice of the Secret Service that he board *Air Force One,* worried that Robert Kennedy, and other detractors in the White House, would interpret his flight to Washington as either callous or cowardly. The nation needed a commander in chief, but Johnson was initially paralyzed by fear.

President Kennedy's death changed the dynamic between RFK and LBJ. While he was alive, JFK had managed to control his brother's deep resentment toward Johnson. The need to serve one president had forced Johnson and Robert Kennedy to keep their personal hostility in check. With JFK dead, there was nothing to restrain their mutual enmity. "After Dallas, when Bobby Kennedy looked at Lyndon Johnson, he saw a usurper in the Oval Office; when Johnson looked at Bobby, he saw a pretender to the Presidency," observed Clark Clifford.[11]

While Johnson worked hard to maintain a cordial relationship with Mrs. Kennedy, those close to the family continued to treat him with contempt. Aware of Johnson's desperate need for their approval, the Kennedy clan deliberately denied him the acceptance he craved. In the spring of 1964, the Kennedys gathered at a swanky Washington restaurant for a birthday party honoring Jackie Kennedy. "Almost anyone that was anyone in Washington was present and they were swarmed about Mrs. Kennedy," O'Donnell recalled. Johnson stood in a corner having a drink. "No one," he said, "spoke to him except in a ceremonial fashion." Later, in the car ride back to the White House with O'Donnell and Larry O'Brien, Johnson said, "Despite what they think, I suppose I still am the President of the United States."[12]

Johnson was less worried about the personal slights than he was about Robert Kennedy's political ambitions. Would he assemble a shadow government and start laying the groundwork for a presidential campaign in 1968? Aides claimed that LBJ became obsessed with RFK after he left the cabinet and won election to the Senate in 1964.

In the months after the assassination, RFK was overcome by two emotions: a profound sense of loss and grief at the death of his brother and a simmering anger toward the man who, at least temporarily, had assumed his job. The Senate provided him with a power base outside the White House. For those who knew him best, RFK was a man transformed. While still intense and driven, he revealed a gentleness and a reflectiveness absent from his personality before November 1963.

Politically, RFK was more of a threat to Johnson than ever. As Kennedy emerged from his brother's shadow and developed his own voice, he found a large following among young people and liberals. As Kennedy grew in stature, he sometimes overshadowed the president, even as Johnson was at the peak of his powers. As Johnson started cutting back on Great Society programs to pay for his expanded war, Kennedy emerged as one the president's toughest and most articulate critics.

There was plenty to criticize. By 1967, the pent-up anger of the civil rights movement exploded in an orgy of violence that tore through dozens of American cities. Most of all, there was Vietnam: a nagging distraction in 1963 that LBJ had turned into a massive land war in Asia. In August, Johnson sent 45,000 more troops to Vietnam and asked for higher taxes to finance the war. The horror of the war, flashed into the homes of most Americans on evening newscasts, was matched by that of racial violence in the nation's cities. Flames tore through thirty cities. Between unrest over urban upheaval, the war, and the need to raise taxes, the president's popularity all but vanished. By October 1967, only 31 percent of the nation approved Johnson's handling of the war.

By 1967, Kennedy became a magnet for those disaffected with Johnson and his policies. What started out as a bitter personal squabble between two powerful figures soon changed into a titanic struggle for the soul of the Democratic Party and the future of liberalism. Lyndon Johnson looked to the past for his inspiration, defending his policies as a continuation of the government activism of the New Deal and the muscular containment policies of Harry Truman and John F. Kennedy. Robert Kennedy became the spokesman of the so-called New Politics, an amorphous coalition of young people, intellectuals, the poor and disenfranchised. They were bound together as much by anger about the war and hostility toward Johnson as by a shared coherent philosophy. Overall, however, they wanted to move the party further to the left: more spending on social programs, less focus on middle-class entitlements, and an end to the war.

For a brief period, it looked like the 1968 Democratic primaries would serve as a political battleground for the two visions of the party's future. By 1968, many Democratic leaders were urging RFK to challenge

LBJ in the upcoming primaries, but he refused, reluctant to be drawn into a nasty personal battle with the incumbent president. But after Minnesota, Senator Eugene McCarthy exposed LBJ's political weakness by nearly winning the New Hampshire primary on March 12, 1968. RFK switched course, and announced his candidacy four days later. "The thing I feared from the first day of my presidency was actually coming true," LBJ confided to Doris Kearns Goodwin. "Robert Kennedy had openly announced his intention to reclaim the throne in the memory of his brother. And the American people, swayed by the magic of the name, were dancing in the streets."[13]

The showdown between the two rivals was not to be. On March 31, torn between his generals who demanded more troops for the war and a frustrated public calling for withdrawal, Johnson told a national television audience that he would not seek reelection. On June 4, after winning the crucial California primary, Kennedy was shot and killed by Sirhan Sirhan, a Palestinian who opposed the senator's pro-Israeli position.

In the end, JFK's death made the Johnson presidency possible, but it also doomed it to failure. The tragic circumstances that allowed LBJ to ascend to the office would make him one of the most influential, but also one of the most tragic, of modern presidents. "Johnson, although a man of immense ego, felt threatened both by his unnatural accession and by the spoken and unspoken comparisons to Kennedy," observed Hubert Humphrey. Johnson was the "heir to the presidency," but he also desperately wanted "to be the heir to the affection of the Kennedy insiders as well as of the nation. When it was not readily forthcoming, he tried more desperately to succeed; and both his virtues and his flaws were larger than life."[14]

Johnson's extraordinary talent was on full display in those first twenty-four hours. He skillfully molded the outpouring of grief following Kennedy's death into a powerful political weapon, and his sure-footed handling of the transition inspired trust in his leadership. In those critical first hours, the public witnessed LBJ's ability to take charge of a difficult situation, establish priorities, and keep focused on a handful of basic tasks. He never lost sight of the need to communicate with the public, and he skillfully used the media for that purpose.

There were, however, also troubling hints

of what was to come. What seemed like minor failings on November 22, 1963, would emerge as major character flaws and eventually destroy his presidency. Johnson had hoped to surpass the achievements of his hero, Franklin D. Roosevelt. Instead, he presided over the unraveling of the Roosevelt coalition and the erosion of public faith in government.

# ACKNOWLEDGMENTS

I could not have written this book without the support of the University of Oklahoma and the History Channel, the dedication of skilled archivists, the insight of many colleagues and scholars, and the encouragement of friends.

As always I am indebted to my friend and mentor James T. Patterson, who read an early draft of the book and made many insightful comments. Gary Ginsberg offered perceptive comments and valuable support. Nick Davatzes also offered helpful comments and encouragement. At Basic Books, Lara Heimert guided the project from beginning to end. She read the manuscript with great care and offered incisive criticism and thoughtful commentary. Sandra Beris, and the entire production team at Basic Books, have turned a rough manuscript into a polished book in record time.

At the John F. Kennedy Presidential

Library, Maura Porter made me aware of the recently declassified interview with General Godfrey McHugh. Laurie Anderson and Maryrose Grossman helped process my requests for photos. At the Lyndon Baines Johnson Library, Claudia Anderson responded to my numerous requests for information. The archivists who staff the reading room at the LBJ library are among the most knowledgeable, polite, and helpful in the business. They make the library one of my favorite places to work. Suzy Taraba, chief archivist at Wesleyan University, provided me with an early peek into the papers of William Manchester. I'm grateful to the family of William Manchester for granting me permission to quote from the collection.

At History, Nancy Dubuc and David McKillop had enough confidence in the project to approve a two-hour special based on the book. Executive producer Paul Cabana has skillfully overseen the production. The project has been placed in the able hands of Emmy Award–winning producer Anthony Giacchino.

My friends have sustained me over the past year with their affection and support. I can't name them all, but a few come immediately to mind: Jim and Katie Ryan,

Debbie and Max Raines, Abbe Raven and Marty Tackel, Ross Baker, Greg Kerr, David Courier, Charlie Mustachia, Carolyn Morgan, Mindy Jones, Salil Mehta, Tripp Hall, Robert Griswold, Bill Miller, Matt Miller, Bill Rindfuss, Maged Shenouda, Sam Stoia, Joao Delinger, David Sampliner, Lisa Dallos, Ken Orkin, and Andrew Hurwitz.

This book is dedicated to the Honorable David L. Boren, president of the University of Oklahoma. David Boren has devoted his life to public service. In a remarkable career that has spanned four decades, he has served as governor, a United States senator, and now the leader of Oklahoma's premier university. Along the way, he has touched the lives of thousands of people. He changed my life in 1997 when he invited me to become the first dean of a new Honors College. Over the past decade, I have watched him transform the university with his bold vision, his unique political skills, and his remarkable energy. He is relentless and uncompromising in his dedication to students. He can be a tough and demanding boss, but he is also man with an open mind and a big heart. He talks often about tolerance and compassion, and he practices what he preaches everyday.

# NOTES

**Preface**

1. Theodore H. White, *The Making of the President 1964* (New York: New American Library, 1965), 186.
2. Manchester to Valenti, April 12, 1965, Box 1, "Manchester File," Special File on the Assassination, Lyndon Baines Johnson Library (SFA-LBJL), Austin, TX.
3. Andrew Glass, "LBJ Depicted as Fleeing Dallas," *Washington Post,* January 24, 1967, A1.
4. Arthur M. Schlesinger Jr., *Robert Kennedy and His Times* (New York: Ballantine Books, 1978), 819.
5. In describing the plane ride back to Washington, for example, the draft quoted Mrs. Kennedy as saying to Malcolm Kilduff, "You make sure, Mac — you go and tell the President — don't let Lyndon Johnson say that I sat with him and Lady Bird and they comforted me all during

the trip. You say — you say that I came back here and sat with Jack." The published version simply says, "You make sure, Mac — you go and tell them that I came back here and sat with Jack." See Untitled Document, Box 3, "President Johnson's Statements and Schedule," SFA-LBJL.

6. Max Holland, *The Kennedy Assassination Tapes: The White House Conversations of Lyndon B. Johnson Regarding the Assassination, the Warren Commission, and the Aftermath* (New York: Knopf, 2004), 359; Jeff Shesol, *Mutual Contempt: Lyndon Johnson, Robert Kennedy, and the Feud That Defined a Decade* (New York: Norton, 1997), 357.

7. Untitled Document, Box 3, "President Johnson's Statements and Schedule," SFA-LBJL.

8. Bishop to Valenti, January 10, 1966, "Name File, Bishop," LBJL.

9. Watson to President, May 24, 1966, "Name File, Bishop," LBJL.

10. Bishop to Salinger, November 29, 1963, "Name File, Bishop," LBJL.

11. "Beleaguered Author," *New York Times,* December 17, 1966, 19; "Battle of the Book," *Time,* December 23, 1966.

12. Jim Bishop, *The Day Kennedy Was Shot*

(New York: Crown Publishers, 1983), 307.

## Chapter 1

1. "Lyndon Johnson on the Record," *Texas Monthly,* December 2001, 107; Randall B. Woods, *LBJ: Architect of American Ambition* (New York: Free Press, 2007), 415.
2. Lyndon Baines Johnson, *The Vantage Point: Perspectives of the Presidency, 1963–1969* (New York: Holt, Rinehart and Winston, 1971), 6; James Reston, *The Lone Star: The Life of John Connally* (New York: Harper and Row, 1989), 268.
3. Johnson, *The Vantage Point,* 6.
4. Joe Belden, "Yarborough Lacks Majority Support for Renomination, *The Texas Poll,* July 12, 1963, VP Papers, Series 3, Box 202, "Politics," Lyndon Baines Johnson Library (LBJL), Austin, TX.
5. Reston, *The Lone Star,* 269.
6. John Connally, *In History's Shadow: An American Odyssey* (New York: Hyperion, 1994), 61.
7. Woods, *LBJ,* 35.
8. Robert Mann, *The Walls of Jericho: Lyndon Johnson, Hubert Humphrey, Richard Russell, and the Struggle for Civil Rights* (New York: Harcourt Brace, 1996), 65.
9. Fletcher Knebel, "Lyndon Johnson: Trained for Power," *Look,* December 31,

1963, 23.

10. Rowland Evans and Robert Novak, *Lyndon B. Johnson: The Exercise of Power* (New York: New American Library, 1966), 105.

11. Clark Clifford, *Counsel to the President: A Memoir* (New York: Random House, 1991), 385–386.

12. Robert Caro, *The Years of Lyndon Johnson: Master of the Senate* (New York: Knopf, 2002), 624.

13. Jeff Shesol, *Mutual Contempt: Lyndon Johnson, Robert Kennedy, and the Feud That Defined a Decade* (New York: W. W. Norton, 1998), 34.

14. Ibid., 34, 37.

15. Mann, *The Walls of Jericho,* 275.

16. "Lyndon Johnson on the Record," 107.

17. Woods, *LBJ,* 357.

18. Mann, *The Walls of Jericho,* 276; Arthur M. Schlesinger Jr., *Robert Kennedy and His Times* (New York: Ballantine Books, 1978), 224.

19. Woods, *LBJ,* 361–362.

20. "Lyndon Johnson on the Record," 107; Schlesinger, *Robert Kennedy and His Times,* 224–227; W. J. Rorabaugh, *The Real Making of the President: Kennedy, Nixon, and the 1960 Election* (Lawrence:

University of Kansas Press, 2009), 90.

21. Sally Bedell Smith, *Grace and Power: The Private World of the Kennedy White House* (New York: Random House, 2004), 15.

22. John Connally, "Why Kennedy Went to Texas," *Life,* November 1967, 86.

23. "Lyndon Johnson on the Record," 107.

24. Transcript, Lyndon Baines Johnson Oral History Special Interview, March 8, 1969, by Jack Valenti and Bob Hardesty, LBJL; Connally, "Why Kennedy Went to Texas," 86.

25. Smith, *Grace and Power,* 424.

26. Connally, "Why Kennedy Went to Texas," 86.

27. Transcript, Lyndon Baines Johnson Oral History Special Interview, March 8, 1969, by Jack Valenti and Bob Hardesty, LBJL.

28. Smith, *Grace and Power,* 431.

29. Gerald Bruno Papers, Box 6, "JFK Administration Trips: 11/21/63–11/22/63," John F. Kennedy Presidential Library (JFKL), Boston, MA.

30. "Leaders Charge Connally at Fault," *Dallas Morning News,* November 21, 1963.

31. Arthur M. Schlesinger Jr., *A Thousand Days: John F. Kennedy in the White House* (Boston: Houghton Mifflin, 1965), 1021.

32. Connally, "Why Kennedy Went to

Texas," 100; Elizabeth Forsling Harris, "Looking Back in Sorrow," *Washington Post Magazine,* November 20, 1988, 24.

33. "Split State Party Continues Feuds," *Dallas Morning News,* November 22, 1963, 1.

34. Ibid.

35. Reston, *The Lone Star,* 269; "Lyndon Johnson on the Record," 107.

36. "Lyndon Johnson on the Record," 107.

37. Malcolm Kilduff, Oral History, no. 2, 32, JFKL.

38. Johnson, *The Vantage Point,* 1.

39. "Kennedy Killed by Sniper As He Rides in Car in Dallas," *New York Times,* November 23, 1963, 2.

40. Reston, *The Lone Star,* 272–273.

41. Johnson, *The Vantage Point,* 4.

42. Johnson, *The Vantage Point,* 4; Dave Powers Interview, William Manchester Papers, Wesleyan University Special Collections and Archives (WM-WU), Middletown, CT.

**Chapter 2**

1. Charles Roberts, *The Truth About the Assassination* (New York: Grosset and Dunlap, 1967), 11; Charles Roberts, Oral History, Part I, 3, Lyndon Baines Johnson Library (LBJL), Austin, TX.

2. An FBI summary of the motorcade noted "that the distance from the airport to the Trade Mart where the President was to speak was four miles. The actual route selected by the political advance man was a distance of 10 miles so that more persons could see the President." Brennan to Sullivan, December 1, 1963, Hoover's Official and Confidential Files, Folder 92 — Lyndon Baines Johnson, JFK Assassination Records, National Archives (JFK-NA), College Park, MD.

3. Brennan to Sullivan, December 1, 1963, Hoover's Official and Confidential Files, Folder 92 — Lyndon Baines Johnson, JFK-NA. Kennedy aides often joked about "Kennedy weather." "The weather always cleared up for the President. One time in Louisville it had been raining three weeks and then he stepped out of the plane and immediately it cleared." Lawrence O'Brien and Kenneth O'Donnell Interview, William Manchester Papers, May 4, 1964, Wesleyan University Special Collections and Archives (WM-WU), Middletown, CT.

4. Lem Johns Interview, November 19, 1964, WM-WU.

5. Lyndon B. Johnson, *The Vantage Point: Perspectives of the Presidency, 1963–1969*

(New York: Holt, Rinehart and Winston, 1971), 1–5; *New York Times,* November 23, 1963, 2.

6. Vincent Bugliosi, *Reclaiming History: The Assassination of President John F. Kennedy* (New York: W. W. Norton, 2007), 33; Jack Valenti, "One Day's Passage of Power," *Washington Post,* November 21, 1963.

7. Ralph Yarborough Interview, April 6, 1964, WM-WU.

8. Yarborough Interview, second interview, November 11, 1964, WM-WU.

9. Kenneth O'Donnell, Oral History, 41, LBJL; Hugh Sidey Interview, WM-WU.

10. Clark Clifford, *Counsel to the President: A Memoir* (New York: Random House, 1991), 389.

11. Randall B. Woods, *LBJ: Architect of American Ambition* (New York: Free Press, 2007), 377.

12. Robert Dallek, *Flawed Giant: Lyndon Johnson and His Times, 1961–1973* (New York: Oxford University Press, 1998), 9.

13. Dallek, *Flawed Giant,* 9–12.

14. Jeff Shesol, *Mutual Contempt: Lyndon Johnson, Robert Kennedy, and the Feud That Defined a Decade* (New York: W. W. Norton, 1998), 100.

15. Sally Bedell Smith, *Grace and Power:*

*The Private World of the Kennedy White House* (New York: Random House, 2004), 175; Jim Bishop, *The Day Kennedy Was Shot* (New York: Crown Publishers, 1983), 395.

16. Woods, *LBJ,* 381; Tip O'Neill, *Man of the House: The Life and Political Memoirs of Speaker Tip O'Neill* (New York: Random House, 1987), 182.

17. Arthur M. Schlesinger Jr., *Robert Kennedy and His Times,* 693.

18. Robert Dallek, *Lyndon Johnson and His Times, 1961–1973* (New York: Oxford, 1998), 34.

19. Shesol, *Mutual Contempt,* 66; George Reedy, Oral History, XXI, 5, LBJL.

20. Dallek, *Flawed Giant,* 35.

21. "Kennedy Denied Talk of Dropping Johnson," *New York Times,* November 23, 1963, 9.

22. Charles Bartlett, Oral History, 79, John F. Kennedy Presidential Library (JFKL), Boston, MA; Tom Wicker, "Lyndon Johnson vs. the Ghost of Jack Kennedy," *Esquire,* November 1965, 149–150.

23. James T. Patterson, *Grand Expectations: The United States, 1945–1974* (New York: Oxford, 1997), 527.

24. Wicker, "Lyndon Johnson vs. the Ghost

of Jack Kennedy," 149.

25. Alan L. Otten, "Kennedy's O'Donnell Escapes Limelight Yet Wields Great Power," *Wall Street Journal,* April 11, 1963, 1.

26. Richard Reeves, *President Kennedy: Profile of Power* (New York: Simon and Schuster, 1993), 104.

27. Kenneth P. O'Donnell and Dave Powers, *"Johnny, We Hardly Knew Ye"* (Boston: Little, Brown, 1970), 216–217; Arthur M. Schlesinger Jr., *Robert Kennedy and His Times* (New York: Ballantine, 1978), 224.

28. Reeves, *President Kennedy,* 119.

29. Woods, *LBJ,* 382.

30. Shesol, *Mutual Contempt,* 75; Doris Kearns Goodwin, *Lyndon Johnson and the American Dream* (New York: Harper and Row, 1976), 167–168.

31. Shesol, *Mutual Contempt,* 110.

32. Bartlett, Oral History, 156–157, JFKL.

33. Robert W. Richards, "Where's Lyndon?" *Copley News Service,* July 24, 1962, VP, Box 185, "Vice-President — Office of," LBJL.

34. Charles Muehlstein to LBJ, September 23, 1961, VP, Box 119, "Vice-President — Office of," LBJL; Robert Swanson, February 9, 1962, VP, Box 119, "Vice-President — Office of," LBJL.

35. LBJ to Busche, August 14, 1962, VP, Box 119, "Vice-President — Office of," LBJL.

36. Woods, *LBJ*, 402; Schlesinger, *Robert Kennedy and His Times,* 621, 671.

37. "Transcript from Mrs. Johnson's Tapes Relating to November 22, 1963," *Warren Commission,* V, 565; "Notes taken during interview with Mrs. Johnson," June 15, 1964, Box 1, "Manchester," Box 3, Special File on the Assassination (SFA-LBJL).

38. Robert Mann, *The Walls of Jericho: Lyndon Johnson, Hubert Humphrey, Richard Russell, and the Struggle for Civil Rights* (New York: Harcourt Brace, 1996), 57.

39. Clifford, *Counsel to the President,* 392.

40. Jan Jarboe Russell, *Lady Bird: A Biography of Mrs. Johnson* (New York: Scribner, 1999), 20–21.

41. Yarborough Interview, April 6, 1964, WM-WU.

42. Theodore White Notes, December 19, 1963, WM-WU.

## Chapter 3

1. "Statement of SAIC Rufus Youngblood," Report of the Secret Service on the Assassination of President Kennedy, November 29, 1963, Box 3, Special File on the Assassination, Lyndon Baines Johnson Li-

brary (SFA-LBJL), Austin, TX.

2. Rufus Youngblood, *20 Years in the Secret Service: My Life with Five Presidents* (New York: Simon and Schuster), 65–66.

3. Ibid., 66.

4. Rufus Youngblood, Oral History, 34, LBJL; Youngblood, *20 Years in the Secret Service,* 67–68.

5. Youngblood, *20 Years in the Secret Service,* 77.

6. Ibid., 83.

7. Ibid., 85.

8. "Notes taken during interview with Mrs. Johnson," June 15, 1964, Box 1, "Manchester," SFA-LBJL.

9. "Lyndon Johnson on the Record," *Texas Monthly,* December 2001, 107.

10. "Statement of SAIC Rufus Youngblood," Report of the Secret Service on the Assassination of President Kennedy, November 29, 1963, Box 3, SFA-LBJL; "Notes taken during interview with Mrs. Johnson," June 15, 1964, Box 1, SFA-LBJL.

11. Ralph Yarborough Interview, April 6, 1964, William Manchester Papers, Wesleyan University Special Collections and Archives (WM-WU), Middletown, CT.

12. "Transcript from Mrs. Johnson's Tapes

Relating to November 22, 1963," *The Report of the President's Commission on the Assassination of President John F. Kennedy* (Doubleday: New York, 1964), V, 565. Hereafter referred to as *Warren Commission.*

13. *Warren Commission,* 48–50; Mimi Swartz, "The Witness," *Texas Monthly,* November 2003, 114. The detail about Mrs. Kennedy saying that "I have his brains in my hand" was omitted from the official Warren Commission report, but can be found in earlier drafts. See J. Lee Rankin Papers, Box 19, JFK Assassination Records, National Archives (JFK-NA), College Park, MD.

14. Theodore White Notes, December 19, 1963, WM-WU.

15. Paul Landis, November 30, 1963, *Warren Commission,* Vol. XVIII, Exhibit 1024, 755.

16. Dave Powers Interview, April 8, 1964, WM-WU; Kenneth P. O'Donnell and Dave Powers, *"Johnny, We Hardly Knew Ye"* (Boston: Little, Brown, 1970), 29.

17. "Statement of SAIC Clinton J. Hill," Report of the Secret Service on the Assassination of President Kennedy, November 29, 1963, Box 3, SFA-LBJL.

18. Paul Landis, November 30, 1963, *War-*

ren Commission, Vol. XVIII, Exhibit 1024, 755; Emory Roberts Interview, December 4, 1964, WM-WU.

19. Swartz, "The Witness," 114; White Notes, December 19, 1963, WM-WU.

20. CBS Interview: "Tragedy and Transition," Transcript, May 2, 1970, Box 2, LBJL.

21. "Statement of SAIC Rufus Youngblood," Report of the Secret Service on the Assassination of President Kennedy, November 29, 1963, Box 3, SFA-LBJL. There was little interaction between agents protecting Johnson and those covering the president. "Although we belong to the same service, we really do not know them and there is a definite separation there," Agent Lem Johns told William Manchester. "We ride in separate cars and on a separate plane, and we are not welcome in their posts and their security room." Lem Johns Interview, November 19, 1964, WM-WU.

22. Lyndon B. Johnson, The Vantage Point: Perspectives of the Presidency, 1963–1969 (New York: Holt, Rinehart and Winston, 1971), 8; Fletcher Knebel, "After the Shots: The Ordeal of Lyndon Johnson," Look, March 10, 1964, 27.

23. Yarborough Interview, April 6, 1964,

WM-WU.

24. Johnson, *The Vantage Point*, 8–9.
25. "Statement of SAIC Rufus Young-blood," Report of the Secret Service on the Assassination of President Kennedy, November 29, 1963, Box 3, SFA-LBJL; Youngblood, *20 Years in the Secret Service*, 114.
26. Knebel, "After the Shots," 27; Young-blood, *20 Years in the Secret Service*, 115.
27. "Statement of SAIC Rufus Young-blood," Report of the Secret Service on the Assassination of President Kennedy, November 29, 1963, Box 3, SFA-LBJL.
28. Youngblood, *20 Years in the Secret Service*, 115.

**Chapter 4**

1. "Notes taken during interview with Mrs. Johnson," June 15, 1964, Box 1, Special File on the Assassination, Lyndon Baines Johnson Library (SFA-LBJL), Austin, TX.
2. "Transcript from Mrs. Johnson's Tapes Relating to November 22, 1963," *Warren Commission*, V, 565.
3. "Lyndon Johnson on the Record," *Texas Monthly*, December 2001, 107.
4. "Statement of SAIC Rufus Youngblood," Report of the Secret Service on the Assassination of President Kennedy, November

29, 1963, Box 3, SFA-LBJL; "Transcript from Mrs. Johnson's Tapes Relating to November 22, 1963," *Warren Commission,* V, 565; Rufus Youngblood, *20 Years in the Secret Service: My Life with Five Presidents* (New York: Simon and Schuster, 1973), 116.

5. Emory Roberts Interview, December 4, 1964, Wesleyan University Special Collections and Archives (WM-WU), Middletown, CT.

6. *Warren Commission,* 53–54; "Warren Commission Drafts," J. Lee Rankin Papers, Box 19, JFK Assassination Records, National Archives (JFK-NA), College Park, MD.

7. Emory Roberts Interview, December 4, 1964, WM-WU.

8. Kenneth P. O'Donnell and Dave Powers, *"Johnny, We Hardly Knew Ye"* (Boston: Little, Brown, 1970), 31.

9. Ralph Yarborough Interview, April 6, 1964, WM-MU.

10. Mimi Swartz, "The Witness," *Texas Monthly,* November 2003, 114.

11. Vincent Bugliosi, *Reclaiming History: The Assassination of President John F. Kennedy* (New York: W. W. Norton, 2007), 54; Ralph Yarborough April 6, 1964, WM-MU; Paul Landis, November 30, 1963,

*Warren Commission,* Vol. XVIII, Exhibit 756.

12. Jack Price Memo, November 27, 1963, 2–3, WM-WU.

13. "Johnson Takes Oath," *Los Angeles Times,* November 23, 1963, 1; Bugliosi, *Reclaiming History,* 58; *Warren Commission,* 53–54.

14. *Warren Commission,* 56.

15. Mrs. John Connally, "Since That Day in Dallas," *McCall's,* August 1964, 79.

16. Elizabeth Forsling Harris, "Looking Back in Sorrow," *Washington Post Magazine,* November 20, 1988, 24.

17. Roberts, *Warren Commission,* XVIII, Exhibit 735; Jerry Kivett Statement, November 29, 1963, Box 3, 2, SFA-LBJL; Youngblood, *20 Years in the Secret Service,* 116.

18. Fletcher Knebel, "After the Shots: The Ordeal of Lyndon Johnson," *Look,* March 10, 1964, 28; Roberts Interview, December 4, 1964, WM-WU; Youngblood, *20 Years in the Secret Service,* 116.

19. Youngblood, *20 Years in the Secret Service,* 116.

20. Lyndon B. Johnson, *The Vantage Point: Perspectives of the Presidency, 1963–1969* (New York: Holt, Rinehart and Winston,

1971), 9.

21. CBS Interview: "Tragedy and Transition," Transcript, May 2, 1970, Box 2, LBJL; Max Holland, *The Kennedy Assassination Tapes: The White House Conversations of Lyndon B. Johnson Regarding the Assassination, the Warren Commission, and the Aftermath* (New York: Knopf, 2004), 363.

22. "Dictated by Congressman Brooks to Marie Fehmer aboard Air Force #1, en route to Washington, D.C., November 22, 1963," Box 3, "Daily Diary backup material," SFA-LBJL.

23. Jack Valenti, "The Unforgettable Afternoon," *New York Times,* November 22, 1998, 17.

24. Ruth C. Silva, *Presidential Succession* (New York: Greenwood Press, 1968), 20–30.

25. "Confidential Draft Release: The White House," VP, Box 119, "Vice President — Office of," LBJL.

26. Ibid.

27. Lem Johns Interview, August 8, 1978, WM-WU; House Select Committee on Assassinations, Record Number 180–10074–10079, Box 196, JFK-NA.

28. Youngblood, *20 Years in the Secret Service,* 116–117.

29. Henry Gonzales Interview, June 25, 1964, WM-MU.

30. Homer Thornberry, Oral History, 26–27, LBJL.

31. Emory Roberts Interview, December 4, 1964, WM-WU; "Transcript from Mrs. Johnson's Tapes Relating to November 22, 1963," *Warren Commission*, V, 565.

32. "Statement of SAIC Rufus Young-blood," Report of the Secret Service on the Assassination of President Kennedy, November 29, 1963, Box 3, SFA-LBJL; Jan Jarboe Russell, *Lady Bird: A Biography of Mrs. Johnson* (New York: Scribner, 1999) 220–221.

33. Knebel, "After the Shots," 28.

**Chapter 5**

1. William Manchester, *The Death of a President: November 20–November 25, 1963* (New York: Harper and Row, 1967), 230; Roy Kellerman, *Warren Commission*, II, 96.

2. Kenneth P. O'Donnell and Dave Powers, *"Johnny, We Hardly Knew Ye"* (Boston: Little, Brown, 1970), 32.

3. O'Donnell and Powers, *"Johnny, We Hardly Knew Ye,"* 32.

4. According to his Warren Commission testimony, O'Donnell said "it looked very,

very serious" and added that "it looked pretty black." (*Warren Commission,* VII, Exhibits 450–451). In later reflections on that day, O'Donnell claimed to have told LBJ that he believed Kennedy might be dead. "In my first conversation with President Johnson I said, 'it looks bad. I think the President is dead,' " he told William Manchester (Kenneth O'Donnell Interview, August 6, 1964, Wesleyan University Special Collections and Archives [WM-WU], Middletown, CT. No one else in the room, however, recalled O'Donnell mentioning that Kennedy might be dead. Agent Johns supports LBJ's account that all O'Donnell said was that JFK's condition was "bad." "Statement of SAIC Thomas L. Johns," Report of the Secret Service on the Assassination of President Kennedy, November 29, 1963, Box 3, Special File on the Assassination, Lyndon Baines Johnson Library [SFA-LBJL], Austin, TX).

5. Emory Roberts Interview, December 4, 1964, WM-WU.

6. O'Donnell and Powers, *"Johnny, We Hardly Knew Ye,"* 33.

7. Rufus Youngblood, *20 Years in the Secret Service: My Life with Five Presidents* (New York: Simon and Schuster, 1973), 117.

8. "Transcript from Mrs. Johnson's Tapes Relating to November 22, 1963," *Warren Commission,* V, 566; Jack Brooks, Oral History, 28, LBJL.

9. Jan Jarboe Russell, *Lady Bird: A Biography of Mrs. Johnson* (New York: Scribner, 1999), 187, 195; "Transcript from Mrs. Johnson's Tapes Relating to November 22, 1963," *Warren Commission,* V, 566; James Reston, *The Lone Star: The Life of John Connally* (New York: Harper and Row, 1989), 282.

10. "Transcript from Mrs. Johnson's Tapes Relating to November 22, 1963," *Warren Commission,* V, 566; Mimi Swartz, "The Witness," *Texas Monthly,* November 2003, 114.

11. "Dictated by Cliff Carter to Marie Fehmer aboard Air Force #1 en route to Washington, D.C., November 22, 1963," Box 1, "Appointment File — Diary Backup," LBJL.

12. Lyndon B. Johnson, *The Vantage Point: Perspectives of the Presidency, 1963–1969* (New York: Holt, Rinehart and Winston, 1971), 10.

13. Lem Johns Interview, November 19, 1964, WM-WU.

14. Fletcher Knebel, "After the Shots: The

Ordeal of Lyndon Johnson," *Look,* March 10, 1964, 28.

## Chapter 6

1. "Secret Service Report on the Assassination of President Kennedy," March 19, 1964, *Warren Commission,* XVII, Exhibit 1026; O'Donnell Testimony, *Warren Commission,* VII, Exhibit 451.
2. William Manchester, *The Death of a President* (New York: Harper and Row, 1967), 188; Vincent Bugliosi, *Reclaiming History: The Assassination of President John F. Kennedy* (New York: W.W. Norton, 2007), 71; *Warren Commission,* 55.
3. Jack Price Memo, November 27, 1963, 5, Wesleyan University Special Collections and Archives (WM-WU), Middletown, CT.
4. Father Oscar Huber, "President Kennedy's Final Hours," December 8, 1963, WM-WU; Patrick Huber, "Father Oscar Huber, the Kennedy Assassination, and the News Leak Controversy: A Research Note," *Southwestern Historical Quarterly,* January 2007, 382–384.
5. Huber, "President Kennedy's Final Hours," December 8, 1963, WM-WU.
6. Theodore White Notes, December 19, 1963, WM-MU.

7. Huber, "President Kennedy's Final Hours," December 8, 1963, WM-WU; Bishop, *The Day Kennedy Was Shot*, 223–224.

8. Manchester, *The Death of a President*, 215; Bugliosi, *Reclaiming History*, 70.

9. "JFK Aide and Confidant, David Powers, Dead at 85," *The Boston Herald*, March 28, 1998, 2.

10. "Transcribed Tapes, 11/22/63," Dave Powers Papers, Box 9, 12–13, John F. Kennedy Presidential Library (JFKL), Boston, MA.

11. Copy of Memorandum by Dave Powers," WM-WU; Dave Powers Interviews, April 8, 1964, and August 10, 1964, WM-WU; "Transcribed Tapes, 11/22/63," Powers Papers, Box 9, 12–13, JFKL.

12. "Statement Regarding Assassination of the President of the USA, President Kennedy, November 22, 1963," 4:45 p.m., Records of the Secret Service, Box 3, Folder: CD-2–34030, JFK Assassination Records, National Archives (JFK-NA), College Park, MD.

13. Jimmy Breslin, "A Death in Emergency Room No. One," *Saturday Evening Post*, December 14, 1963, 30–31.

14. Jim Bishop, *The Day Kennedy Was Shot* (New York: Crown Publishers, 1983), 232.

15. *Warren Commission*, 55.

16. At 12:39 p.m., Clinton Hill called Gerald Behn, the head of the Secret Service in Washington, to inform him of the "double tragedy." Both Kennedy and Connally were shot and "the situation was extremely critical," he said. A few minutes later, Kellerman came out of the operating room and said, "Clint, tell Gerry that this is not for release and not official, but the man is dead." See Clinton Hill, *Warren Commission*, XXVIII, 743.

17. *Warren Commission*, 57; Lyndon Johnson Statement, Box 3, Special File on the Assassination, Lyndon Baines Johnson Library (SFA-LBJL), Austin, TX; Johnson, *The Vantage Point*, 10.

18. Emory Roberts Interview, December 4, 1964, WM-WU; Emory Roberts, "Activity of Section," November 22, 1963, Records of the Secret Service, Box 1, JFK-NA.

19. "Dictated by Cliff Carter to Marie Fehmer aboard Air Force #1 en route to Washington, D.C., November 22, 1963," Box 1, "Appointment File — Diary Backup," LBJL.

20. Clifton Carter Interview, WM-WU.

21. Rufus Youngblood, *20 Years in the Secret Service: My Life with Five Presidents* (New York: Simon and Schuster, 1973), 118;

Kenneth P. O'Donnell and Dave Powers, *"Johnny, We Hardly Knew Ye"* (Boston: Little, Brown, 1970), 33–34.

22. O'Donnell and Powers, *"Johnny, We Hardly Knew Ye,"* 33–34.

23. Charles Roberts, Oral History, 1, 9, LBJL.

24. Dean Rusk, *As I Saw It* (New York: Penguin, 1991), 296.

25. Ibid., 321.

26. Max Holland, "The Key to the Warren Report," *American Heritage,* November 1995, 50; George Ball, *The Past Has Another Pattern: Memoirs* (New York: W. W. Norton, 1983), 311.

27. Evan Thomas, "The Real Cover-Up," *Newsweek,* November 22, 1963, 66; George Ball Interview, April 10, 1964, WM-MU.

28. Thomas, "The Real Cover-Up," 66.

**Chapter 7**

1. Lyndon B. Johnson, *The Vantage Point: Perspectives of the Presidency, 1963–1969* (New York: Holt, Rinehart and Winston, 1971), 10.

2. Kenneth P. O'Donnell and Dave Powers, *"Johnny, We Hardly Knew Ye"* (Boston: Little, Brown, 1970), 34.

3. Jim Bishop, *The Day Kennedy Was Shot*

(New York: Crown, 1983), 267.

4. O'Donnell and Powers, *"Johnny, We Hardly Knew Ye,"* 33; Johnson Statement to the Warren Commission, Box 3, Special File on the Assassination, Lyndon Baines Johnson Library (SFA-LBJL).

5. Rufus Youngblood, Warren Commission, Hearings, II, 152–153.

6. O'Donnell and Powers, *"Johnny, We Hardly Knew Ye,"* 33–34.

7. Kenneth O'Donnell Interview, August 6, 1964, William Manchester Papers, Wesleyan University Special Records and Archives (WM-WU), Middletown, CT.

8. Godfrey McHugh, Oral History, John F. Kennedy Presidential Library (JFKL), Boston, MA, 18.

9. Charles Roberts, *The Truth About the Assassination* (New York: Grosset & Dunlap, 1967), 107.

10. McHugh, Oral History, 28, JFKL.

11. Emory Roberts Statement, November 29, 1963, Box 3, SFA-LBJL; Emory Roberts Interview, December 4, 1964, WM-MU; Warren Taylor Statement, November 29, 1963, Box 3, SFA-LBJL.

12. Emory Roberts Interview, December 4, 1964, WM-MU.

13. Vincent Bugliosi, *Reclaiming History: The*

*Assassination of President John F. Kennedy* (New York: W. W. Norton, 2007), 81.

14. Johnson, *The Vantage Point,* 11; "Johnson Feared a Plot in Dallas," *New York Times,* December 24, 1963, 6; Malcolm Kilduff, Oral History, March 15, 1976, 36, JFKL; Malcolm Kilduff Interview, May 2, 1964, WM-WU.

15. "Johnson Feared a Plot in Dallas," *New York Times,* December 24, 1963, 6. The original news stories quote Johnson as saying "worldwide conspiracy." Kilduff later admitted that he made the decision to drop the use of the word "communist," fearing that it would have been too inflammatory at the time. Kilduff Interview, May 2, 1964, WM-WU.

16. Johnson, *The Vantage Point,* 11; Lady Bird Johnson, *Warren Commission,* V, Exhibit 566.

17. Rufus W. Youngblood, *20 Years in the Secret Service: My Life with Five Presidents* (New York: Simon and Schuster, 1973), 120.

18. Fletcher Knebel, "After the Shots: The Ordeal of Lyndon Johnson," *Look,* March 10, 1964, 28; Youngblood, *20 Years in the Secret Service,* 120.

19. William Manchester, *The Death of a*

*President* (New York: Harper and Row, 1967), 237.

20. Johnson, *The Vantage Point,* 12; Lady Bird Johnson Statement, *Warren Commission,* V, Exhibit 565.

21. Gary L. Donhardt, *In the Shadow of the Great Rebellion: The Life of Andrew Johnson, Seventeenth President of the United States* (New York: Nova Science Publishers, 2007), 61–62.

22. Doris Kearns Goodwin, *No Ordinary Time: Franklin & Eleanor Roosevelt: The Home Front in World War II* (New York: Simon & Schuster, 1994), 602–604.

23. "White House Gets Word Via Newsman," *Washington Post,* November 23, 1963, A3.

24. Thomas J. Banta, "The Kennedy Assassination: Early Thoughts and Emotions," *The Public Opinion Quarterly,* Summer 1964, 216–224.

25. "TV Coverage of JFK's Death Forged Medium's Role," *Denver Post,* November 16, 2003, F1.

26. Only two of 1,384 respondents had not heard of the shooting. See Bradley S. Greenberg, "Diffusion of News of the Kennedy Assassination," *The Public Opinion Quarterly,* Summer 1964, 225–232.

27. "First, 'Is It True?,' " *New York Times,* November 23, 1963, 5.

28. "People Across U.S. Voice Grief and Revulsion," *New York Times,* November 23, 1963, 11.

29. "Millions Feel Full Impact of Tragedy and Witness History's Grim Unfolding," *New York Times,* November 24, 1963, 9.

30. Roberts, *The Truth About the Assassination,* 16.

31. Knebel, *After the Shots,* 27.

32. George Reedy Interview, June 23, 1964, WM-WU.

## Chapter 8

1. Kilduff watched LBJ pull away from Parkland Hospital; he then walked into the temporary press room to make the announcement. Since the press conference started at 1:33 p.m., it is clear that Thornberry's estimate that they left the hospital at 1:30 p.m. was the most accurate.

2. Fletcher Knebel, "After the Shots: The Ordeal of Lyndon Johnson," *Look,* March 10, 1964, 29

3. James Swindal Interview, April 29, 1964, Wesleyan University Special Collections and Archives (WM-WU), Middletown, CT.

4. Rufus Youngblood, *20 Years in the Secret*

*Service: My Life with Five Presidents* (New York: Simon and Schuster, 1973), 123.

5. Lyndon B. Johnson, *The Vantage Point: Perspectives of the Presidency, 1963–1969* (New York: Holt, Rinehardt and Winston), 13.

6. Jack Valenti, "The Unforgettable Afternoon," *New York Times,* November 22, 1998, w17.

7. "Transcript from Mrs. Johnson's Tapes Relating to November 22, 1963," *Warren Commission,* V, 566.

8. "Liz Carpenter's Recollections of President Kennedy's Assassination, December, 1963, Box 4, Special File on the Assassination, Lyndon Baines Johnson Library (SFA-LBJL); Liz Carpenter Interview, June 10, 1964, WM-WU.

9. Youngblood, *20 Years in the Secret Service,* 125; Knebel, "After the Shots," 28.

10. Jack Brooks, Oral History, 31, Lyndon Baines Johnson Library (LBJL), Austin, TX.

11. Notes taken during interview with Mrs. Johnson, June 15, 1964, Box 1, Special File on the Assassination, Lyndon Baines Johnson Library (SFA-LBJL); Marie Fehmer, Oral History, 53, LBJL.

12. Evan Thomas, *Robert Kennedy: His Life*

(New York: Simon and Schuster, 2000), 117.

13. Arthur M. Schlesinger Jr., *Robert Kennedy and His Times* (New York: Ballantine, 1978), 655.

14. "Statement of Special Agent Clinton J. Hill," November 30, 1963, Records of the Secret Service, Box 7, JFK Assassination Records, National Archives (JFK-NA), College Park, MD.

15. John McCone Interview, April 10, 1964, WM-WU.

16. William Manchester, *The Death of a President* (New York: Harper and Row, 1967), 257.

17. Johnson, *The Vantage Point,* 13; Manchester, *The Death of a President,* 269; McCone Interview, April 10, 1964, WM-WU.

18. Schlesinger, *Robert Kennedy and His Times,* 656.

19. President Johnson's Statements and Schedule, Box 3, SFA-LBJL.

20. Nicholas Katzenbach Interview, June 5, 1964, WM-WU.

21. Fehmer, Oral History, 53 LBJL; "Bundy notes," December 4, 1963, WM-WU.

22. Johnson, *The Vantage Point,* 13–14; McCone Interview, April 10, 1964, WM-WU. Manchester made no mention of

McCone's comments, even though he had conducted the interview. The notes of his interview with McCone were also unavailable to other researchers writing about the assassination until they were opened in 2008. Over time, the RFK side of the story gathered new details. In his 1964 interview with Manchester, Katzenbach pointed out that Kennedy's tone was "very matter of fact, and flat." There was no hint that he opposed LBJ's request, or that he had any opinion about when or where the swearing in should take place. However, in his memoirs, published in 2008, Katzenbach suggested that Kennedy disapproved of Johnson's request. "They want to swear him in right away, in Texas. That's not necessary, is it?" he quotes RFK as saying. "No," Katzenbach claimed he responded. "Not necessary." He believed that RFK "wanted President Kennedy to return to Washington on *Air Force One* as if he were still president. I think too that swearing in JFK's successor in Texas was an offensive idea to him," he wrote. See Nicholas Katzenbach, *Some of It Was Fun: Working with RFK and LBJ* (New York: W. W. Norton, 2008), 130–131.

23. "Tragedy and Transition," CBS Inter-

view, Transcript, May 2, 1970, Box 2, LBJL.

24. Evan Thomas, "The Real Cover-Up," *Newsweek,* November 22, 1963, 66.

25. Thomas, *Robert Kennedy: His Life,* 284.

26. Randal B. Woods, *LBJ: Architect of American Ambition* (New York: Free Press, 2006), 405.

27. "Notes made by Marie Fehmer aboard Air Force #1, November 22, 1963, en route to Washington, D.C.," Appointment File — Diary Backup, Box 1, LBJL.

28. Kenneth O'Donnell and Dave Powers, *"Johnny, We Hardly Knew Ye"* (Boston: Little Brown, 1970), 7–8.

## Chapter 9

1. Jack Price Memo, November 27, 1963, 9, Wesleyan University Special Collections and Archives (WM-WU), Middletown, CT; Testimony of Roy Kellerman, *Warren Commission,* II, 96; Jim Bishop, *The Day Kennedy Was Shot* (New York: Crown Publishers, 1983), 283.

2. Roy Kellerman Testimony, *Warren Commission,* II, 96–97; Bishop, *The Day Kennedy Was Shot,* 284; Vincent Bugliosi, *Reclaiming History: The Assassination of President John F. Kennedy* (New York: W. W. Norton, 2007), 92.

3. Dave Powers Memo, WM-WU; Lawrence O'Brien and Kenneth O'Donnell Joint Interview, May 4, 1964. WM-WU.

4. Price Memo, November 27, 1963, 9, WM-WU; Charles Roberts, *The Truth About the Assassination* (New York: Grosset & Dunlap, 1967), 18.

5. Godfrey McHugh, Oral History, 44–46, John F. Kennedy Presidential Library (JFKL) Boston, MA.

6. Lyndon B. Johnson, *The Vantage Point: Perspectives of the Presidency, 1963–1969* (New York: Holt, Rinehart and Winston, 1971), 14.

7. Marie Fehmer Interview, June 11, 1964, WM-WU.

8. Johnson, *The Vantage Point,* 14; "Transcript from Mrs. Johnson's Tapes Relating to November 22, 1963," *Warren Commission,* V, 566–567.

9. Johnson, *The Vantage Point,* 14; "Transcript from Mrs. Johnson's Tapes Relating to November 22, 1963," *Warren Commission,* V, 566–567.

10. "Transcript from Mrs. Johnson's Tapes Relating to November 22, 1963," *Warren Commission,* V, 566–567; Theodore White Notes, December 19, 1963. WM-WU.

11. William Manchester, *The Death of a*

*President* (New York: Harper and Row, 1967), 318.

12. Kenneth P. O'Donnell and Dave Powers, *"Johnny, We Hardly Knew Ye"* (Boston: Little, Brown, 1970), 37.

13. Kenneth O'Donnell, Oral History, 42, Lyndon Baines Johnson Library (LBJL), Austin, TX.

14. Godfrey McHugh Interview, May 6, 1964, WM-WU.

15. McHugh Interview, May 6, 1964, WM-WU; James Swindal Interview, April 29, 1964, WM-WU.

16. McHugh, Oral History, 46–47, JFKL.

17. McHugh Interview, May 6, 1964, WM-WU.

18. McHugh, Oral History, 46, JFKL.

19. Ibid., 47.

20. Malcolm Kilduff Interview, May 2, 1964, WM-WU; Jack Valenti, *This Time, This Place: My Life in War, the White House, and Hollywood* (New York: Harmony, 2007), 26.

21. Kilduff Interview, May 2, 1964, WM-WU.

22. McHugh, Oral History, 47, JFKL.

23. General Godfrey McHugh, Telephone Interview, May 11, 1978, House Select Committee on Assassinations, Record Number: 180–10078–10465, Box 173,

File Number 009414, JFK Assassination Records, National Archives (JFK-NA), College Park, MD.

24. McHugh Interview, May 6, 1964, WM-WU.

25. Christopher Anderson, *Jackie After Jack: Portrait of the Lady* (New York: William Morris, 1998), 28.

26. "In Fact, It's Fiction," *Daily News*, February 22, 1998, 3.

27. Edwin O. Guthman and Jeffrey Shulman, editors, *Robert Kennedy in His Own Words* (New York: Bantam Books, 1988), 22; Randall B. Woods, *LBJ: Architect of American Ambition* (New York: Free Press, 2006), 606–607.

28. O'Donnell and Powers, *"Johnny, We Hardly Knew Ye,"* 38; Manchester, *The Death of a President,* 319; Chester Clifton Interview, April 21, 1964, WM-WU.

29. O'Donnell, Oral History, 43–45, LBJL.

30. O'Donnell and Powers, *"Johnny, We Hardly Knew Ye,"* 38.

31. O'Donnell Interview, November 23, 1964, WM-WU; O'Donnell, Oral History, 45, LBJL.

32. O'Donnell and Powers, *"Johnny, We Hardly Knew Ye,"* 40.

33. Johnson, *The Vantage Point,* 15.

34. Ibid.

## Chapter 10

1. Charles Roberts, *The Truth About the Assassination* (New York: Grosset & Dunlap, 1967), 109.
2. Bill Moyers, "Untitled Speech," Moyers Papers, Box 80, "Miscellaneous Loose Material," Lyndon Baines Johnson Library (LBJL), Austin, TX.
3. "Notes made by Marie Fehmer aboard Air Force #1, November 22, 1963, en route to Washington D.C.," Box 1, Appointment File — Diary Backup, LBJL.
4. Sarah Hughes, Oral History, 19, LBJL; Kenneth O'Donnell, Oral History, 43–44, LBJL.
5. Arthur Schlesinger Jr. Journal, November 25, 1963, 366, Wesleyan University Special Collections and Archives (WM-WU), Middletown, CT.
6. Kenneth O'Donnell, Oral History, 43–44, LBJL.
7. Merriman Smith, "The Murder of the Young President," United Press International, November 23, 1963.
8. Jack Valenti, "One Day's Passage of Power," *Washington Post,* November 21, 1993.
9. Sarah Hughes, Oral History, 20, LBJL.

10. Roberts, *The Truth About the Assassination,* 114; Smith, "The Murder of the Young President"; James Swindal Interview, April 29, 1964, WM-MU; Godfrey McHugh, Oral History, 49, John F. Kennedy Presidential Library (JFKL), Boston, MA.

11. Cecil Stoughton, Oral History, 27, LBJL.

12. Ibid., 27–28.

13. Rufus Youngblood, *20 Years in the Secret Service: My Life with Five Presidents* (New York: Simon and Schuster, 1973), 130; "Cecil Stoughton: photographed moment Lyndon Johnson was sworn in as president," *TimesOnline,* November 6, 2008, http://www.timesonline.co.uk/tol/comment /obituaries/article5091605.ece.

14. "Transcript from Mrs. Johnson's Tapes Relating to November 22, 1963," *Warren Commission,* V, 566.

15. "Notes taken during interview with Mrs. Johnson," June 15, 1964, Box 1, Special File on the Assassination, Lyndon Baines Johnson Library (SFA-LBJL).

16. Charles Roberts, "Eyewitness in Dallas," *Newsweek,* November 5, 1966, 28; Roberts, *The Truth About the Assassination,* 111.

17. " 'He's Dead,' Whispered Aide." *Los*

*Angeles Times,* November 24, 1963, J1.

18. Moyers, "Untitled Speech," Moyers Papers, Box 80, "Miscellaneous Loose Material," 2, LBJL.

19. Stoughton, Oral History, 32–33, LBJL.

20. Ibid., 34.

21. Ibid., 35.

22. Richard B. Trask, *That Day in Dallas: Three Photographers Capture on Film the Day President Kennedy Died* (Danvers, MA: Yeoman Press, 1998), 52.

23. Jack Valenti, "The Unforgettable Afternoon," *New York Times,* November 22, 1998, w17.

24. *TimesOnline,* November 6, 2008.

## Chapter 11

1. Cliff Carter, Oral History, 10, Lyndon Baines Johnson Library (LBJL), Austin, TX.

2. "Tragedy and Transition," CBS Interview, Transcript, May 2, 1970, Box 2, LBJL.

3. Carter, Oral History, 12, LBJL.

4. Doris Kearns Goodwin, *Lyndon Johnson and the American Dream* (New York: Harper and Row, 1976), 177–178.

5. Kearns Goodwin, *Lyndon Johnson and the American Dream,* 175.

6. Helen O'Donnell, *A Common Good: The Friendship of Robert F. Kennedy and Ken-*

*neth P. O'Donnell* (New York: William Morrow, 1998), 335.

7. Bill Moyers, "Untitled Speech," Moyers Papers, Box 80, "Miscellaneous Loose Material," 3, LBJL.

8. Lem Johns Interview, November 19, 1964, Wesleyan University Special Collections and Archives (WM-WU), Middletown, CT.

9. Max Holland, *The Kennedy Assassination Tapes: The White House Conversations of Lyndon B. Johnson Regarding the Assassination, the Warren Commission, and the Aftermath* (New York: Knopf, 2004), 26–36.

10. Malcolm Kilduff Interview, May 2, 1964, WM-WU; Fletcher Knebel, "After the Shots: The Ordeal of Lyndon Johnson," *Look,* March 10, 1964, 33. Knebel quotes Johnson, but it sounds more like Valenti than LBJ.

11. Liz Carpenter Interview, June 10, 1964, WM-WU.

12. Lyndon B. Johnson, *The Vantage Point: Perspectives of the Presidency, 1963–1969* (New York: Holt, Rinehart and Winston, 1971), 16.

13. Jack Valenti, *A Very Human President* (New York: Norton, 1975), 50–51.

14. Holland, *The Kennedy Assassination*

*Tapes,* 40.

15. Charles Roberts, *The Truth About the Assassination* (New York: Grosset & Dunlap, 1967), 112.

16. Chester Clifton Interview, April 21, 1964, WM-WU.

17. Holland, *The Kennedy Assassination Tapes,* 44–45.

18. Rufus Youngblood, *20 Years in the Secret Service: My Life with Five Presidents* (New York: Simon and Schuster, 1973), 132–133; Knebel, "After the Shots," 33.

19. Gerald Posner, *Case Closed: Lee Harvey Oswald and the Assassination of JFK* (New York: Anchor, 2003), 265–272; Vincent Bugliosi, *Reclaiming History: The Assassination of President John F. Kennedy* (New York: W. W. Norton, 2007), 64, 78.

20. Posner, *Case Closed,* 271–272.

21. Bugliosi, *Reclaiming History,* 111–13.

22. George Ball, *The Past Has Another Pattern: Memoirs* (New York: W.W. Norton, 1983), 311.

23. Ball, *The Past Has Another Pattern,* 312; Clifton Interview, April 21, 1964, WM-WU.

24. Ball, *The Past Has Another Pattern,* 312.

25. Valenti, *A Very Human President,* 48; Carpenter Interview, June 10, 1964, WM-

WU; Holland, *The Kennedy Assassination Tapes,* 46.

26. Carpenter Interview, June 10, 1964 WM-WU; Holland, *The Kennedy Assassination Tapes,* 46.

27. Holland, *The Kennedy Assassination Tapes,* 47–48.

28. Kilduff Interview, May 2, 1964, WM-WU.

29. Swindal Interview, April 29, 1964, WM-WU; Brennan to Sullivan, "Protection of the President," December 1, 1963, "Hoover's Official and Confidential Files, Folder 92 — Lyndon B. Johnson, JFK Assassination Records, National Archives (JFK-NA), College Park, MD; McGeorge Bundy Interview, April 9, 1964, WM-WU.

30. David Powers Interview, April 8, 1964, WM-WU.

31. Kilduff Interview, May 2, 1964, WM-WU.

32. Johnson, *The Vantage Point,* 16; Valenti, *A Very Human President,* 52.

33. Transcript, Lyndon Baines Johnson Oral History Special Interview, 3/8/69, by Jack Valenti and Bob Hardesty," LBJL.

34. Lawrence O'Brien and Kenneth O'Donnell Joint Interview, May 4, 1964, WM-WU; Carpenter Interview, June 10, 1964, WM-WU; "Transcript from Mrs.

Johnson's Tapes Relating to November 22, 1963," *Warren Commission,* V, 567.

35. Salinger told Manchester, "I had already fired Kilduff . . . Ken O'Donnell did not want him there. He did not feel that Kilduff was loyal to the President — Kilduff has a loose mouth, and was talking a great deal outside the White House and making disparaging remarks about the President. Kenny just felt that Kilduff was not loyal." See Pierre Salinger Interview, Numbered Files, JFK Task Force, Box 290, JFK-NA.

36. Kilduff Interview, May 2, 1964, WM-WU.

37. Kilduff Interview, May 2, 1964, WM-WU; Godfrey McHugh Interview, May 6, 1964, WM-WU.

38. Roberts, *The Truth About the Assassination,* 112–113.

39. O'Donnell, Oral History, 46, LBJL.

40. Roberts, *The Truth About the Assassination,* 116; Charles Roberts, "U.S. Leaderless for 2 Hours on Fatal Day," *Washington Post,* April 6, 1967, F1.

41. "Growing Rift of LBJ and Kennedys," *U.S. News & World Report,* January 2, 1967, 26.

42. William Manchester, *The Death of a*

*President* (New York: Harper and Row, 1967), 311.

**Chapter 12**

1. James Swindal Interview, April 29, 1964, Wesleyan University Special Collections and Archives (WM-WU), Middletown, CT.
2. Lyndon B. Johnson, *The Vantage Point: Perspectives of the Presidency, 1963–1969* (New York: Holt, Rinehart and Winston, 1971), 16.
3. "Lyndon Johnson," *International Herald Tribune,* November 23, 1963, 1.
4. "Liz Carpenter's Recollections of President Kennedy's Assassination," December 1963, Box 4, Special File on the Assassination, Lyndon Baines Johnson Library (SFA-LBJL), Austin, TX; Carpenter Interview WM-WU; Jack Valenti, *A Very Human President* (New York: Norton, 1975), 55.
5. Jack Valenti, *A Very Human President,* 56.
6. Arthur M. Schlesinger Jr., *Robert Kennedy and His Times* (New York: Ballantine Books, 1978), 675; Robert Dallek, *Flawed Giant: Lyndon Johnson and His Times, 1961–1973* (New York: Oxford University Press, 1998), 50.
7. Godfrey McHugh, Oral History, 59,

John F. Kennedy Presidential Library (JFKL) Boston, MA; Kenneth O'Donnell, Oral History, 47, LBJL.

8. "Interview with Roy Kellerman, 8/24/77 and 8/25/77, Holiday Inn North, St. Petersburg, Florida," House Select Committee on Assassinations, Record 180–10105–10163, Box 52, JFK Assassination Records, National Archives (JFK-NA), College Park, MD.

9. Malcolm Kilduff Interview, May 2, 1964, WM-WU.

10. Kilduff Interview, May 2, 1964, WM-WU.

11. O'Donnell, Oral History, 47–48, LBJL.

12. Randall B. Woods, *LBJ: Architect of American Ambition* (New York: Free Press, 2007), 421.

13. Rufus Youngblood, *20 Years in the Secret Service: My Life with Five Presidents* (New York: Simon and Schuster, 1973), 134–135.

14. Hubert Humphrey, *The Education of a Public Man: My Life and Politics* (Minneapolis: University of Minnesota, 1992), 260.

15. Fletcher Knebel, "Lyndon Johnson: Trained for Power," *Look,* December 31, 1963, 21.

16. Loudon Wainwright, "A Confession on

the Presidency," *Life,* January 22, 1965, 23; Horace Busby, *The Thirty-first of March* (New York: Farrar, Straus and Giroux, 2005), 160.

17. Johnson, *The Vantage Point,* 17.

**Chapter 13**

1. George Ball, *The Past Has Another Pattern: Memoirs* (New York: W. W. Norton, 1983), 313; Schlesinger Journal, November 23, 1963, 5:15 a.m., 363, Wesleyan University Special Collections and Archives (WM-WU), Middletown, CT.

2. Robert McNamara Interview, May 27, 1964, WM-WU.

3. George Ball Interview, April 10, 1964, WM-WU; Ball, *The Past Has Another Pattern,* 313.

4. Louisville *Courier-Journal* Correspondent, November 18, 1964, WM-WU.

5. Fletcher Knebel, "After the Shots: The Ordeal of Lyndon Johnson," *Look,* March 10, 1964, 33.

6. Merle Miller, *Lyndon: An Oral Biography* (New York: Ballantine Books, 1981), 323.

7. McGeorge Bundy Interview, June 2, 1964, WM-WU.

8. Jim Bishop, *The Day Kennedy Was Shot* (New York: Crown Publishers, 1983), 430–431.

9. "Texan Asks Unity," *New York Times,* November 23, 1963, 1.

10. A few days later, Hoover wrote in a memorandum that LBJ said that "I was more than head of the FBI — I was his brother and personal friend." See Hoover Memorandum, November 29, 1963, "Hoover's Official and Confidential Files, Folder 92 — Lyndon Baines Johnson," JFK Assassination Records, National Archives (JFK-NA), College Park, MD; Randall B. Woods, *LBJ: Architect of American Ambition* (New York: Free Press, 2007), 433–434.

11. Bishop, *The Day Kennedy Was Shot,* 453–454; "Memo for Record from Senator," November 23, 1963, 9. WM-WU.

12. Robert Dallek, *Flawed Giant: Lyndon Johnson and His Times, 1961–1973* (New York: Oxford University Press, 1998), 157; Carl Solberg, *Hubert Humphrey: A Biography* (New York: Norton, 1984), 240.

13. "Memo for Record from Senator," November 23, 1963, 13–14, WM-WU.

14. Ibid., 14–16.

15. Max Holland, *The Kennedy Assassination Tapes: The White House Conversations of Lyndon B. Johnson Regarding the Assassination, the Warren Commission, and the*

*Aftermath* (New York: Knopf, 2004), 60–61.

16. Ibid., 61–62.

17. Ted Sorenson, *Counselor: A Life at the Edge of History* (New York: HarperCollins, 2008), 364.

18. Bishop, *The Day Kennedy Was Shot,* 461; Cliff Carter, Oral History, 12–13, Lyndon Baines Johnson Library (LBJL), Austin, TX.

19. Busby, *The Thirty-First of March,* 150.

## Chapter 14

1. Lady Bird Johnson, *A White House Diary* (Austin: University of Texas, 2007), 7–8.

2. "The Elms," Reference File, Lyndon Baines Johnson Presidential Library (LBJL), Austin, TX.

3. Jan Jarboe Russell, *Lady Bird: A Biography of Mrs. Johnson* (New York: Scribner, 1999), 226–227.

4. "First Lady's First Day," *Los Angeles Times,* March 1, 1964, A6.

5. Fletcher Knebel, "After the Shots: The Ordeal of Lyndon Johnson," *Look,* March 10, 1964, 33; Merle Miller, *Lyndon: An Oral Biography* (New York: G.P. Putnam's, 1990), 324.

6. Horace Busby, *The Thirty-first of March* (New York: Farrar, Straus and Giroux,

2005), 152.

7. Miller, *Lyndon: An Oral Biography*, 324.

8. Busby, *The Thirty-first of March*, 152–153.

9. Ibid.

10. According to the Warren Commission, Connally was struck by the same bullet that tore through Kennedy's neck. Busby, *The Thirty-first of March*, 153.

11. Ibid.

12. Carr testified before the Warren Commission that he called District Attorney Henry Wade and told him of Johnson's concerns. Wade assured Carr that he had no intention of referring to an international plot in the indictment. Oswald, he said, would be charged with murder. See "Testimony of Waggoner Carr, *Warren Commission,* V, 258–259.

13. Fletcher Knebel, "After the Shots," 33.

14. Busby, *The Thirty-first of March,* 154.

15. Miller, *Lyndon,* 324–325.

16. Busby, *The Thirty-first of March,* 156.

17. Ibid, 154.

18. Ibid, 154–155.

19. Ibid, 155.

20. Jim Bishop, *The Day Kennedy Was Shot* (New York: Crown Publishers, 1983), 592–593.

21. Clifton Carter, Oral History, 14, LBJL.

22. Carter, Oral History, 14, LBJL.

23. Jack Valenti, "Lyndon Johnson: An Awesome Engine of a Man," in *Lyndon Johnson Remembered: An Intimate Portrait of His Presidency* (Lanham, MD: Rowan & Littlefield, 2003), 37.

24. Jack Valenti, *This Time, This Place: My Life in War, the White House, and Hollywood* (New York: Harmony, 2007), 31.

25. Ibid., 32.

26. Jack Valenti, *A Very Human President* (New York: Norton, 1975), 152–153.

27. Hubert Humphrey, *Education of a Public Man: My Life and Politics* (Minneapolis: University of Minnesota Press, 1992), 266.

## Chapter 15

1. Godfrey McHugh, Oral History, 54–55, John F. Kennedy Presidential Library (JFKL), Boston.

2. William Manchester, *The Death of a President* (New York: Harper and Row, 1967), 415–416.

3. Theodore White Notes, December 19, 1963, Wesleyan University Special Collections and Archives (WM-WU), Middletown, CT.

4. Arthur M. Schlesinger Jr., *Robert Kennedy and His Times* (New York: Ballantine Books, 1978), 675; Godfrey McHugh

Interview, May 6, 1964, WM-WU.

5. Kenneth P. O'Donnell and Dave Powers, *"Johnny, We Hardly Knew Ye"* (Boston: Little, Brown, 1970), 38.

6. Jeff Shesol, *Mutual Contempt: Lyndon Johnson, Robert Kennedy, and the Feud That Defined a Decade* (New York: W. W. Norton, 1998), 116.

7. Lawrence O'Brien, Oral History, VI, 48, Lyndon Baines Johnson Library (LBJL), Austin, TX.

8. Shesol, *Mutual Contempt,* 138.

9. Dave Powers Interview, April 8, 1964, WM-WU.

## Chapter 16

1. Max Holland, *The Kennedy Assassination Tapes: The White House Conversations of Lyndon B. Johnson Regarding the Assassination, the Warren Commission, and the Aftermath* (New York: Knopf, 2004), 74; "Daily Diary Supplement, November 23–30, 1963," Daily Diary, Box 1, Lyndon Baines Johnson Library (LBJL), Austin, TX.

2. Emory Roberts, Activity Report, November 23, 1963, Records of the Secret Service, Box 1, JFK Assassination Records, National Archives (JFK-NA), College Park, MD; "President's Daily Diary,

November 22–30, 1963," Daily Diary, Box 1, LBJL.

3. Orville Freeman Memo, November 23, 1963, 5:15 p.m., Wesleyan University Special Collections and Archives (WM-WU), Middletown, CT.

4. Jeff Shesol, *Mutual Contempt: Lyndon Johnson, Robert Kennedy, and the Feud That Defined a Decade* (New York: W.W. Norton, 1998), 119.

5. Merle Miller, *Lyndon: An Oral Biography* (New York: Ballantine Books, 1981), 331.

6. Arthur M. Schlesinger Jr., *Robert Kennedy and His Times* (New York: Ballantine Books, 1978), 676; William Manchester, *The Death of a President* (New York: Harper and Row, 1967), 454.

7. President Johnson's Statements and Schedule, Box 3, Special File on the Assassination, Lyndon Baines Johnson Library (SFA-LBJL), Austin, TX.

8. Mildred to Mr. President, November 23, 1963, 8:05 a.m., Appointment File, Diary backup, November 23, 1963, Box 1 LBJL.

9. "Parties' Outlook for 1964 Altered," *New York Times,* November 23, 1963, 6.

10. Ibid.; "California Reappraisal of 1964 Downgrades Democrats' Hopes," *New York Times,* November 24, 1963, 11;

"New Era: Johnson at Helm," *New York Times,* December 1, 1963, 24.

11. "News of Assassination Causes Shock and Disbelief," *Washington Post,* November 23, 1963, A4; "Congress Chiefs Visit President," *New York Times,* November 24, 1963, 9.

12. John McCone, "Memorandum for the Record," November 25, 1963, Meeting Notes File, Box 1, LBJL.

13. Ibid.

14. "Daily Diary Supplement, November 23–30, 1963," Daily Diary, Box 1, LBJL.

15. Dean Rusk, *As I Saw It* (New York: Penguin, 1991), 321.

16. Robert Dallek, *An Unfinished Life: John F. Kennedy, 1917–1963* (New York: Little, Brown, 2003), 685–86.

17. Jack Valenti, *A Very Human President* (New York: Norton, 1975), 152.

18. "Memorandum for the Record, "South Vietnam Situation," November 25, 1963, Meetings Notes File, Box 1, LBJL.

19. "Lyndon Baines Johnson Oral History Special Interview," August 12, 1969, LBJL.

20. *New York Times,* November 24, 1963, 25.

21. Johnson used an IBM machine designed for taking dictation to record his phone

conversations. Oddly enough, the conversation with Hoover was taped, and secretaries prepared a transcript and then destroyed the tape. This was the only recording that was destroyed (Holland, *The Kennedy Assassination Tapes,* 69).

22. Holland, *The Kennedy Assassination Tapes,* 71.

23. Ibid., 72–73.

24. Holland, *The Kennedy Assassination Tapes,* 71–73. Over the next few days, Hoover would continue to provide Johnson with false and misleading information. On November 29, the FBI director wrote a long memo about his conversation with LBJ. "The President asked how many shots were fired, and I told him three. He asked if any were fired at him. I said no, that three shots were fired at the President and we have them." He went on to say that "the President was hit by the first and third bullets and the second hit the Governor; that there were three shots; that one complete bullet rolled out of the President's head; that it tore a large part of the president's head off; that in trying to massage his heart on the way into the hospital they loosened the bullet which fell on the stretcher and we have that." In fact, the Warren Com-

mission concluded that one bullet missed its target, one bullet struck both Kennedy and Connally, and the third shot hit Kennedy in the head. The bullet the FBI recovered came from the stretcher used to carry Connally into the hospital. Nothing "rolled out" of Kennedy's head. See Hoover Memorandum, November 29, 1963, "Hoover's Official and Confidential Files, Folder 92 — JFK Assassination Records," National Archives (JFK-NA), College Park, MD.

25. A note in the president's daily diary read, "President called Mr. Meany per Justice Goldberg's request to tell him that he would like to meet with him and his colleagues and for the President to say he knows he can count on Mr. Meany & the labor movement." (Daily Diary Supplement, November 23–30, 1963, Daily Diary, Box 1, LBJL. Humphrey called the White House to say that Meany was glad to get the telegram to view the president's body, but he "thought it would be good if the balance of the Executive Committee were sent similar telegrams." (Walter Jenkins to President, November 23, 1963, Diary Backup, Appointment File, November 23, 1963, Box 1, LBJL.)

26. George Reedy, Memorandum, Novem-

ber 23, 1963, Diary Backup, Appointment File, November 23, 1963, Box 1, LBJL; Daily Diary, November 23, 1963, Daily Diary, Box 1, LBJL.

## Chapter 17

1. Arthur Schlesinger Jr. Journal, November 23, 1963 — 5:15 am, 363, Wesleyan University Special Collections and Archives (WM-WU), Middletown, CT.
2. Sally Bedell Smith, *Grace and Power: The Private World of the Kennedy White House* (New York: Random House, 2004), 444–445.
3. Ibid., 446–447.
4. Lady Bird Johnson, *A White House Diary* (Austin: University of Texas, 2007), 7; "Memo for Record from Senator," November 23, 1963, 12, WM-WU.
5. Godfrey McHugh, Oral History, 56–57, John F. Kennedy Presidential Library (JFKL), Boston, MA.
6. Lady Bird Johnson, *A White House Diary,* 7.
7. Orville Freeman Memo, November 23, 1963, 5:15 p.m., WM-WU.
8. Juanita Roberts, Memo, November 23, 1963, Diary Backup, Appointment File, Box 1, Lyndon Baines Johnson Library (LBJL), Austin, TX; "First Lady's First

Day," *Los Angeles Times,* March 1, 1964, A6.

9. HB to The President, "Visit with Eisenhower," November 23, 1963, Appointment File, Diary Backup, Box 1, LBJL.

10. "President to Address Joint Congressional Session Wednesday," *Washington Post,* November 24, 1963, 1.

11. Dwight D. Eisenhower Interview, August 27, 1964, August 27, 1964, WM-WU.

12. John McCone, "Memorandum for the Record," November 25, 1963, Meeting Notes File, Box 1, LBJL.

13. Chief, SR/CI to Assistant Deputy Director, "Possible KGB Role in Kennedy Slaying," November 23, 1963, Russ Holmes Work File, Record Number: 104–10436–10026, JFK Assassination Records, National Archives (JFK-NA), College Park, MD.

14. John McCone, "Memorandum for the Record," November 25, 1963, Meeting Notes File, Box 1, LBJL; Max Holland, *The Kennedy Assassination Tapes: The White House Conversations of Lyndon B. Johnson Regarding the Assassination, the Warren Commission, and the Aftermath* (New York: Knopf, 2004), 69. The Warren Commission would later conclude there was no evidence to prove that either

the Soviets or the Cubans were involved in Oswald's plot to assassinate Kennedy.

15. Ball, *The Past Has Another Pattern, Memoirs* (New York: Norton, 1983), 316.
16. Schlesinger Journal, November 23, 1963, 364, WM-WU; Eisenhower Interview, August 27, 1964, WM-WU.
17. Schlesinger Journal, November 23, 1963, 364, WM-WU.
18. Ibid.
19. Ted Sorenson, *Counselor: A Life at the Edge of History* (New York: HarperCollins, 2008), 377–378.
20. Schlesinger Journal, November 25, 1963, 366, WM-WU.

**Conclusion**

1. Tom Wicker, "Lyndon Johnson vs. The Ghost of Jack Kennedy," *Esquire,* November 1965, 149.
2. *New York Daily News,* November 27, 1963, 1–2.
3. Freeman Memo, November 23, 1963, 5:15 p.m., Wesleyan University Special Collections and Archives (WM-WU), Middletown, CT; "Johnson Orders Day of Mourning," *New York Times,* November 24, 1963, 1, 7.
4. Stewart Alsop, "Johnson Takes Over: The Untold Story," *Saturday Evening Post,*

February 15, 1964, 17–23; Randall B. Woods, *LBJ: Architect of American Ambition* (New York: Free Press, 2006), 423.

5. *Wall Street Journal,* November 29, 1963; "Transfer of Power Brutal," *Cleveland Ohio Plain Dealer,* December 4, 1963; "An Impressive Start," *The Plain Dealer,* November 27, 1963, 14.

6. Stewart Alsop, "Johnson Takes Over: The Untold Story," 17–23; Doris Kearns Goodwin, *Lyndon Johnson and the American Dream* (New York: Harper and Row, 1976), 178.

7. "The Nation," *Los Angeles Times,* December 1, 1963, M4.

8. Steven M. Gillon, *The American Paradox: A History of the United States Since 1945* (Boston: Houghton Mifflin, 2003), 197.

9. Kearns Goodwin, *Lyndon Johnson and the American Dream,* 170.

10. Liz Carpenter Interview, June 10, 1964, WM-WU.

11. Clark Clifford, *Counsel to the President: A Memoir* (New York: Random House, 1991), 395.

12. *"Johnny, We Hardly Knew Ye,"* Working Drafts, Kenneth O'Donnell Papers, Box 13, John F. Kennedy Presidential Library (JFKL), Boston.

13. Kearns Goodwin, *Lyndon Johnson and the American Dream,* 342–343.

14. Hubert Humphrey, *The Education of a Public Man: My Life and Politics* (Minneapolis: University of Minnesota Press, 1992), 288–289.

# NOTE ON SOURCES

Shortly after the assassination, President Lyndon Johnson created a special committee headed by Chief Justice Earl Warren to investigate the murder. On September 24, 1964, only ten months after the events in Dallas, the President's Commission on the Assassination of President Kennedy, popularly known as the Warren Commission, issued its exhaustive report, which included an 888-page summary, 26 volumes of supporting documents, testimony, or depositions of 552 witnesses, and more than 3,100 exhibits. The Warren Commission summary report and its supplemental volumes remain the best source of information on the events of November 22, 1963.

In trying to understand Lyndon Johnson's mindset on that day, and afterward, Max Holland's *The Kennedy Assassination Tapes* (New York: Knopf, 2004) is essential reading. Holland has meticulously transcribed hundreds of hours of taped phone conversations, including a few from *Air Force One* on the day of the assassination. He provides readers with a revealing and unvarnished portrait of LBJ.

Johnson discussed his reaction to the shooting in his memoir — *The Vantage Point: Perspectives of the Presidency, 1963–1969* (New York: Holt, Rinehart and Winston, 1971). In this self-serving account, LBJ simply repeats the brief statement he provided to the Warren Commission. He opened up a little more in a 1970 interview with Walter Cronkite for a CBS special titled "Tragedy and Transition." The full transcript of the interview is housed at the Lyndon Baines Johnson Presidential Library. Lady Bird's observations of that day, which she later recorded and turned into a book — *A White House Diary* (Austin: University of Texas, 2007) — are much more revealing. The original recordings can be found at the LBJ library.

Among secondary sources, Robert Dallek's *Flawed Giant: Lyndon Johnson and His Times, 1961–1973* (New York: Oxford University Press, 1998) remains the best, most balanced, and thoughtful account of LBJ's presidency. I also relied on Randall Wood's excellent *LBJ: Architect of American*

*Ambition* (New York: Free Press, 2006) for biographical information on Johnson. Doris Kearns Goodwin's portrait of the president in *Lyndon Johnson and the American Dream* (New York: Harper & Row, 1976) is still relevant today. Jeff Sheshol offers the best treatment of the LBJ-RFK rivalry in *Mutual Contempt: Lyndon Johnson, Robert Kennedy, and the Feud That Defined a Decade* (New York: Norton, 1997).

There are a handful of memoirs about that day that are helpful to researchers. Jack Valenti has recorded his memories on a number of occasions, most prominently in two books: *A Very Human President* (New York: Norton, 1975) and *This Time, This Place: My Life in War, the White House, and Hollywood* (New York: Harmony, 2007). Horace Busby, who spent much of the evening of November 22 with LBJ, wrote a manuscript that remained unpublished at the time of his death in May 2000. Fortunately, his son, Scott Busby, discovered the papers and later published them as *The Thirty-First of March: An Intimate Portrait of Lyndon Johnson's Final Days in Office* (New York: Farrar, Straus and Giroux, 2005). Most useful for my purposes was a book by Secret Service agent Rufus Youngblood, *20 Years in the Secret Service:*

*My Life with Five Presidents* (New York: Simon & Schuster, 1973).

Secondary sources, however, are of limited value in trying to re-create the events of a single twenty-four-hour period. The Secret Service agents who protected LBJ on that day provide the most complete and detailed account of his actions. The agency itself took statements from these individuals and pulled them together into a lengthy report, "Report of the U.S. Secret Service on the Assassination of President Kennedy."

Given the extraordinary amount of interest in the assassination, the Lyndon Johnson Presidential Library has pulled together all the relevant materials into a series of well-organized boxes. The collection is titled "Special File on the Assassination of President John F. Kennedy." These boxes contain not only all the declassified Secret Service reports but also notes, memoranda, and personal reflections of all the witnesses to the assassination and its aftermath.

One of the most valuable resources contained in the special files is President Johnson's daily diary, which provides a detailed account of his actions during the entire weekend. Included in the daily dairy is a "backup" file. Archivists have sifted through the collections and copied documents that provide background information on events recorded in the diary. For example, the diary will note that LBJ met with former President Dwight Eisenhower on Saturday, November 23. The backup file will contain briefing notes that were prepared for the meeting, and any scribbling LBJ made about his discussion.

The LBJ library also houses a number of valuable oral histories that shed light on that day. Among the most useful were the reflections of those who were with Johnson that day: Jack Brooks, Clifton Carter, Homer Thornberry, Marie Fehmer (Chiarodo), and Judge Sarah Hughes.

Some resources in the Kennedy Presidential Library and Museum are helpful in understanding the background of the Texas trip, but few deal with LBJ after the assassination. The papers of Jerry Bruno, who served as the advance man for the Texas trip, offer insight into the clashing political agendas. Dave Powers and Kenneth O'Donnell reveal some interesting details in the background material and working drafts of their book *"Johnny, We Hardly Knew Ye."*

In 1992 Congress passed the President John F. Kennedy Assassination Records Collection Act, which made the National Archives in College Park, Maryland, the central repository for all documents related to the assassination. At last count, the collection consisted of more than 4.5 million pages of records, photographs, motion pictures, sound recordings, and artifacts. In theory, all the materials housed at the Johnson and Kennedy libraries are also stored in the National Archives. Because of its massive size, however, the National Archives collection is disorganized and difficult to navigate.

Nevertheless, there are some very useful materials in the archives that cannot be found anywhere else. The papers of J. Lee Rankin, who served as general counsel to the Warren Commission, contain drafts of the report, along with the editorial comments of committee members. The papers of the Secret Service include agent testimony and rare photos of the assassination scene. J. Edgar Hoover's "Official and Confidential" file on Lyndon Johnson sheds insight on the discussions the two men had in the days following the shooting. The investigative files of the House Select Committee on Assassinations (HSCA), created by Congress in 1976 to reexamine the shootings of JFK and Martin Luther King, Jr., contain interviews with key witnesses.

Two new sources that only became available in 2008 allowed me to provide a fresh look at the day's events. The family of William Manchester granted me access to the original notes of the interviews that Manchester conducted in 1964–65 for his controversial book, *The Death of the President.* Chosen personally by Mrs. Kennedy to write the authorized account of the assassination, Manchester had remarkable access to all the key players.

The detailed notes of his interviews, housed at Wesleyan University's Olin Library, provide a valuable window into the events that transpired in the first twenty-four hours of the Johnson presidency. The major players come alive in these pages, and so do the private grievances and political intrigues that thrived just beneath the surface of that grief-stricken day. Many of the participants also turned over to Manchester private notes and memoranda that were not made available to the Warren Commission. This collection is an essential resource for anyone trying to understand the events of November 22, 1963.

Complementing the Manchester papers is a lengthy and revealing interview with Brigadier General Godfrey McHugh, President Kennedy's Air Force aide, opened by the Kennedy library in 2008. McHugh was a central player in the drama that unfolded on *Air Force One* as it carried JFK's body and LBJ back to Washington. He had participated in other oral history projects, and he spoke at length with Manchester. But in this interview, conducted in 1978, McHugh made new and explosive accusations about LBJ's behavior in the hours after the assassination. If what McHugh said is true, it adds a new dimension to the dramatic events that day and sheds a revealing light on Johnson and his response to the assassination.